THE HOME COMPUTER HANDBOOK

THE HOME COMPUTER HANDBOOK

By
Edwin Schlossberg
John Brockman
and Lyn Horton

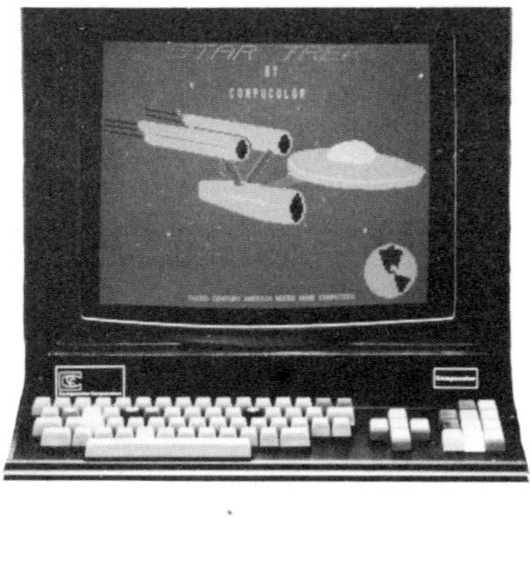

STERLING PUBLISHING CO., INC. NEW YORK

Books by Edwin Schlossberg and John Brockman

THE 1977/78 CB GUIDE
THE HOME COMPUTER HANDBOOK (with Lyn Horton)
THE POCKET CALCULATOR GAME BOOK

Cover photograph courtesy of Radio Shack.™

Published by Sterling Publishing Co., Inc.
Two Park Avenue, New York, N.Y. 10016
Manufactured in the United States of America

Library of Congress Catalog Card No.: 77-95272
Sterling ISBN 0-8069-3096-9 Trade
3097-7 Library

Contents

Introduction

You are interested in the phenomenon of the home computer. Why? Is it because you're an electrical engineer and want to share your work experiences with your family? Or are you a business executive who constantly finds himself using larger computers and has always had an urge to "play" with one at home? Are you a student who senses that computers are going to play a larger and larger role in our lives and so wants to get in on the ground floor? Or are you someone who has always been fascinated with assembling intricate pieces of electrical equipment? Or do you like to play games and think that it would be more fun to use a home computer? Or are you someone who likes to know about what's new in the world and so you want to know about this new electronic marvel? If you are any or all of these people then this book is for you.

Each year we all experience the tremendous excitement created by new pieces of hardware. One year it was electric knives; another year it was special shower heads. Last year and the year before that it was CB radios and calculators. Now and for the immediate future this excitement will be focused upon the home computer. But what do you need a home computer for? What can you do with it that you can't do without it? These are two of the questions that this book is about to answer.

The introduction of new technologies makes each one of us increasingly capable of knowing and being in the world at the same level as everyone else. That is, whereas many years ago education and access to information belonged to the privileged world of the aristocracy, today it is possible to become a Citizens Band radio operator and have your own radio station, or to create your own entertainment network through the use of video games, or to develop a home computer system which provides you with your own personal information system (with access to materials available on large computer systems or to other home computer systems).

The home computer is a new technological phenomenon made possible by the invention, in 1971, of the microprocessor, an information-processing device the size of a flake of detergent which can do the work of the best computer produced a decade or so ago. *The New York Times,* in a front-page article (May 4, 1976), reported, "The computer, once an awesome, mysterious and incredibly expensive machine of superhuman powers, has become the hottest new toy of electronic hobbyists, some of whom predict that within a few years computers will be commonplace in American homes."

Nearly 100 million people in the United States already own products using microprocessors, products which did not even exist five years ago. Most familiar are pocket calculators, digital watches, and electronic games played through home television sets. There is every reason to believe that the home computer (which is based on the use of the microprocessor) will surpass all these products and become as widespread in ownership and use as radio and television—and in a very short period of time.

It is interesting to realize that the home computer systems now selling for $600 in retail outlets have many of the same capabilities as any giant computer seen in science-fiction movies, magazines, and display windows of downtown office buildings. The difference lies in its ultraminiaturization in the scale of the number of operations it can perform and the fact that you, the private consumer, will be the operator. There is nothing new concerning what these computers can do. The key lies in new applications for their decentralized use in homes throughout the nation. The challenge to the industry is in projecting and devising software (computer programs) which will allow you to apply this new equipment for use in your daily life.

Home computers are not part of a larger network. They operate independently of any other system and work on the information, plans, games, and ideas of their owners. At present retail prices, any interested person can own a home computer and have a self-contained computer center. The number of people that are sharing such an interest is rapidly growing. And this is just the beginning.

The Home Computer: A New Automatic Tool

It is useful at the outset to examine the nature of the home computer in terms of how we will employ it as a tool. The key word is "automatic." Many of today's tools are automatic to the degree that very little time, energy, or study is required for you to operate them. Consider the automobile. Everybody drives automobiles, but only a relatively few people know how an automobile works and how to fix one.

A classic example of the automatic nature of contemporary tools is the thermostat in your home, a device that responds to the conditions within itself and around itself and adjusts itself accordingly. When the temperature drops, the circuit in the furnace is activated, turning on the furnace to heat the room. What happens in the thermostat mirrors the operation of a computer, the only difference being that the thermostat is programmed by the manufacturer. Responding to heat is the same as responding to a direction, or a piece of information. It is the same as if you yourself had to close the switch when the room got too warm and open it when it got too cold, except that the thermostat does it over and over again without your having to stoke the furnace or turn any switches. A computer is simply a set of circuits that can be organized to respond to information in the same way that the furnace and the thermostat work. Instead of using heat as the "information," the computer uses information in the form of words and numbers. The logic, however, is the same.

In setting up your home computer, you create the conditions that make it "choose" between one set of information and another, just as the thermostat "chooses" between hot and cold. But remember that it is the nature of the metal used to control the thermostat that expands and contracts that makes the "choice." It is not some "knowing thing." The computer is not some knowing thing. It is simply a set of circuits that can be set up to make either/or decisions on the basis of the limits that the program sets for it. The thermostat is set to go on when it goes below 55 degrees, and off when it goes above 65 degrees. If you want to play chess, you can program your computer to move the king one place to the left when opposing queen is on a nearby square or a square of the same color. The computer does not know anything except what you tell it to know.

The programmed computers that are already in your home are those devices that respond to conditions according to specific rules that have already been decided, as the thermostat's metal responds to hot and cold. Any kind of device that responds to conditions in an environment is called a "feedback" device. It is feedback, or response to conditions, that makes devices automatic. The fact that the metal expands with heat and contracts with cold makes it usable as a feedback device. A float in a water tank that hits a bell when the water falls below a certain level is a feedback device. In a sense, these feedback devices are computers—they respond to the environment and alter conditions on the basis of that response—*but they are not programmable*. This means that they are set by the manufacturers to perform in a specific way. You cannot adjust and define the way in which they will respond. You can change the temperature range of the thermostat, but you cannot change the chemistry of the metal and thereby its response. Each of the feedback devices is "dedicated" to its use and is not programmable by you, the user.

In your home today, there are several computing devices that are dedicated computing devices. Some of them are based on microprocessors. For example, you might have a programmable microwave oven that does what you want when you want. However, these devices are not home computers although they (a) are in your home and (b) are computers. The term "home computer" applies to a device that you can program, into which you can describe what you want to do, in a computer language, and get a response on this basis. A plethora of programs (software) for specific home computer uses are already on the market. You can buy these in cartridge form and simply insert them into your system, and, as your sophistication grows, you can begin to create your own programs.

The home computer is currently being tested for its potentials. In this regard, the computer hobbyist is playing a major role as the "hands on" operator to test home computer systems. The engineers, electronics buffs, and programmers who have taken up home computing as a hobby are building foundations for future home computer use. According to Nels Winkless, editor of *Personal Computing,* ". . . the amateurs are developing a profound feeling in their bones for computer logic, for the basic ideas that make computers tick. People who grew up with the Model T are at ease with mechanical systems in which energy is harnessed to do useful and interesting jobs for people. The kids who grow up with ALTAIR and its ilk will be at ease with logic systems in which information is harnessed to do useful and interesting jobs for people."

During the past two or three years, a new market has developed. A new generation of home computerists is emerging, consisting of a wide variety of people who do not possess computer expertise. In contrast to the hobbyist—an individual who can build, test, and debug a set—the new so-called "second-level" market consists of businessmen, homemakers, lawyers, teachers, doctors, students, and other people who are not interested in technical aspects so much as in the results that can be expected from their use of the home computer.

Several new organizations have formed to supply the growing needs of the home computerist. One of these is the regional Personal Computer Fair which has occurred in several cities in the east, including New York and Boston, and in the west in Los Angeles. There is also a computer network for home computerists called PCNET set up in Palo Alto to provide a way for home computerists to communicate and interact via telephone lines. A growing number of home computerists have become interested in developing a National Computer Club. Home computer book clubs, magazines and other entities will, undoubtedly, grow very rapidly and will supplant the computer hobbyists' outlets for interest and communication.

Home Computer Clubs

For the hobbyist and general user alike, there is a growing network for the exchange of information and ideas about home computing. The center of this network is the home computer club. In 1975, the Southern California Computer Society was founded by a few members. By March 1976, membership reached 3,000. By July 1976, 10,000 people were enrolled in 150 clubs across the United States. These figures reinforce predictions that within five years, club membership will total 200,000 to 300,000.

Membership in a club provides excellent access to information as well as a sense of shared experience. Many clubs now publish newsletters, another useful source of information. Such newsletters tell of club activities and provide information on new products and programs.

Home Computer Conventions

In much the same way that CBers are flooding to CB breaks and jamborees, home computer people gather at conventions. The first major home computer convention was held in Albuquerque, New Mexico, in 1976 for over 1,000 owners and users of the ALTAIR home computer system. A recent 1977 convention attracted more than 5,000 people—evidence of the increased general level of interest.

Home Computer Stores

There are now about 300 retail outlets for computers in the United States. The first such store, the Computer Store, was opened in 1975 by MITS as an outlet for its products. The majority of stores are individually owned, although there is a BYTE Shop chain in the West, and the Computer Store chain in the Northeast.

In general, computer stores offer the following: (a) several lines of computers; (b) parts; (c) peripherals; (d) prototyping equipment; (e) storage devices; (f) software; (g) custom interfacing; (h) repair service; (i) testing equipment, such as logic monitors, logic probes, pulse generators, and frequency counters; (j) tools, such as solder irons; (k) books and magazines; and (l) consultation and advice.

The stores usually have various home computer systems hooked up for the benefit of potential buyers. They are often havens for enthusiasts, providing an environment in which computer products and the state of the art can be discussed, and where the beginner can plug into computer jargon and learn how to proceed to pursue an interest in home computers.

Publications

Two books published in 1973 helped to get across the home computer idea to hobbyists. *My Computer Likes Me When I Speak Basic,* by Bob Albrecht, aims "to bring computers to the people." David Ahl's book *101 Basic Computer Games* contains schema for programming for games. The latter book helped many perceive the possibilities for recreational and entertainment uses for the computer.

For the most part, however, books on home computing are hardware-oriented. They provide an overview of the computer industry, describe the basic terminology and structure of the computer, discuss programming techniques, and explain the designing of home computer systems. Further examples are *An Introduction to Microcomputers,* a three-volume work by

Adam Osborne; and *Microcomputer Dictionary and Guide,* by Charles Sippl and David Kidd.

No movement ever gets off the ground without an avalanche of periodicals. A number of recent publications have come into being to supply eager readers with up-to-date information on home computers. In 1975, Carl Helmers and Wayne Green created *BYTE,* which now has a circulation of over 65,000. *BYTE* contains technical articles, new products surveys, reviews of books on computers and languages, news of activities of clubs and computer organizations, articles on software, etc. At this time, there are more than 20 amateur computer publications published by clubs and computer manufacturers including,

Interface Age, originally published by the Southern California Computer Society and now independent, contains general information on computing.

Dr. Dobb's Journal of Computer Calisthenics and Orthodontia focuses on software.

Personal Computing is a general-information magazine for home computerists.

Creative Computing focuses on computer applications in games, music, and art.

PCC, from People's Computing Company in Menlo Park, California, is a casual newsprint general-information magazine.

Popular Electronics & Radio Electronics features news concerning breakthroughs in the computer industry.

Using This Book

The following chapters describe the home computer and the world that has grown up around it, as well as what it can do and what you can do with it.

Chapter One introduces the wide range of possibilities for the home computer—present to future. Chapter Two provides an introductory vocabulary to enable you to deal with the language of home computers. Chapter Three is a handy question-and-answer section dealing with the fundamentals of the home computer and how it works. Chapter Four discusses the heart of the home computer, the microprocessor. Chapter Five presents information about the microprocessor in greater detail and goes on to present the state of the art of home computer product technology. Chapters Six and Seven are thorough and somewhat technical chapters on home computer operations and on programming languages and the binary system. Chapter Eight presents information you will need when considering the purchase of your own home computer system. Chapter Nine details how you will use your system today and presents scenarios for new uses still in developmental stages.

The Appendices include a complete glossary of home computer terms, a buyer's guide to home computer systems and peripheral equipment, and lists of books, magazines, companies, clubs, and stores. Finally, for those who are interested, a history of computers is provided.

In introducing the main concepts in this book, we have found it necessary to present similar information in more than one context and in varying degrees of complexity. This kind of repetition is helpful in learning about and understanding these new ideas.

Eventually, the home computer will be as common as the automobile: most people will "drive" them, some will repair and build them, and others will do both. This book is written for all those people. If, however, your main interest is in the uses of the home computer—i.e., the "outside"—skip over those chapters dealing with the inside. You are probably a home computer "driver" rather than a builder or repairer.

This book is a manual for a tool that will be fully realized only as it becomes an expression of its users' needs, abilities, and ideas. In addition, it is a guide book to the new world of home computers, a world in which very few people (even "experts") have been involved for more than five years. It is a world that requires, for admission, the spirit of discovery as well as imagination.

1

Possibilities—Present to Future

A tool which can be adapted to the needs of its user suggests a tool that can have an infinite variety of applications. To realize these possible applications, software will have to be developed which will enable the user to direct the home computer to do the tasks envisioned. Since home computers are so new, the applications to date are only beginning to be tested and developed. But it is a certainty that many of the tasks that now take up untold hours of our days will be accomplished through the use of the home computer.

As a way to understand this and to get a feel for the range of possibilities, we have made a descriptive list of some of the possible uses for home computers. It is not an exhaustive list since there will be as many uses as there are users! In addition to the use by an individual, there are the uses that can be developed by linking several home computers together using telephone lines and a device called a MODEM. In this way, several home computerists can interact their systems with each other or with a larger computer.

The following descriptions will give you a sense of how home computers will be used in the near future:

(1) *Medical Monitoring*

A total health-care package featuring computerized checks of bodily functions. Instead of going to a doctor, you may have monitoring apparatus in your home to check heartbeat and pulse rate, and even take blood tests. You will be able to transmit this information to your doctor or hospital, thus practicing continual preventive medicine. You will also be able to connect into the local health-information network to which you can address questions about any problems you may experience.

Your home computer system may also be able to help you deal with emotional or psychological problems. You will be able to describe situations that are disturbing you to a psychological information bank and receive suggestions of possible therapeutic actions.

(2) *Information Searches*

Ask the computer any question based on fact and receive an immediate answer.

(3) *Complete Travel Programs*

The computer will read out information regarding flights, schedules, rooms, prices, availability, and facilities for travel services throughout the world. You will book your own program without leaving home.

(4) *Reservation Service*

Reservations will be made for any events requiring reserved seating. Restaurant reservations can be made via computer. You will be able to read a diagram of the restaurant and even select the table of your choice.

(5) *Total News Service*

The home computer will be on-line with all the world's news services. You will be able to have the latest information from any part of the world as it happens.

(6) *Governmental Information Service*

Local, state, and federal government will be able to make data banks of information available to home computer operators.

(7) *Polling Service*

Government, news media, and private sector can use the home computer network for instant polling and questionnaires.

(8) *Stock-Market Service*

Continual monitoring of the performance of all listed and over-the-counter stocks.

(9) *Instant Secretarial Service*

You will be able to program a letter format to be typed out by machine.

(10) *Companion Sorting*

A personalized computer-dating service.

(11) *Educational Programs*

Learning programs with subjects such as languages and math for children and for adults.

(12) *Decentralized Businesses*

By using the home computer there will be a radical reorganization of many businesses. Most people will not have to go to an office.

(13) *Personal Mapping Service*

Anticipatory design of personal experience. You will find out in advance if the parks are crowded, if there are fish in the stream, the ratio of males to females at a social event, etc.

(14) *Personal Library Service*

The home computer can be used to keep track of your personal files, records, book collections, tapes, and recordings.

(15) *Recipe Computations*

The exact amounts to be used in recipes can be computed for any number of people.

(16) *Tax Service*

The home computer will be programmed as an accounting aid in the preparation of your tax returns.

(17) *Graphic Art*

The home computer can be programmed in a myriad of ways to produce beautiful artistic displays over color television monitors.

(18) *Personal Security System*

By storing heights, weights, and diameters of all your acquaintances, the home computer will tell you who is at your doorstep—friend (who will be identified), or stranger (whose dimensions will be revealed).

(19) *Household Budget Planning*

All aspects of your household budget and income can be programmed to maximize efficient use of available funds.

(20) *Intelligent Answering Service*

The home computer will be able to recognize each caller's voice (if it has been stored) and give your personal message.

(21) *Personal Banking Service*

The home computer will soon replace the need for paper checks. Most financial transactions will take place through the computer. Bank balances will be instantly available and up-to-date.

(22) *Replacement of Mail*

Mail may become obsolete. Home computers will allow for the instant input/output of any kind of information, either written or photographic. Records of same will be permanently stored in the computer's memory. You will receive and send letters through your home computer, dialing the address and then typing the information on the keyboard and transmitting it over telephone lines.

(23) *Education*

Children will use the home computer for programmed instruction as well as plugging into school networks.

(24) *Robots*

Robots, or automated machines that will carry out tasks, are in the not-too-distant future. Your home computer will provide you with the means of becoming familiar with the procedure of programming such a robot and fully automating your environment.

(25) *Automobile Use*

Home computers are being used to automate the use of your car. Already, manufacturers are installing microprocessors in automobiles to regulate gas, to adjust to changing environmental conditions, to avoid skidding, etc. In the not-too-distant future, it will be possible to program your car to take a trip to the market. Your car will respond to the traffic and environmental conditions and deliver you to a specified location. Home computers are also being used to provide test equipment to enable you to easily carry out a complete diagnosis of your vehicle.

(26) *Electronic Equipment Monitoring*

Your home computer will run the lawn mower and vacuum cleaner, keep the air conditioner operating at optimal levels, and turn on the coffee pot in the morning.

In addition, your home computer can be used to monitor a variety of functions in the home that are usually "worry" items. This includes providing active security measures such as turning lights on and off, turning radios on, and duplicating your activities so that potential burglars cannot tell whether or not you are home.

(27) *Nutritional Planning*

Your home computer can be used to plan the family diet, taking into consideration nutritional needs as well

SAMPLE HOME COMPUTER USE
FOOD / DIET CONTROL

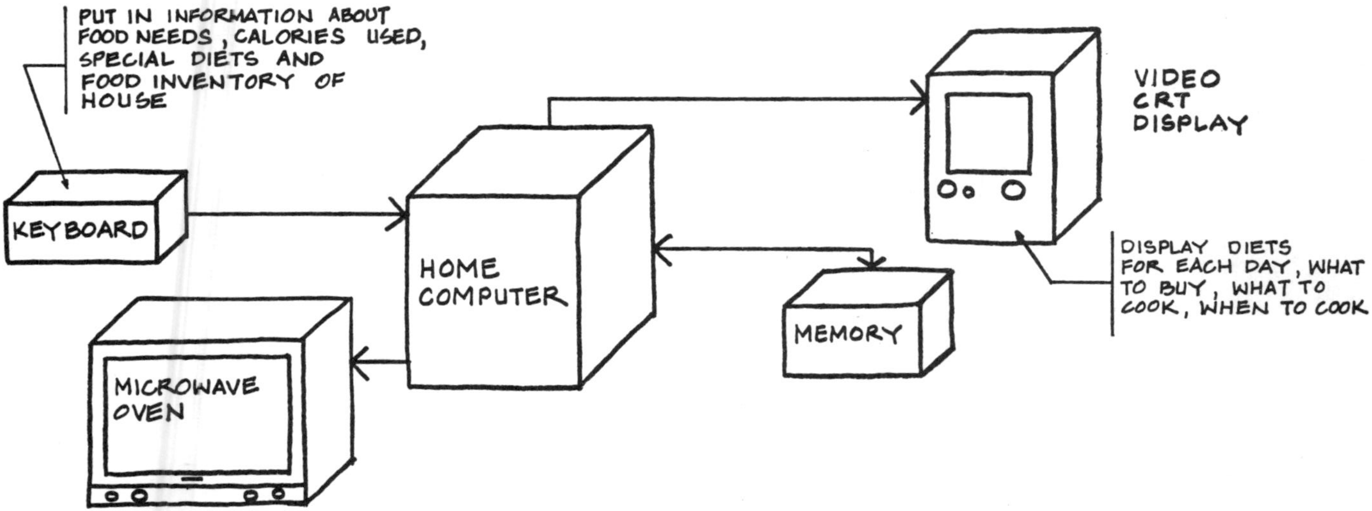

as what each member of the family likes to eat. The home computer can store food preferences and caloric needs and daily expenditures for each member of the family. For example, a husband may expend 2,500 calories daily during the week, and 4,500 daily on weekends. Your home computer can thus recommend meals for weekdays and for the weekend. It can inventory the foods in the house and print out a list of what you need to buy. If programmed and hooked up to the supermarket computer, it can order foods and have them delivered. It can sound alarms as to when foods should be prepared, preheat the oven, cook the food, and let you know when it is ready. There are facets of this process that will involve your personal participation, but for the most part the procedures will be automated.

(28) *Energy Conservation*

Your home computer can be effectively used to plan and operate a personal energy-conservation program. Your home computer, which uses very little electricity, can monitor the amount of electricity other energy sources consume. The computer will turn down the hot-water heater between certain hours, lower the thermostat, reduce the cooling activity of the refrigerator depending on use, turn off outside lights, and perform other energy-conserving tasks.

The home computer can also help harness solar energy in a particular location. For example, by feeding information into the computer, a homeowner can learn how many hours of sunlight there are in a year, temperature ranges for the year, and the amount of energy used in heating and cooling. The computer can calculate the benefits of installing a solar energy system. If a go-ahead decision is made, the computer can assist in operating solar-heating devices and regular backup heating systems as necessary.

(29) *Environmental Monitoring*

Your home computer will allow you to monitor the air and water in your environment and take whatever

SAMPLE HOME COMPUTER FUEL/TEMPERATURE MONITOR

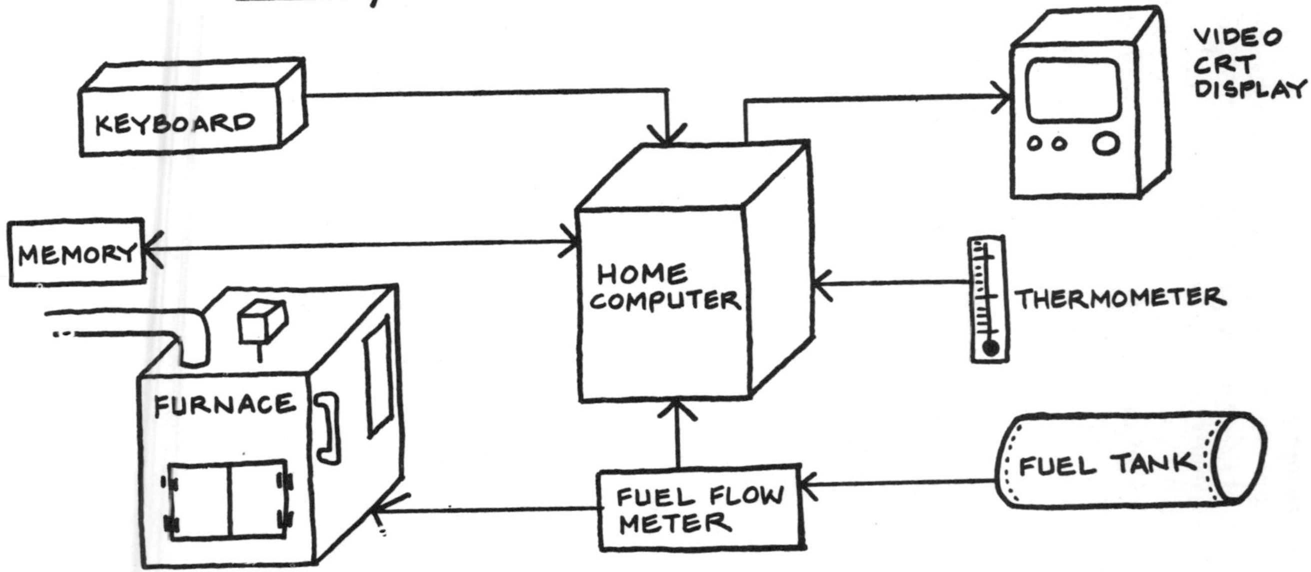

actions are possible to remedy pollution. You will be able to monitor for tornadoes and other potential dangers, such as fires and floods. Potential dangers are lessened since the home computer can act without being dependent upon human interaction. It can turn off electricity in case of a fire, turn off natural gas, shut down the furnace, etc. The home computer can monitor electrical utility power so that in the event of a brownout, the computer can turn off appliances that would be damaged.

(30) *Games*

A wide variety of games can be programmed on your home computer: electronic Ping-Pong, sophisticated word games, contests of intellectual skill. You can play games directly on or with your computer, or use your computer in conjunction with game boards or other game material. For a complete list of currently available computer games, see Chapter 9.

2

Key Words for Home Computers

Before beginning the discussion about home computers, it is necessary to become familiar with the terms most often used. The world of home computers is an original one: new words are invented and old words are redefined to describe new uses and needs. For a more extensive listing of computer terminology and definitions, see the Glossary in Appendix A.

access: the ability to interact with a computer through a device such as a keyboard, or a TV and a keyboard, etc.

address: the location in the memory of the computer where a particular *bit* of information is stored. The address requires information to find it as well as the information that is stored at that address.

binary numbers: Binary means two. The number system with which the computer operates is usually binary, using the numbers 1 and 0. This is done because the computer stores information in the format wherein a particular place is either "on" or "off." 1 is on, and 0 is off.

bit: the term used to indicate a piece of information denoting whether a place is on or off. Each bit requires a place in which a circuit is either on or off.

byte: usually 8 bits of information. Eight bits of information are assembled together to make a word or an instruction. In general, 8 bits is enough to characterize one word, and this is called a byte.

code: the particular way in which information is entered into the computer. For example, if information entered is of a binary nature, it will be a binary code.

computer: A machine duplicates a mechanical process. For instance, the typewriter prints letters that would take longer to do with a pen; the machine duplicates the process ordinarily done by hand. In a similar way, the computer duplicates decisions that would ordinarily be made by a person. The information, fed into the computer, is stored on a tape, or in the electronic duplicate of a tape—a *microprocessor*. The computer then stores as information the process by which a programmer makes decisions about that information. This is the *program*. The computer decides (programs) using the same logic as the programmer. A computer, then, is actually a very fast "pencil" that remembers how the programmer writes and, to a certain degree, what the programmer would say and how it would be said. So, a computer reflects the logic of its operator, but it will not simply turn on and "do something." The operator must figure out a task and then devise a way to tell the computer to do it. Instructions must be broken down into simple and easily followed commands. These commands need to be adjusted to the type of computer, the type of language, and the type of input/output devices that are available.

computer language: The computer is organized to follow instructions by the way it is programmed. It can follow only very clear instructions. Thus, languages have been developed which help the programmer describe what the computer should do in a clear and precise manner.

CPU: central processing unit. This is the center of the computer through which the information flows. It is the place where the program is realized, the place where the information about the environment is operated on through your programming instructions.

data: all the types of information that the computer uses, such as words, numbers, and sometimes patterns in a visual display system.

digital: A "digital" computer uses the numbers 1 and 0 as symbols and operates on the fact of the direct relationship between these numbers and the on or off condition at a specific place in the computer or circuitry. An "analog" computer operates on a wide range of conditions, one of which is the amount of voltage. A thermostat is an analog computational device. A calculator or a home computer is usually a digital device in that each circuit can be only on or off and cannot have a variety of conditions (such as a range of heat or cold, as in the thermostat).

disc: The computer stores its bits on a variety of materials, one of which is a recordlike surface called a disc. The computer can then play the disc and find the information just as you would play a record for a specific song.

hardware: all the manufactured equipment that is used as a tool. For example, the actual keyboard, microprocessor, or video display are all hardware.

input: the information fed into the computer. In the thermostat, the input is the temperature. In most home computers, it is a flipped switch, words typed on a keyboard, or information previously stored in the memory (such as the disc described above).

input/output devices (I/O devices): the pieces of hardware that allow the user to put information into the computer for processing. The microprocessor is so tiny that there would be no way for you to write on it or in it. Thus, you need a device to get the information into the machine and back out. No matter how small the size of the microprocessor, the I/O devices will always be large enough to allow visual inspection and/or tactile manipulation.

interface: Between the *input/output devices* and the microprocessor there must be connections and wires that allow the signals to be read and utilized. These places, called the interfaces, are where the information from the keyboard becomes usable to the microprocessor. They are also called "ports."

keyboard: A computer keyboard is similar to a typewriter and, in fact, many typewriters are adapted for use with home computers. The difference is that the information is translated by a device that transforms each word into a series of electrical signals that open and close the places in the computer in order to store information and instructions.

languages: The computer has several languages. One set that exists only within it is called machine language. This is usually in a binary form. Another set, computer language, is the language you use to instruct and inform the computer about the things you want to do. The computer makes the translation from your instructions to the on/off states within the machine using machine language.

mainframe: a term that refers to the *CPU* part of the hardware. The mainframe does not encompass any of the *input/output devices.*

memory: The memory of a computer system is not like human memory. The memory consists of a series of *bytes* of information that have been assembled along two major themes: (1) the information as to how to use all the information that comes in; and (2) the new information that is to be used by the computer. The memory can be a disc, a tape, or some other device that can register and then return information. Instead of thinking of it as a memory, think instead of the metal in the thermostat; the memory of the computer is like the chemical structure of the metal in the thermostat in that it stores how we want the computer to operate and on which signals (such as heat and cold).

microcomputer: Over the past 15 years, the technology to create circuitry that can store signals has become very sophisticated. With each new advance, there is an increase in efficiency and a decrease in size. The microcomputer comes after the computer and the minicomputer. All have had approximately the same capability but in an ever-decreasing size. So now a microcomputer has the same capability of a minicomputer five years ago and a computer ten years ago. Almost all home computers are microcomputers.

microprocessor: It is the logic circuit on which the computer bases its operations. In other words, the microprocessor is the computing device which stores the computer programs. As such, it has replaced room-sized installation of vacuum-tube equipment. Technically, the microprocessor is a series of very small intersections of currents such that each point can either be on, off, or either on or off. The system uses binary math, a system based on two numbers (0 and 1) rather than the usual ten. The range of conditions allows for an enormous number of possibilities. A single microprocessor the size of half a stick of gum can contain 3,000 transistors along with other components that are the equivalent of a room-size computer of ten years ago.

peripherals: another term for *input/output devices.*

program: a description of the logical sequence of instructions that must be fed into the computer and which provides the basis on which the computer processes information.

software: all the instructions, programs, computer languages, and operations that happen between the user and the hardware. The software of a system is often as complicated to design as the hardware, but because of the growing numbers of highly trained people entering the computer field, there has developed a library of software that allows anyone to have access to the use of computers.

terminal: another term for a *peripheral* or *input/output device,* except that in some circumstances the terminal has a microprocessor of its own and becomes an "intelligent terminal." A "dumb terminal" is an I/O device used with a larger CPU, but one which has no microprocessing capability. Most of the time, the word "terminal" is used by those dealing with larger systems than home computers.

3

The Home Computer: What It Is and How It Works

It is incorrect to look at the home computer as a machine that is smarter than you are, or one that can perform supernatural tasks such as looking into your brain and providing the "right" answer, regardless of what the question might be. The computer (and especially the home computer) is a simple tool that has only a minute fraction of the sophistication of your brain in its normal operations. The home computer can carry out logical functions provided you supply the logic and method of procedure and feed it the information.

The following section presents the most frequently asked questions about home computers along with their answers.

What is the difference between a computer and a calculator?

A calculator is a machine that takes information in the form of numbers and utilizes it according to fixed rules that are part of the logical machinery (in older calculators) or circuitry (in newer calculators). A computer uses information in the same way but the way it utilizes it is determined by the program used. Because it is not preset, the computer is a reflection of the logic of its program, whereas the calculator simply utilizes numbers that the user presents in a standard manner.

What is a digital computer?

A digital computer is a type of electronic device that is capable of doing arithmetic and logical operations on information supplied and handled in the form of digits. These digits are stored and handled electronically in a microprocessor.

What is a microprocessor?

A microprocessor is made of a semiconductor chip which contains the electronic circuitry necessary for digital arithmetic and logical operations. The semiconductor chip is made of semiconducting material, usually a combination of a metal and silicon; the circuitry is imprinted on it by a process called photolithography which employs light as a precise, efficient transfer medium. The chip is mounted in what is called a dual in-line package (DIP), which connects it with the rest of the circuitry in the computer. The development of semiconducting material could not begin until transistor circuitry was developed in 1948. Transistors were to be used as a replacement for cumbersome vacuum tubes. The transistor's development led the way for miniaturization of electronic circuitry, which resulted in the integrated circuit, and more recently, in 1971, in the microprocessor. The microprocessor has not only been incorporated into computer hardware but also provides decision-making capability for electronic appliances, such as sewing machines, ovens, etc. The miniaturization of electronic circuitry has meant, from an industrial standpoint, that there is a decrease in cost and increase in availability of the microprocessor; and from a technological standpoint in the computer industry, the microprocessor, when put into a computer, permits messages to have a much shorter distance to travel from point of input to point of output in order to be processed.

What is hardware?

"Hardware" is a term used to describe the physical equipment that makes up all computer systems. Home

MICROPROCESSORS, HOME COMPUTER SYSTEMS AND THEIR APPLICATION

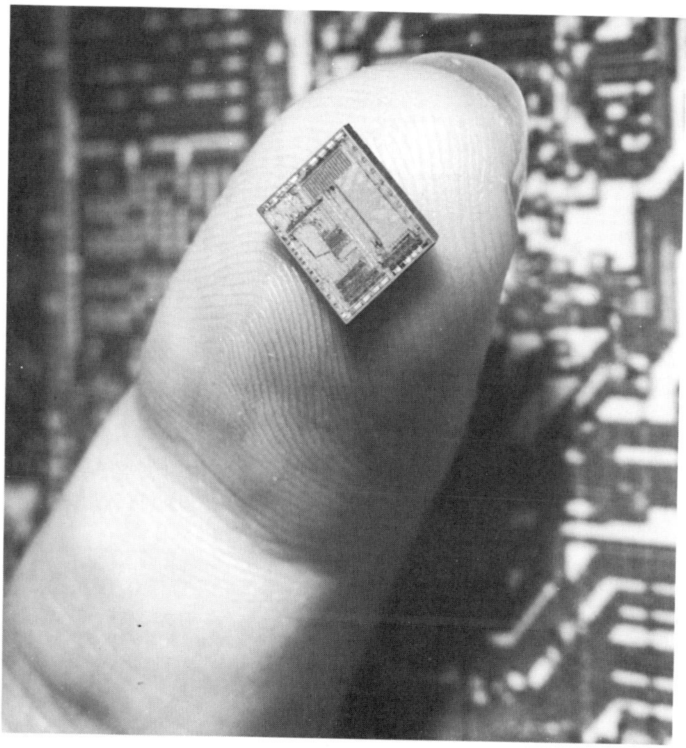

A microprocessor is a semiconductor chip which contains the electronic circuitry necessary for digital arithmetic and logical operations. (Intel 8748 LSI)

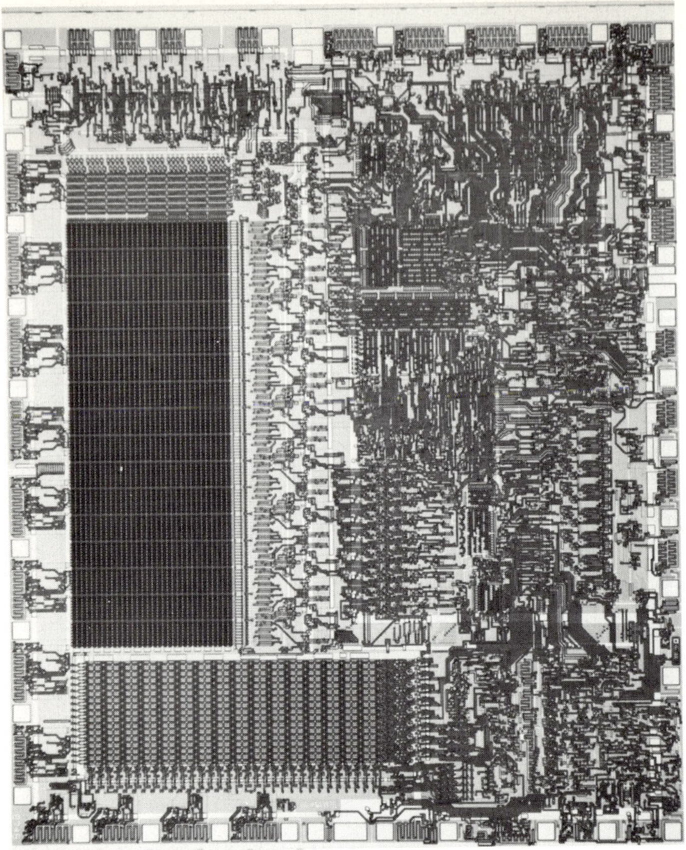

The chip is made of a semiconductor material (combination of a metal and silicon); the circuitry is imprinted on it by photolithography. (Intel 8748 LSI)

The chip is mounted in a dual in-line package (DIP) which connects it with the rest of the circuitry. (Intel 8748 LSI)

(Above)
The microprocessor unit (MPU), also known as the central processing unit (CPU), controls the processing of data and the execution of instructions. (Cromemco)

(Opposite)
A storage device, also known as memory, can be placed apart from the microprocessor. It stores information in the form of signals which the computer can access. This "Programmable Read-Only Memory" (PROM) is a semiconductor chip storage device which can be programmed in the computer operation. (Cromemco)

COPYRIGHT 1975 BY CROMEMCO
8K BYTESAVER
COMPONENT SIDE
ON

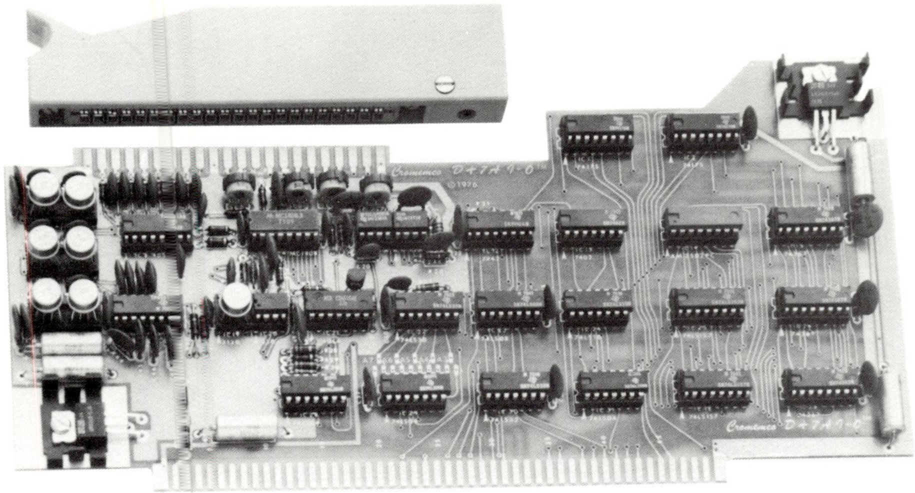

Between the input/output devices and the microprocessor there must be connections that allow the signals to be utilized. These connections, called interfaces, are where the information from the keyboard becomes usable to the microprocessor. Interface logic connects the computer processing unit with the outside world. (Cromemco)

An input/output device (I/O) usually exists outside the mainframe computer. I/O devices are the means by which information/data gets in and out of the computer. One type of input device is the keyboard. (Imsai)

Another output device is Dot-Matrix printer or line printer where the information is printed at high speed on computer paper. (Dot-Matrix impact printer, Model 40C, by Electronic Product Associates, Inc.)

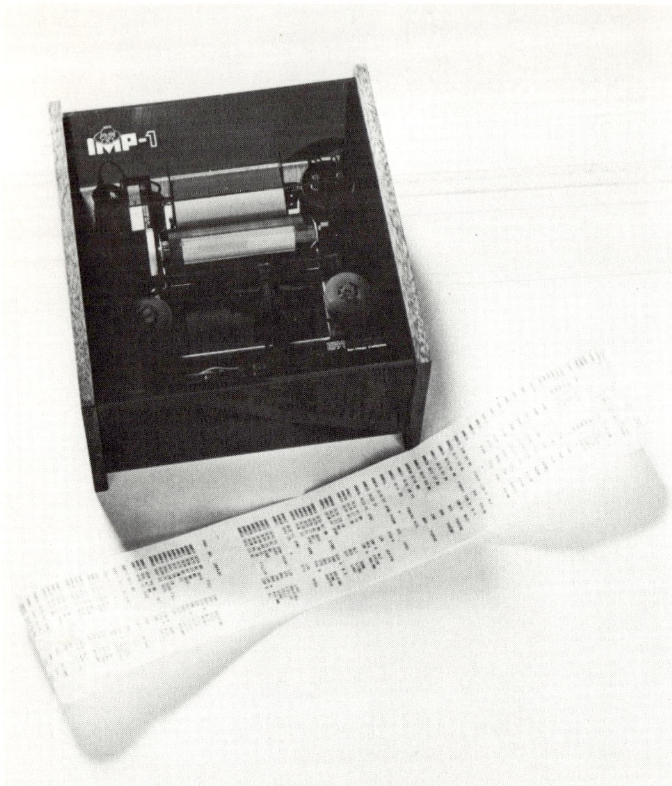

Output can also be stored on a thin magnetic record-like recording device called a floppy disc. You can then play the disc and find the information just as you would play a record.

Output devices which receive the processed data from the computer processing unit serve as a means for the computer user to see the results of the processed input. One type is the cathode-ray-tube (CRT) display unit.

Memory cassettes are like regular tape cassettes, but are adapted for use with the microprocessor.

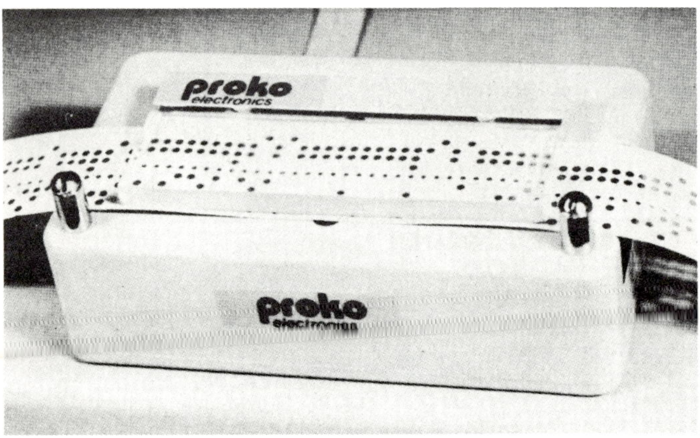

The paper tape reader codes the information in lines on a piece of paper tape punched by a special machine.

The MITS Altair 8800b home computer uses the Intel 8080 chip. I/O is through switches and lights requiring programming by user. Peripheral devices can be easily interfaced. It uses 8k Altair Basic and costs about $840 (kit) and $1,100 (assembled).

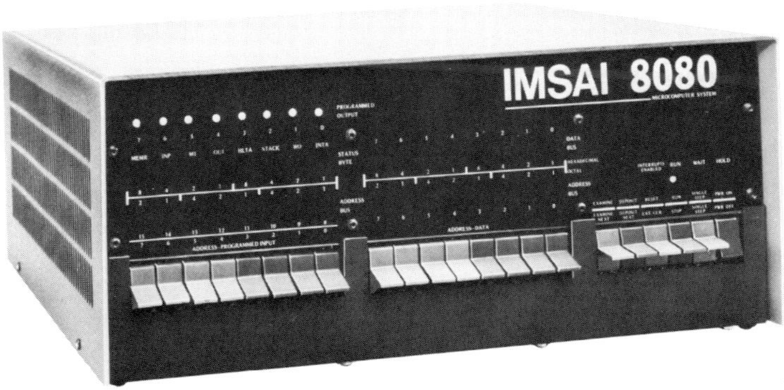

The Imsai 8080 IMS Associates uses the Intel 8080 chip. I/O is through switches and lights requiring programming by user. Peripheral devices can be interfaced with possible expansion to 65k memory dynamic RAM. Programming design uses Imsai Assembly Language or Basic and costs about $700 (kit) and $930 (assembled).

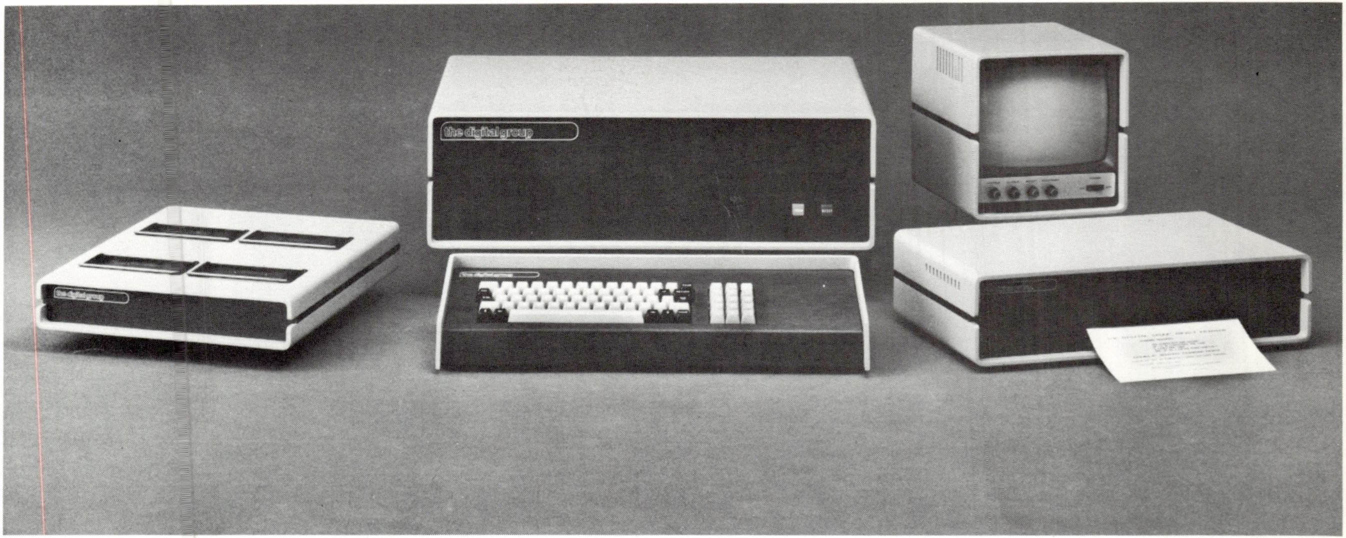

The System 4 by the Digital Group includes input devices (keyboard and tape cassette) and output devices (video display and line printer). It uses z80 chip and has I/O interfaces. It costs about $2,700 (kit) and $3,300 (assembled).

This intelligent terminal, the Sol-20 by Processor Technology Corp., uses the Intel 8080 or 8080a chip and is an intelligent I/O device. It can be interfaced with S-100 bus systems and can interface with other I/O devices. The memory is expandable to 16k RAM and costs about $1,000 (kit) and $1,500 (assembled).

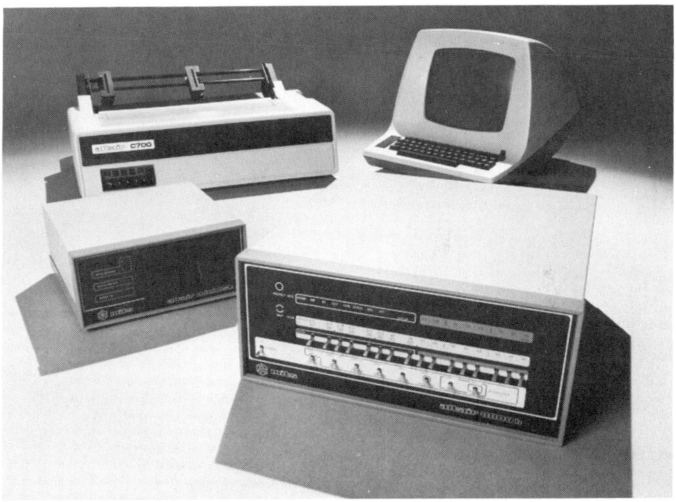

This system includes Altair 8800b, the Lear Siegler video display, the Centronic C-700 line printer and the Altair mini-disc. This is a compatible system and costs about $5,400 (assembled).

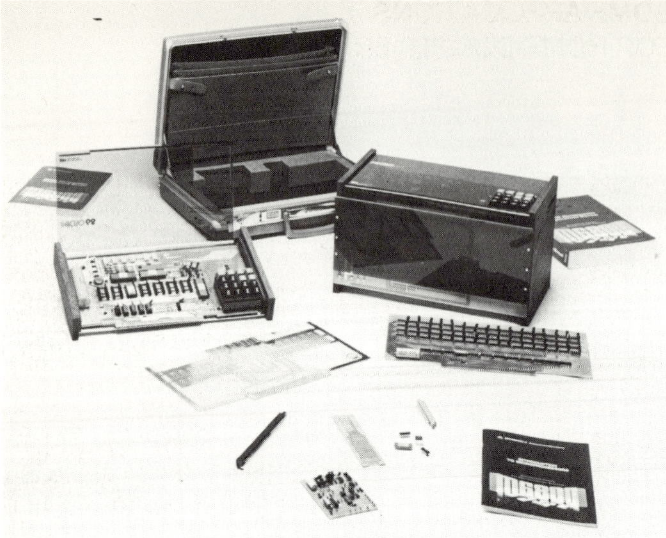

This is the M-68, Micro 68B home computer from Electronic Product Associates, Inc. It has a main CPU unit and includes components of PC board, manuals and carrying case. This is a system designed for the more sophisticated home computerist who can do programming. It costs about $1,900 (assembled).

The Poly 88 system 16 from Polymorphic Systems Inc. uses the Intel 8080 chip and includes input devices (keyboard and cassette tape), output device (video terminal) and includes 11k Basic. It can be expanded to other I/O interfaces and costs about $2,000 (assembled).

Stock market service: continual monitoring of the performance of all listed and over-the-counter stocks. (Apple II by Apple Computer Company)

Graphic art: The home computer can be programmed in myriad ways to produce beautiful, artistic displays over color television monitors. (Apple II by Apple Computer Company)

Games: A wide variety of games can be programmed on the home computer. You can play games directly on or with your computer, or use it in conjunction with game boards or other game materials. (Compucolor 8001 by Compucolor Corporation)

computer hardware does not differ in principle from hardware in other computer systems. It is simply more compact and therefore easier to handle. Home computer hardware consists of a group of separate units integral to the functioning of the computer. These units are within the microprocessing unit (MPU). They include the microprocessor, main memory, interface logic for input and output, timing circuitry, and circuitry for transporting signals from one unit to another (called a bus). The microprocessor unit (MPU), also known as the central processing unit (CPU), can consist of one or more semiconductor chips.

The CPU controls the processing of data and the execution of instructions to the computer. The CPU has specific areas of function, one of which is the arithmetic logic unit (ALU). The ALU has been referred to as the heart of the computer, for without it no operations could be performed.

How is a home computer usually organized?

A basic home computer system consists of a mainframe device (containing the microprocessor and other circuitry), a storage device, an input device (keyboard, cassette tape, etc.) and an output device.

What is a storage device? Is it memory?

A storage device, also known as memory, is equipment apart from the microprocessor, in which information can be held in the form of signals and from which the computer can access information for processing. Storage devices are usually in the form of auxiliary

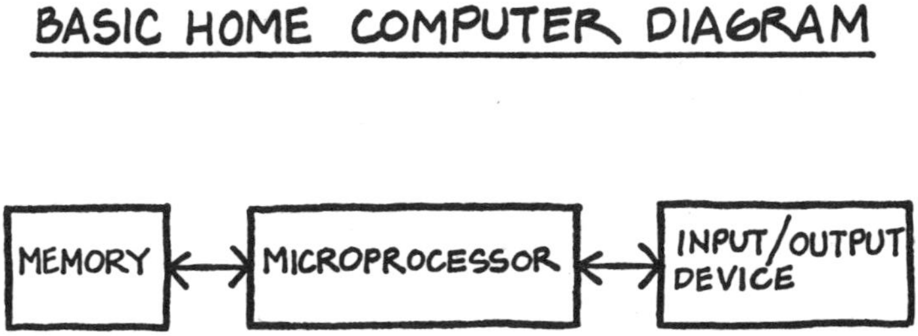

mass-storage units. The memory units external to the central microprocessor are necessary because of the limited capacity of the temporary storage devices in the central microprocessor, which itself must be programmed in order for operations to be carried out quickly. Some storage devices are called "read-only memory" (ROM), which is implemented on a semiconductor chip containing logic circuitry that cannot be changed in computer operation. They are useful because what is retained there does not disappear when the power is turned off. Other storage devices are called "random access memory" or "read-write memory" (RAM), which is often implemented on several semiconductor chips and can be changed in computer operation, and "programmable read-only memory" (PROM), which has the same principal characteristics as ROM but can be changed by the computer user. Interface logic, also implemented on chips, connects the CPU with the outside world.

What is an input/output (I/O) *device?*

An input/output device, also known as an I/O device, usually exists outside the mainframe computer. It is a device by which you can communicate with the logic of the computer. I/O devices are the means by which information or data gets in and out of the computer. Some types of input devices are keyboards, either typewriter or touchtone telephone. In addition, there are special readers which can input information by using punched cards, punched paper tape, or magnetic tape. Output devices which receive the processed data from the computer processing unit serve as a means for the computer user to see the results of the processed input. Some types of output devices are the cathode-ray-tube (CRT) display unit and the line printer

What is a peripheral device?

A peripheral device is any equipment that exists outside the mainframe computer and works with it. It can act as a separate device for storage, for data input, or for display or printing of output. It can also be equipment that aids in the coding of a program or the loading of a program in the computer.

What are the most common hardware setups for home computing?

A home computer with lights and switches. A home computer with a keyboard and video CRT display.

What is home computer software?

Computer hardware cannot function without computer software. Software is the logical organization of information that makes the computer work, and with which the user communicates to the computer. Computer software is either in the form of data (numbers, letters, symbols—configurations that a computer can process as well as produce as a result of processing), or of instructions (the coded information that tells the computer what arithmetic or logical operations to perform). The most common configuration of software for all computers is the program.

How do you communicate with a home computer?

You communicate with a home computer in two basic ways. First, you instruct the computer as to how to use the information that is given to it. This is like telling someone the rules of a game. It is done in programming language. Second, you enter information into the computer. This is like playing a game in which the computer uses the information in terms of the "rules" that were initially entered.

Can you talk directly to a computer in English?

Some computers can operate with direct language communication, but the majority use a series of languages that have been developed and that force you into thinking in accurate and logical steps. These are computer languages, and the communicating is done with a machine that understands you only insofar as it has been accurately programmed.

How does the computer transfer language inside itself into information?

The computer uses what are called *bits* and *bytes.* A bit means one circuit that is either on or off. A byte is a string of bits that makes up one whole word or instruction. Usually, there are eight bits for each byte.

What is input/output?

Input is conveyed to a computer using an input device that sends signals to the logical areas of the computer. Input is your way of telling the computer what to do. It can be in the form of instructions or, subsequently, it can be in combination with data. Output is the result of computer operations. Output is received as signals to an output device. The signals are then automatically translated to a form you can understand. I/O can be of several types. Output can be on a video screen, it can be printed on a line printer, it can be punched onto a card or paper tape, or it can be stored on recording tape or on magnetic tape, or on a thin record-like recording device, called a floppy disc. Input can also be in any of these forms, and it can be entered from a teletypewriter which is just like a typewriter but has all the special words of computer language already on it.

What is a program?

A program is a logical series of events designed for storage in the computer. It includes instructions for data manipulation and arithmetic and logical calculations. It is stored in the computer's main memory.

The idea of a computer having a stored program was first introduced by John von Neumann, Arthur Burks, and Herman Goldstine in 1946 in a paper entitled "A Preliminary Discussion of the Logical Design of an Electronic Computing Instrument." For a computer to have a stored program means that the computer will have a way to solve problems that the programmer has already worked out. Programs are written in program or computer language.

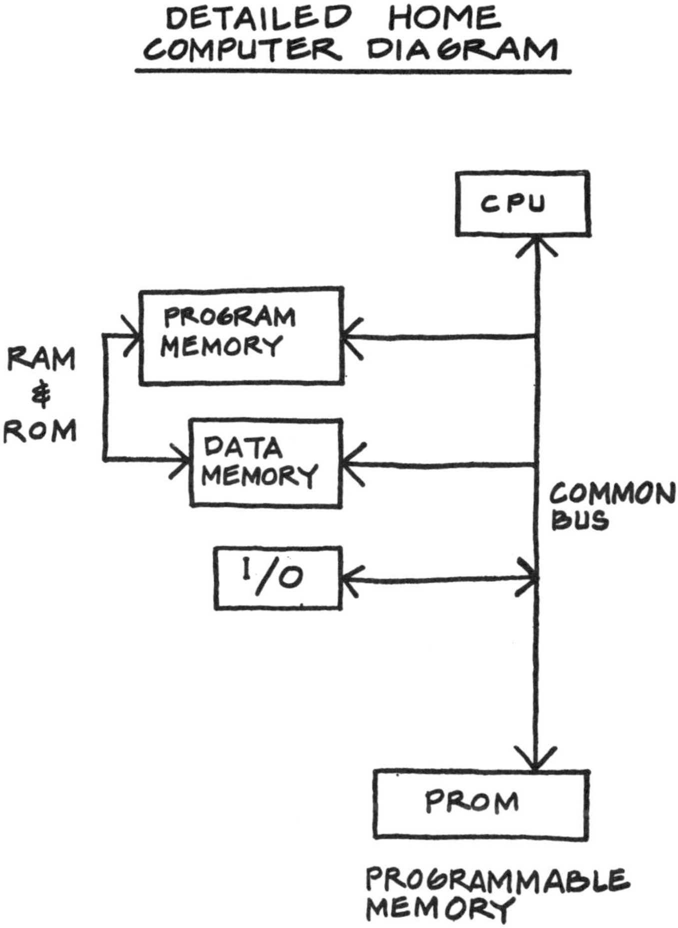

How do you figure out a program?

In order to figure out how to design your own program, it is necessary to be able to describe all the logical steps required to accomplish a task. For example, if you want to program the computer to find all the prime numbers, you must describe a process whereby the computer will recognize and then print out a prime number. How can this be done? First, you can define a prime number to the computer (any number that can be evenly divided only by itself and 1 is a prime number), and so on.

As a beginner home computerist, you can select programs that are commercially marketed and later figure out ways to design your own programs.

Do programs always come out correct?

No. The most interesting and difficult part of using a computer is figuring out how to design and use programs. Many home computerists buy pre-programmed cassettes which already have programs on them. All you do is feed the information into the computer using this cassette and enter your information. The information you enter is always in the form of numbers which change, or change from one program run to another. For example, if you are playing chess with a computer, the information you feed it in the first round will change the second round, and so on. You can also make changes in the program by introducing routines or subroutines.

What is a routine/subroutine?

A routine is a sequenced group of instructions which is not part of the main program. Routines are used to do specific tasks that are frequently performed. These tasks are not necessarily involved with the problem-solving procedure of the main program, but aid in the processing of it (for example, figuring out all the possible moves for a piece on a chessboard *before* moving).

What is a computer language?

Computer languages were developed to make it easier to use computers. They are continually being refined and improved to make the functioning of computers easier and consequently swifter. Computer languages allow you to communicate with a computer, or allow computers to communicate with each other. A programming or computer language must have a "vocabulary" that follows a specific set of rules.

Are there different kinds of computer languages?

Computer languages are designed for specific purposes. A language that is used in computing for business purposes is different from a language used in computing for science or engineering purposes. This means that computer languages have different "vocabularies" and "grammar": they will differ in the number of symbols (letters, numbers, punctuation symbols, etc.) that are permissible; they will differ in the number of mathematical operations that can be specified; they will differ in the ways in which instructions are stated, etc.

There are high-level languages, interpretive languages, assembly languages, and machine languages. All languages, with the exception of machine languages, must be translated by another kind of program into a form that the computer can understand. This means translating from words into bits and bytes. This form is machine code. Machine language is already written in machine code. The kinds of translating programs used are: compilers, which are used to translate high-level languages into machine code; assemblers, which are used to translate assembly language into machine code; and interpreters, which are used to translate interpretive language into machine code.

What are assembly languages?

Assembly languages are used in the design of individual-purpose programs. Assembly languages have a special format. Programs in assembly language are easier to write than programs in machine language because there is less room for error. Assembly languages are used to write source programs (the rules of operations), which the high-level languages are also used to write. The source program is translated into an object program by an assembler program. The object program is written in machine code and can be immediately loaded into the computer's memory.

What are interpretive languages?

Interpretive languages allow a source program to be translated by an interpreter for use in a computer. The interpreter translates the interpretive-language source program into machine code and, instead of producing an object program, lets the program be immediately operated on by the computer. Interpretive-language programs are used for solving difficult problems and for running short programs.

What are machine languages?

Machine languages are written in binary code, using 1's and 0's. Binary machine code is what the computer understands immediately without any additional translation. Machine languages can be used for writing programs for which another language does not seem appropriate. Writing a machine-language program is a personal choice. The program must conform specifically with the design of your computer hardware. Writing machine-language programs is difficult and time-consuming because you are apt to make mistakes manipulating 1's and 0's.

What are high-level languages?

High-level languages are designed for certain kinds of problem-solving. Some examples of them are:

FORTRAN (Formula Translator) is used to solve scientific and engineering problems. It was one of the first languages to be originally developed by IBM in 1963. Now, it is one of the most popular languages used in science, engineering, and business. It is made up of a combination of mathematical and English statements. Its use by a computer requires that a program written in FORTRAN be translated into machine code by a compiler program.

FORTRAN IV is a refinement of the original FORTRAN. It employs a wider range of symbols and instruction statements. It allows for more accuracy and flexibility because program statements and numbers can be longer. Its use also requires a compiler.

BASIC (Beginners Algebraic-Symbol Interpreter Compiler) was developed at Dartmouth by J. G. Kemeny and T. E. Kurtz. It resembles FORTRAN in its problem-solving orientation and is easy to use by those who are not versed in computers. It is often used in time-sharing systems where a number of remote terminals are linked up to one computer for business and commercial purposes. With BASIC, program statements can be written in any order because each statement is given a number for identification purposes. Conversational statements, several statements for one instrument, etc. can also be used. BASIC is good for home computer programming because it is easy to learn and can be used for many purposes. BASIC programs have been written for the purposes of accounting, business, science, education, engineering, and game-playing. They can also be used for controlling air-conditioning and heating systems and for home-entertainment systems. Programs written in BASIC can be easily changed in case of error. The usage of a BASIC program by a computer requires that it be translated into machine code by a compiler program.

COBOL (Common Business-Oriented Language) is a problem-oriented, procedure-oriented language. ("Procedure-oriented" means that program statements must be written in a specific order.) It was developed for commercial problem-solving. It uses English statements. It must be translated into machine code by a compiler program before the computer can use it.

PL/1 (Programming Language 1) was designed for solving problems that involve both science and business. It combines characteristics of FORTRAN and COBOL. It requires being translated into machine code by a compiler program.

APL was designed by Kenneth Iverson in 1962 for mathematical problem-solving. Today, it has a wider range of application for business and economic problem-solving. An advantageous characteristic of APL is its precision in making statements. It requires compiler translation.

APL-PLUS is a refinement of APL designed for use by time-sharing systems.

ALGOL (Algorithmic Language) resembles FORTRAN and PL/1. It is a scientific language and is noted for its conciseness in expression of arithmetic and logical statements. It requires compiler translation.

SNOBOL is a list-processing language used with large computers. A list-processing language helps to process data in terms of lists, for example by recognizing patterns in a large group of data. Other list-processing languages are LISP, used for processing symbolic lists, and SLIP.

JCL is used with the IBM 360 or 370 computers.

SIMSCRIPT and GPSS (General-Purpose Simulation System) are languages used for simulation systems. They are specifically used to aid in the making of physical models.

How does the computer process information?

Most of the questions and answers above deal with how one uses a home computer. The next step is how the computer processes information. This is "inside" talk as opposed to "outside" talk. Inside talk describes what happens in the electronics and the logical operations in the microprocessor, and in the rest of the units of the home computer.

The central processing unit (CPU) of the home computer contains specific areas of circuitry that perform certain functions:

The data counter (DC) stores the address of the location of the data memory word that is input to the computer.

The program counter (PC) stores the address of the location of the instruction memory word that is input to the computer.

The accumulator(s) (AC) stores the contents of the data memory word accessed out of memory to be operated on by the arithmetic logic unit, described below.

The instruction register (IR) stores the contents of the instruction memory word accessed out of memory to be used in the operation on data in the ALU.

The arithmetic logic unit (ALU) is a group of logic circuits. It must be able to perform binary addition, Boolean logic operations, and other operations. The ALU can deal only with bytes and no smaller data units. (This is why the smallest unit accessible from memory is a memory byte.)

The control unit (CU) ensures that the operations of

the ALU occur in the proper sequence and time. When the CPU carries out instructions, it works in two time periods (clock cycles): the *instruction fetch* and *the instruction execute.* Both these operations require the interaction of all the areas in the CPU; the interaction is controlled by the CU. In an instruction fetch, the memory address in the PC is output to memory. The contents of the memory are returned to the CPU and stored in the AC. The CU then gets the data from the AC and instruction from the IR, decodes it, and sends it to the ALU in proper sequence and time to be operated on.

What the ALU produces as a result of its operations will be stored in an AC so that the rest of the program can continue. The results produced by the ALU are also checked by conditional status flag bits in the CPU. These flag bits are set by a specific kind of instruction integrated into the program sequence. The status flags, once set, will determine when and if another program procedure should be taken. This allows for more than one possible result of ALU operations according to one instruction. The flags are: the Carry status flag, used in arithmetic operations involving many bytes; the Zero status flag, used to signal what procedure should be taken if ALU results are 0 or not; the Sign status flag, used to determine the algebraic sign of a result; the Overflow status flag, used for determining if an operation results in a group of bits that cannot fit into the allowable bit space; and the Parity status flag, used to determine if there has been an error in the transfer of character codes from memory.

The CPU can carry out as many instructions as are allowed by the instruction set, predetermined by the configuration of the computer machinery. A typical microcomputer instruction set will include instructions for processing data and input and output of data. In a microcomputer whose word size is 8 bits, for example, there are 256 possible instructions that can be input to the computer. This means that there are 256 possible combinations of 8 bits and that these combinations can be arranged in forms that designate instruc-

DETAILED HOME COMPUTER PROCESS DIAGRAM

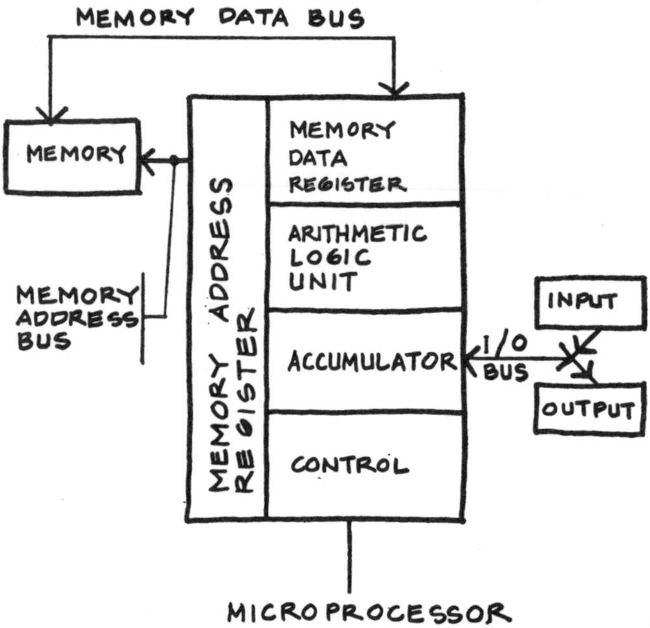

tions. These instructions will demonstrate the complexity of a program; they will constitute the instructions that the program can have in it.

Programs are usually designed around the instruction set. It is important not to waste memory space. Some of the instructions included in a typical program are:

—those which move data to and from memory and to and from other parts of the computer

—those which indicate arithmetic operations and Boolean logic operations

—those which contact specific parts of the CPU

—those which implement a change in program sequence

—those which move data (within the CPU) without the use of memory

—those which operate on data without the use of memory

—those which will find and solve the problems created by an interruption in computer operation

—those which indicate the execution of a branch routine

—the one which will stop the computer from operating: HALT.

These instructions are carried out on cue from input to the computer from an input device. The results of the instructions in combination with data constitute the output. Instruction sets vary from home computer to home computer according to the manufacturer.

A program, as explained earlier in the chapter, designates what the computer should do to perform an operation. The program includes the instructions necessary for the solution of a problem, already designed by a programmer. A program will be stored in the computer memory. Also stored in the memory are all the data necessary for the instructions to be carried out. When the computer operator inputs instructions to a computer, the operator is signaling the computer to recall from memory what it has been programmed to do. Input then instructs the computer to go to a certain place in memory, retrieve what is there, and take what is in the memory to the microprocessor, where it is operated on as has been designated by the program. Accessing data from the memory also requires the operation of the CPU, but this is automatic and not of concern to the operator.

Memory and Memory Address

Memory words are indicated by their address. The memory address specifies their location in memory. The memory address takes the form of a code number. In a program, memory addresses are referred to rather than the memory word itself. Accessing a memory word means obtaining its contents from memory by inputting to the computer the address of its location, which could be in one of several of the computer storage areas. The contents of the memory word are then taken electronically to the computer processing unit to be operated on.

There are several kinds of memory location addresses. An *indirect address* specifies a memory location whose contents are another address. This is used in cases where an instruction contains many bits. A *direct address* specifies a memory location that contains the data to be operated on. An *immediate address* means that what would be an address in other addressing modes is the data and/or instructions to be operated on.

The flexibility of a computer is determined by the number of addressing modes it can accommodate.

Data can be accessed out of or transferred to memory also using a process called direct memory access (DMA). DMA involves the operation of a special logic mechanism in the home computer. DMA is a high-speed operation where data is transferred to or from auxiliary storage devices and from and to I/O devices. DMA does not require the operation of the CPU.

The different storage areas in the home computer are specified by different ranges of addresses, just as the storage areas outside of the home computer are specified by different ranges of addresses. Each storage area has a limited amount of storage capacity or memory space. This is why auxiliary storage devices are often needed to increase the amount of memory space in the home computer.

The different storage areas in the home computer are as follows:

Read-only memory (ROM) often has a memory space of 1,024 8-bit data units. Once bits are stored in ROM they cannot be erased and will not disappear when the power running the computer is turned off. They are prefabricated circuitry and are acquired in a unit. Their configuration cannot be changed in computer operation. ROM is incorporated into the home computer for storage of basic arithmetic operations (microprogram). ROM is simply the circuitry necessary for the translation of basic operations into a machine code that the microprocessor can use. It is unnecessary to know the logic involved in the translation.

Random-access memory or read-write memory

(RAM) has a larger memory space than ROM, commonly 4,096 bits, often expressed as 4K bits. RAM is different from ROM because it can be changed: new data can be "written in" or stored. RAM can be static, where the contents of memory words will not disappear in computer operation, or dynamic, where the contents of memory words have to be constantly refreshed. RAM is used to store the *macroprogram*—the program designed by the computer programmer. The memory space of RAM is determined by the addressing capability of the home computer.

PROM is a programmable ROM. This means that PROM circuitry can be physically changed by the programmer. PROM is not as reliable as ROM, for it has been discovered that a user's establishment of circuitry patterns can wear out. Once the PROM is programmed through the physical connection of circuits, the program cannot be erased to be replaced by another program.

EPROM is an erasable PROM. EPROM can be reprogrammed as many times as desired. It is erased by using ultraviolet light and programmed in the same way as PROM.

The stack is an area in the home computer that is used for temporary storage in the case of interruption of computer operation or when the main program is interrupted to go on to another routine or smaller program. The stack simply saves the data and instructions being operated on at the time in the microprocessor, when the microprocessor must be used to do something else. What is saved in the stack can be returned to the microprocessor and computer operation can resume in the same fashion as before the interruption occurred.

4

Microprocessors: Computer on a Chip

The key to the world of home computers lies in the development of the microprocessor. This device has allowed for inexpensive computer production in highly miniaturized form.

What is a microprocessor? Let's begin with several simple analogies. First, if you had a dynamic road map of an area, one that you could change as you went along, you could use it both to plan a trip *and* to change conditions on your trip. Each road could be moved, opened, or closed, depending upon when you wanted to travel on it and how much traffic you wanted to confront on your trip.

In another analogy, consider a model railroad. Think of the track as the "programmed" part of the system and the train as information. Suppose you want the train to take six left turns, stop at a station, pick up baggage, take three right turns, and deposit the baggage at another station. All the switches and programs first must be "programmed" to anticipate the train. As the train travels along the track, it will do what you "programmed" it to do. If the programming is correct, the train will do what you expect. If not, you will have to reprogram it, and try again.

A microprocessor has gates through which information passes. The better the microprocessor is, the more controllable the gates are and the faster the information can pass through them. If the gates have many variations and can be reused after the train (i.e. the information) passes by, the microprocessor is very adaptive. When you use a microprocessor, then, you are looking at a two-level model of (1) how information can be used, and (2) the process of using it.

Before the invention of the microprocessor, the gates were controlled through the use of vacuum tubes. These tubes were quite large. A machine that could carry out 100 gated operations would often be the size of a 10x10-foot room. As a result of the development of the microprocessor, that same amount of processing can now take place on a chip which is approximately half the size of a U.S. postage stamp. Soon a microprocessor this size will be able to handle more than 10,000 gated operations.

How does the microprocessor process signals and create gates? Just as wire conducts electricity, the microprocessor has areas etched in its surface which conduct electricity. This surface is made up of layers of material. When one layer is deeply etched, it connects with another layer which makes a circuit. Instead of using thousands of electrons to achieve signaling and gating, the microprocessor is designed to operate with very few electrons in order to reduce its size and increase its efficiency.

The real significance of the invention of the microprocessor is the skill in creating something so accurate and yet so small that it is able to duplicate operations that were originally very large. Anyone can run a model train set. Imagine trying to operate it on the head of a pin! This is what is taking place in a microprocessor, and why it is so amazing.

Semiconductor technology provides the basis for the production of the microprocessor. A semiconductor is a fabricated material that can be treated so that within the area of ½ inch square, some 3,000 operations can be carried out. It is the canvas upon which the microprocessor circuitry is painted. A semiconductor is usually made out of a metal oxide (MOS: metal-oxide semiconductor). The circuits on a semiconductor are made by etching into the surface, according to patterns that are made at a much larger scale, and then photo-reducing to direct these lines onto the very small surface of the semiconductor. This is similar to photography, in which light changes the chemistry in the emulsion and creates a picture. Once the pattern has been etched, connections are made at the edges and the semiconductor is ready to be used as a microprocessor.

As their size is reduced, the efficiency of their production is increased, and the entire design and production phases are accelerated so these electronic devices are continually becoming both less expensive and more sophisticated. Few other areas in our commercial economy show this kind of pattern. And, because this is one of the most interesting and exciting industrial areas, an area ripe with potential, the competition is intense, which also helps lower cost.

Most microprocessors are constructed as explained above, although there are variations between *chips,* as they are called. Since the introduction of large-scale integration (LSI) in 1970, the range of microprocessors has dramatically increased. LSI is the industrial process of making a large pattern and then reducing and transposing it onto the chip using light beams.

Microprocessors are available in two forms. The first is the form in which all the logic, the gates, have been set by the manufacturer. An example of this is the calculator that is not programmable, or the microprocessor that is used in a microwave oven. All the possibilities for the use of these devices are predetermined, preprogrammed, and, therefore the microprocessor is usually referred to as being *dedicated.* The second form of microprocessors is those that are not preprogrammed, not dedicated. They are the microprocessors used in home computers. They allow for the gating logic operations to be inserted, using the appropriate machine language. The microprocessor that has the greatest flexibility of logic sets and operations is the one that will provide you with the greatest utility.

The development of the microprocessor has been rapid. The first successful microprocessor came from Intel Corporation in 1971. It was called the 4004 and operated on a 4-bit mode, which means that it could take and organize 4 bits of information in a word, and use it as a word. Subsequently, Intel developed the 8008 in 1972, a slow but effective 8-bit microprocessor, and the 8080 in 1973. The 8080 and the 8080A have become the industry standards, so to speak, and most designs and applications are based on the model of this very effective and successful microprocessor. Intel, however, was not alone; several other companies—National Semiconductor, Fairchild, Motorola, and others—were working on their own designs. The competition caused rapid developments and improvements in the industry.

In 1974, Intel improved the 8080 and produced the 8080A, in which still more logic was packed into the chip, allowing it to perform more complex programs and also allowing for an easier interface. National Semiconductor improved its IMP-16; a one-chip version was produced and resulted in the PACE, a 16-bit microprocessor. PACE proved not to be as salable as the Intel 8-bit, because it was more expensive and much equipment was already based on a 8-bit microprocessor.

Also during 1974, Motorola developed the M6800, which had the same basic properties of the Intel 8080, and General Instruments produced the 1600 microprocessor, similar to the PACE. Microprocessors different from the already existing products, such as the Fairchild F-8, Rockwell PPS-8, and RCA COSMAC, were also developed.

The microprocessor which proved to be the most attractive for integration into the home computer was the Intel 8080. This is the microprocessor that was used in the ALTAIR 8800, which opened the market for microcomputers in 1975. According to Nels Winkless, editor of *Personal Computing* and a leading industry authority, "Intel's 8080 chip was the first system big enough, reliable enough, cheap enough to find a wide market." The same company has recently introduced yet another generation, the Intel 8748.

Microprocessor manufacturers had a ready market for their product in digital watches and pocket calculators. Naturally, they widened their horizons for the home computer market. The major microprocessor companies—Intel, Texas Instruments, Motorola, Fairchild, National Semiconductor (known in computer lingo as OEMs or original equipment manufacturers)—continue to design microprocessor chip structures which improve upon their original product. This means not only reduction in chip size, but also reduction in chip cost and expansion of the chip's power and efficiency. Datapro Research observes that in 1976, microprocessors for home computers dropped in cost from about $25 to $15; they speculate that in 1978 the cost will drop to $5.

As for cost reduction, the computer processing units costing a few hundred dollars now have the same power as computers that cost a hundred times that much or more a few years ago. Since 1960, the complexity of integrated circuits has doubled every year. This indicates a trend that should continue for even more powerful computers, provided that the microprocessor becomes profitable and a mass-market entity.

As a result of the boom in demand for microprocessors, there has been a rise of the "second tier" microprocessor company. This kind of company, however, is finding it hard to stay in the market because it costs too much to compete with the major companies; research and development are especially costly. There has been a shrinkage of the number of companies in this business from 60 a few years ago to 40 in 1976. In order to survive, they either have to merge with another company that can supply the capital to produce microprocessors, or make specialized products for markets that the larger companies do not supply.

In terms of cost, the decline in the price of microprocessor systems parallels that of the diminishing cost of microprocessors. The Packard Bell 250 model of 15 years ago cost $40,000 and was acclaimed to be the most valuable engineering tool you could own; a modern system with comparable capacities, the Altair 8800 assembled system, costs $1,975, including assembled base unit, memory, video terminal and keyboard, multiplication/division plug-in kit, assembling system for language, and debugging system for testing for hardware/software interaction. Commodore is about to introduce a new complete system for $595! The cost of an entire system will drop greatly in the next fourteen years, just as it has in the past fourteen years, and performance will be equivalent or better.

As a result of this technological revolution, certain industrial shifts have occurred. Some companies, such as NCR, which were producers of mechanical products have been compelled to produce electronic products. IBM, the leading manufacturer of large mainframe computers, steered toward production of a portable desktop computer, the 50-pound IBM 5100, designed specifically for the solution of business, engineering, and scientific problems and costing $9,000 to $20,000. Other companies have reorganized production systems, using the microprocessor as the central unit for factory systems. Winston Bond, writing in the *New Scientist* (November 11, 1976), says: "The rapid development of the microprocessor and the continual fall in its prices has made certain that many other companies will have to face . . . basic problems as the very existence of their products and markets become threatened. The microprocessor provides the possibility of completely changing the nature of many products by making manufacturers able to harness its commercially potent attributes of powerful, miniaturized, distributed, and cheap intelligence."

The microprocessor became part of the everyday world of the consumer by being introduced into familiar objects—but introduced so that their presence was not apparent. Many industries saw that by using a microprocessor as a control unit they could increase the efficiency, dependability and adaptability of their products. A microprocessor that is "dedicated" to adjusting the fuel used in a car, or to timing the amount of heat for cooking a turkey can be very useful. Also, it allows the manufacturer to make a variety of options in its products by simply changing one part—the microprocessor. Instead of redesigning an entire product, only one small "computer-on-a-chip" needs to be replaced and the product will operate differently. For example, if a sewing machine has a microprocessor in it, it can perform a variety of stitches by changing the commands to the microprocessor. If the manufacturer wants to adapt the sewing machine to be used only by, let us say, leather workers, the only change has to be the microprocessor and the instructions it carries.

The microprocessor has been adapted within a wide range of industrial and commercial applications. Wherever there is a control function such as in the thermostat in your home, or in gasoline mixing in your car, or in the operation of your television set in conjunction with a video game, there is the possibility of utilizing a microprocessor and allowing its control function to manipulate the activities. Here are examples of existing applications of microprocessors:

Electronic video games: the first and most obvious use of microprocessors. Such games originated in 1972 with Magnavox's Odyssey, followed by Atari's Pong. In 1976, 3.5 million games were sold. The first games utilized conventional integrated circuits to control the action on the screen. The second wave of games used the microprocessor to control more than one game. The drop in price of the games and the complexity of these games parallels the improvement in microprocessor technology.

Pinball and coin-operated games, AMF's Magic Score: microprocessor integrated into scoring in bowling.

Automobiles: The 1977 Oldsmobile Toronado uses a microprocessor to control spark-plug firings in the engine so that fuel is used more economically. Ford cars will use the microprocessor to shut off cylinders in the engine when their power is not needed (i.e. deceleration), which will save in fuel consumption. Widespread use of the microprocessor in the automobile, however, is not expected to occur until 1980.

Microwave ovens: The Amana Refrigeration "Touchmatic" microwave oven was the first home appliance to use the microprocessor. The microprocessor was the replacement technology for buttons and knobs which control the timing of cooking; an electronic touch keyboard connected with digital display gives precision to cooking timing. The oven is capable of being programmed to defrost and cook.

Cash registers: Products such as the Data Terminal Systems Series 500 are stand-alone electronic cash registers that can be programmed to refer to thousands of prices and categories. They are slowly becoming standard equipment in large supermarket chains across the country.

Computer terminals: The creation of the "intelligent terminal" has occurred, in the sense that mechanisms controlling the terminal itself (display, keyboard, etc.) are controlled by a microprocessor.

FM tuners: In the Sherwood MICRO/CPU FM tuner, the microprocessor allows for better reception.

High-volume-market products: It is projected that many companies will order 50,000 microprocessors per year within the next 3 years for such items as washing machines, televisions, sewing machines, etc.

Digital watches: New advances in this area include the Pulsar watch, which includes a calculator as well as a microprocessor-controlled timing device, and a new watch that allows you to enter a date you want to remember in advance of its occurrence: when the date occurs, the watch flashes.

Telephones: The microprocessor retains up to ten phone numbers in the telephone and the number is automatically dialed when the correct button is pushed; the number can be dialed again if the line is busy.

Taximeters: The Bru-Der Instrument Corporation manufactures a device that allows the meter to show the fares of individual passengers who get into the taxi at different times.

Turntables: The ACCUTRAC 4000 uses a microprocessor to control playing tracks on a record; tracks can be played out of sequence, or repeated.

Postage scales: These scales are programmed with

postage rates, zip codes, and possible package weights so that they can compute postage in response to keyed-in information such as zip codes, class of mail, etc.

Factories: Microprocessors are being used in machine tools. For example, a can-cutting system now exists where microprocessors control the cutting and welding of cans and signal the status of the process to a larger computer system. The larger system, in turn, reports on production statistics. Another example is the RCA solid-state division: microprocessors are in tools which are linked to a supervisory computer which is linked to a larger main computer which makes "real-time" production reports. Also, the microprocessor will increase the automation of production to control smaller systems within the total production system.

Home computers: The home computer will inevitably become a major application for microprocessors. As we have seen, microprocessors have already been introduced into the home through the dedicated uses described above.

The prime mover among home computers manufacturers has been MITS (Micro Instrumentation and Telemetry Systems, Inc.), founded in 1969. Production of the ALTAIR 8800 demonstrated the company's interest in providing an alternative to the calculator. The attraction and appeal of the ALTAIR 8800 was unexpected. According to David Bunnell of MITS: "We'd thought we'd do well to sell four or five hundred units in the first year [1975]—that would have persuaded us that the market was real and worthwhile. In fact, on a single Friday afternoon we received 290 orders by mail and by telephone. Total orders in the first year exceeded 5,000 units."

Since 1975, MITS has developed "add-ons" for its computer: memories, interfacing modules, a mass-memory floppy disc system, as well as an improvement over the 8800 and the 8800B, a new home computer. The original 8800 set the standard for home computer manufacturing. Since its creation, from 1975–76, the number of companies producing home computers has doubled and the number of available products has nearly quadrupled, according to the statistics of a study on home computers done by Datapro Research Corporation in New Jersey.

Some of the original competitors of MITS include IMS Associates, producer of the IMSAI 8080, using the Intel 8080; Southwest Technical Products Corp., producers of the SWTP6800, using the Motorola 6800 microprocessor; and Processor Technology Corp., producer of the SOL terminal computer.

Another kind of company has developed alongside MITS and its competitors. This is the company that produces equipment to be used with home computers to develop an entire home computer system. Such companies produce components compatible with all available systems. They manufacture peripherals, add-in memories, and additional processor boards. These companies represent the birth of the "plug-compatible manufacturers"—PCMs.

Still other companies are developing their own peripherals to complete their systems or are buying peripherals from outside sources to be adapted to their systems.

Microprocessors can be useful in any industrial, educational, or commercial application where control and variation and feedback are important. The industrial corporations that have installed decentralized computing systems, automated assembly lines, or product-control mechanisms have become enthusiastic about the possibilities in this area.

Concerning the implications of the microprocessor into society on the commercial and industrial level, Daniel McGlynn in *Microprocessor: Technology, Architecture and Applications* says: " . . . it is believed that the microprocessor is one of the most significant technological advances in recent years and should have a major influence in the economics and design characteristics of systems in the electronics and data processing industries."

A measure of the significance of microprocessors is the enormous growth in their sales. In 1975, it was a $60-million business worldwide, according to William

Baker of National Semiconductor, who predicts that by 1980 the figure will reach $1.1 billion. Creative Strategies, a market research firm in San Jose, California, observes that the microprocessor business will grow 110% annually through 1980—i.e., from 638,000 units sold in 1975 to 26–35 million units sold in 1980.

The microprocessor is the technology that has made the home computer possible; it has permitted general access to extremely sophisticated equipment. Awareness of its importance will increase as we realize its wide range of possible uses.

5

Home Computer Products: The State of the Art

With each passing day, change in the world of home computers is rapid: the number of patents, inventions, and announcements increases.

The technology used to create the microprocessors around which home computers are organized is as sophisticated as the objects they produce. The scale at which things take place in the production of microprocessors is so small that it has been necessary to invent an entire world of tools for use in this production process.

The production of microprocessors had been focused on the technology of manufacturing the MOS (metal-oxide semiconductor). Although a wide range of types have emerged, there are two microprocessors that have become the standards for the industry and have made the microprocessor world conform to their standards. They are the Intel 8080 and the Motorola MC6800. These microprocessors have a convenient logic that adapts well to BASIC language, and they provide reasonable interface capability. They both use an S-100 bus (the bus is the transfer or exchange carrier route between the I/O devices). This seems to be the best model for the industry.

Other models of MOS microprocessors are the MCS6502, the Fairchild F-8, the National Semiconductor PACE SC/MP, the Signetics 2650, and the Intersil IM6100. Although they all have some applications, they have proved to be less adaptable for many uses and thus have not been adopted by the industry as standards.

It is interesting to consider that such a distinction would take place so quickly and so completely in a new industry. One reason for this is that Intel and Motorola were among the first in the arena. Because of this, they found many others willing to design systems to conform to their specifications. Being first provides a great deal of momentum in an industry which changes equipment and expectations from month to month.

Other criteria exist for choosing among the different kinds of microprocessors. Each microprocessor is distinct in the process used in its fabrication and the resulting scheme of its circuitry. This is obvious because each manufacturer holds some patents on its particular fabricating process and chemical and electrical configurations. Several types of MOS technology dominate the industry. The first process, and the process that, until now, has been the leader, is p-channel MOS technology, developed by Intel for its 8080. P-channel refers to the way the circuit is organized and the number of channels and gates that exist in the circuitry. It is a programmable MOS technology, which distinguishes it from the earlier MOS used for calculators and fixed in terms of programs.

N-channel MOS was an improvement made in the early 1970s. It works at a faster speed and allows for a denser and more elaborate circuit integration. Silicon is used as the semiconductor material. It is the technology used in the Intel 8080.

Then came the CMOS (complementary MOS) microprocessors. These combined the speed and efficiency of the PMOS with the density of the NMOS. However, although they are used extensively in larger machines, their high cost of production has limited their installation in home computers.

CMOS has received quite a bit of attention. It has developed several variations, which include using silicon on sapphire (SOS) as the semiconducting material. These processes have limited application to home computers, since they are more expensive and provide capabilities that are not presently demanded by computers used in the home.

American Microsystems recently announced the introduction of a new process called V-MOS which constructs the microprocessor on a V-shaped model rather than a plane and provides a more active surface (according to the manufacturer) that can be produced at lower cost. As the market and field change with each passing day, we will see whether this invention and the thousands that will appear during the next few years will alter the market.

Two types of processes are used in creating microprocessors. One is the bipolar technology, which requires an elaborate production scheme and results in a somewhat more expanded capability and speed. The other process is known as integrated injection logic (I^2L) and is more compact and faster than either MOS or bipolar technology, and eventually could replace them; however, there are still problems and costs to be worked out in the production end. In all these technologies, the speed of the microprocessor and its production costs and difficulty are weighed to find what type is best for what market. It is a highly volatile field in which a new invention is capable of totally altering the field and creating new lines of products and uses within the course of a single year.

There are a number of differences produced by the various technologies. Each technology requires a varying amount of current to run it. Although the amounts are very small, the differences are significant in large applications. Imagine a turbine that can be spun by being hit with a single stream of pellets, but which is usually powered by thousands of pellets, resulting in a significant waste of energy. The most successful circuitry will utilize the least amount of energy to do the most work.

Each microprocessor is designed to operate on a standard-size word (byte), but some microprocessors need a larger byte size in order to locate and handle instructions. The range is between 8-bit bytes and 16-bit bytes. Obviously, those that can do the same operations with a smaller byte size are the most effective.

Speed of operations is another characteristic variation between microprocessors. They are all in the range of nanoseconds (1/100,000,000 second); however, some microprocessors can handle two-thirds more data in the same amount of time. As a user becomes familiar with a computer, these time variations, at first insignificant, might become meaningful: having to wait a minute for an answer might get tedious. Speed of operations therefore becomes significant.

Each microprocessor searches for and retrieves the location of a piece of information and provides the method of storing it in different ways. That is, one microprocessor might have the location (the address) incorporated into a 4-bit addenda to an instruction, so it might require a full 8-bit byte for an address. Some microprocessors require an added set of instruction modes for each operation; for example, the use of square root in the permanent (ROM) memory might make the programming steps much easier.

Some microprocessors can define and organize the program that they utilize without resorting to introducing a new set of data to define the program to the machine. Eliminating this set makes for a much more efficient microprocessor.

Some microprocessors, developed mainly for use in calculators, can make rapid translation of decimal numbers and arithmetic operations to digital storage and retrieval. Some microprocessors cannot do this, and the steps for programming are very difficult if the task is to do some sort of arithmetic program such as square roots.

The microprocessor is a small, delicate piece of hardware. The ways to get information in and out of it are critical for its successful operation. Sometimes a manufacturer anticipates a certain type of interface device such as a CRT or a teletypewriter and finds that other kinds of information cannot be fed into it. Or, in the case of memory devices, the design of a microprocessor may permit it to accept information from a floppy disc but not from a cassette-type memory. Such restrictions limit the adaptability of a system.

Memory devices store data in the form of information and programs. The computer draws from this data storage to operate. Memories can be constructed in the home computer that recall entire programs and are on call to the microprocessor when the information is necessary. However, in some microprocessors, there is a short-term memory called a stack that allows for immediate use of a few variables in doing a small program. This is similar to the way a pocket calculator recalls the first number that you press from which, for example, a second number is subtracted.

Memories are either prefabricated to contain certain programs and information, or are programmable by the user.

There are several kinds of memories in home computers. ROM (read-only memory) usually uses a PMOS or NMOS microprocessor, but lately such memory systems have begun to be used in the bipolar microprocessor.

ROMs are often programmed by the manufacturer. "Read-only" means that they cannot be altered during operations. They have a common word size (byte) of 8 bits although some are now being made with 12 or 16 bits. The memories have a range of capabilities from 1,000 (K) bits to 64K 8-bit bytes, which means that a large amount of material and programming is already placed in the machine. A typical use of ROM is in microprocessors that are used in microwave ovens, where the user indicates a few variables and the computing is on standard operations. A microcomputer used this way, with a ROM set up with specific operations, is called a dedicated use.

The speed of a ROM depends on its use. In a dedicated system, speed is usually not of significance, but in programmable systems it is important that the ROM work rapidly. The range of access and retrieval is from 100 to 1,000 nanoseconds.

PROM memories are programmable memories which vary in the type of production technology (MOS, PMOS, etc.). The PROM is the area of the home computer that stores the actively engaged program that the user puts into the machine. PROMs usually retain this information only while the home computer is turned on and lose it immediately when the machine is turned off. PROMs are sometimes joined with cassettes or other types of storage tools so that the memory is retained. The PROMs usually have an 8-bit byte and a range of capacities from 8K to 64K, depending on the size and sophistication of the equipment. The speed at which operations take place in the PROM are similar to the speeds of the ROMs and the RAM: 100–1,000 nanoseconds for a storage retrieval event.

RAM (random access memory) is typically an MOS technology, since it functions in a very similar and integral way to the microprocessor itself. The common word size is 8-bit bytes. It can have approximately the same range of storage—8K–64K 8-bit bytes—but the speed of the memory is much accelerated, since it is required to get back and forth within the RAM more rapidly during programming and running than is the case with the ROM. Therefore, the RAM typically operates at speeds up to 2,000 nanoseconds.

As indicated before, the way that the information gets in and out of the microprocessor dictates its effectiveness and efficiency. A microprocessor is a limited piece of equipment if it can have only a few types of I/O devices hooked into and out of it. The range of channels between the memory, the microprocessor, and the I/O devices is critical to the effectiveness of a microprocessor. In some microprocessors, there is the capability of expanding the numbers of channels between the parts of the systems as use demands. This is becoming the way that most microprocessors are designed. However, there are many that are designed with an upper amount that can be integrated. This limits the potential usefulness of that particular microprocessor.

The number of bits of information that can be shunted from one part of the system to another is also a very important difference between microprocessors, since if the number of bits is low then the amount of transfer and the speed of that transfer of information is limited.

In programming a microprocessor, it is necessary to

have an interrupt cycle in the machine in order to be able to change, edit, and interrupt the flow to make corrections or simply to test out a new thought. Without an interrupt system, the microprocessor must always go through an entire program run before changes or editing can take place. Therefore, such a system in the circuitry is essential.

The kind of peripherals with which a microprocessor can interface also determines its usefulness. If the microprocessor can, in a sense, only talk with CRT or with paper tape, the ability to use the machine in varying circumstances or with new equipment as it becomes available is limited. Each microprocessor tends to be designed with a certain set of peripherals (I/O devices) in mind. There are several kinds. The *CRT* (cathode ray tube) is a video input/output device. The *teletype* is like a typewriter. *Printers* print information at high speed on computer paper. *Card readers* take information as presented from punched IBM cards. *Floppy discs* are magnetic recording devices that use a disc rather than a tape and can be used many times. *Memory cassettes* are like regular tape cassettes but are adapted for use with the microprocessor. *Optical character readers* read special patterns on paper (such as those on the sides of supermarket items). *Paper tape readers* are similar to card readers except that the information is coded in lines on a piece of paper tape punched by a special machine.

Each microprocessor is designed to deal with a range of programming languages. This design is reflected by the length of memory word (8 bit, 16 bit, etc.). Each microprocessor can adapt to a unique assembly language, but usually they use similar assembly languages. If a microprocessor uses one language rather than another, it may provide access to a body of programs that have already been created and thus allow the user easy access to more programs. This means less programming to get started with the operations of the computer.

Also, the way in which a microprocessor is designed to handle specific types of languages enables it to have access to programs that, in a sense, put an entire game or set of information into the program. Lately, for example, a great deal of work has been done in BASIC. If the microprocessor in your computer has BASIC as its language, then there is a whole range of available programs, simulator programs, data bases, preprogrammed games, and the like, as well as the important access to debugging programs to see where your computer is making mistakes, or where you are making mistakes in programming.

Knowing the nature of your microprocessor in terms of software is therefore as important as how it is configured for hardware needs.

Depending upon the above factors, you can develop your own home computer system. This means that you will select products on the basis of type of microprocessor used, memory devices that can be used, peripheral devices that can be used, and the software that can be used.

Your home computer system will be chosen also on the basis of the applications you have in mind for it:

—for business: calculating and data processing and information storage

—for entertainment: games, graphics

—for household control of mechanical or electrical appliances, environmental control, etc.

—for personal information storage and processing

—for computing specific kinds of problems, such as development of hardware and software for your own microcomputer system

—for control of peripherals

—for use as intelligent terminals (without extra peripherals or mass-storage units)

—for use in teaching

—for data communications, interfacing with other computers.

Your home computer will vary in cost depending upon the complexity of your system—i.e., the peripheral devices included, the capacity of memory requiring mass-storage units, etc. This, of course, depends upon how you want to use your system.

6

Home Computer Operations and Programming Languages: A Thorough Introduction

The following information is for home computerists who would like to know how the computer handles information and operates internally. It also contains descriptions and characterizations of the available computer languages.

A Program

A stored program means the following: (1) that basic operations are built into the circuitry of a machine and do not have to be re-entered every time the computer is used; (2) these operations are assigned number addresses that can be called for by the machine when needed; (3) the program becomes the arrangement of these number addresses stored in the memory along with data; (4) the specific timing cycles are set up so that what is stored is retrieved in the correct order.

A program means that the computer will have the logical series of operations to solve a problem that the programmer already has worked out. Programs are able to deal with information that includes characters (text), numbers, special symbols, drawings, charts, graphs, etc. Programs are usable not only through the computer but also through input/output devices.

Program Languages

A program (or computer) language is the means by which the computer user communicates with the computer or computers communicate with each other. The fundamentals of a programming language are: (1) that it consists of sets of instructions that follow a specific set of rules and so are sequenced in a specific order (except in the case of BASIC); (2) that it employs the logical capability of the computer.

Instructions in a program have to do with three basic functions and are coded and identified as such: (1) to deal with I/O; (2) to deal with decision-making as in logical operations; (3) to deal with specifically gauged control of information from, to, and through peripherals to be communicated to the computer. Instructions have to be written in accordance with the operable home computer instructions set (i.e., in accordance with hardware capacity). This means that, for example, if there are 256 possibilities for instruction codes using 8-bit word size, then the instructions must be carefully written in accordance with this number of possible combinations. (You do not want to waste memory space in a computer.)

Instruction sets define the operations used in the computer. They may include certain instructions for memory reference, and for data processing. What defines an instruction set of the home computer is the number of bits in a memory word that may be addressed and the addressing range of the instructions.

Designing a program is a process of designing a set of instructions for the computer to carry out in terms of a specified goal. Designing the instructions must be in accord with the language that you will be using in communicating with the computer; some languages are designed to be used for specific purposes. All computer programs (except for machine language programs, which are already in proper form) must eventually be converted into machine language. There are machine languages that can be used directly with certain machines (all computers are not necessarily built the same way, but they follow the same principles). High-level languages, such as a problem-oriented one, cannot go directly into the computer. It must be compiled (translated into machine language) before the computer can understand and use it. A compiler program is used. A compiler can already be stored in the computer for reference, or it can be entered when needed and combined with the machine language to be compiled. So when you use a high-level language, you write a program in that language, and that program is fed into the computer along with a compiler program which translates it into machine language.

Programming, then, is a process of making a program that will be accepted by the computer. Programming necessitates the careful designing of a flow chart, *first*. The flow chart graphically represents the procedure which you want the computer to follow for solving a problem. From the flow chart, you create a source program. The source program is translated into the object program by an assembler (or compiler) program, which is input to the computer.

A source program is written outside of a computer in a source language prior to machine processing. A source language is a symbolic language that has a definite vocabulary and grammar.

The source program and how it is written will *not* resemble the binary-digit object program into which it will be translated. The binary-digit object program is the machine language program, composed of sequences of bits that are understood by the computer.

Machine languages use the binary codes which the computer understands immediately without the language having to be translated. It must conform to the computer machinery that is being used. Programming directly with a machine language is difficult and time-consuming.

A source language in which the source program can be written is an assembly language. Assembly language was created to help programmers program the computer more easily. It is based on eliminating errors which can arise and sometimes go unnoticed if the source language used is actually machine language using binary digits, hexadecimal digits, etc. An assembly-language source program is converted into a binary-digit machine-language object program by the assembler. *The assembler creates the instructions which the home computer understands.* Assembly language has a specific syntax. It must follow certain "rules of grammar" so that it may be understood by the assembler.

The assembler logic has control over how the fields of the assembly-language source programs are read so that the assembler does not mix up the fields. In order for the assembler to calculate the proper binary codes for instructions, the programmer must supply the assembler with information concerning the placement of the object program in the memory.

The assembly process takes three phases to perform before it is finished. The assembly-language source program is coded onto paper tape—using ASCII code, for example. The tape is then fed into the computer and read by the assembler (the assembler makes a table internally that records each of the symbols in the source program). On the second reading of the source program, the assembler punches out an object tape (this is in machine language, a binary-digit code). On the third reading, the assembler produces a listing of the assembled program, which is useful when debugging a program. The object tape produced can then be fed to the computer and executed.

Another means of converting the source program into machine code is by using an interpreter. An interpreter is a program which understands interpretive language. Using an interpreter allows for the direct implementation of a source program in memory such that the source program's instructions (in interpretive language) are translated into machine code and operated on. Interpreters are often used when running short programs.

Specific Programming Languages

According to Charles Sippl, in his *Microcomputer Dictionary,* "Languages are essentially communications devices and must state the action to be taken, the unit of computer so designated, the devices and specific locations for storing, computing, and outputting of information." Languages have been developed to satisfy the needs of computer users. They are constantly being refined and improved. The following is a presentation of different kinds of computer languages:

FORTRAN (Formula Translator)

FORTRAN is a high-level problem-oriented language used for scientific and engineering problems. It is one of the first languages designed. The FORTRAN source program is composed of a combination of mathematical and English statements. It has a character set of 26 letters, 0–9 digits, and special symbols. It specifies five basic operations: $+$, $-$, $\div$, $\times$, and exponentiation with certain symbols. Mathematical operations are defined by writing the mnemonic for the operation in front of the mathematical expression. It contains certain statements for certain operations, i.e. READ, END, PAUSE, DO, FORMAT, etc. It is capable of using positive and negative integers (fixed-point numbers) and decimal numbers (floating-point numbers).

FORTRAN IV is a refinement of the original FORTRAN. It has a larger character set. It also allows for more flexibility and accuracy because statements and numbers are longer.

Using FORTRAN requires a compiler written for the model of computer that is being used. FORTRAN was developed by IBM in 1963 and is the most-used language for scientific and business applications.

BASIC (Beginners Algebraic-Symbol Interpreter Compiler)

BASIC was developed by J. G. Kemeny and T. E. Kurtz, two Dartmouth College professors. It resembles

FORTRAN because it is designed for mathematicians and engineers who are not versed in computer language. It is used in time-sharing systems for business and commercial purposes.

BASIC statements can be written in any order for input. Each line written has a number to show when statements are to be performed in the sequence of the program.

BASIC allows for a great deal of flexibility since it can use conversational statements. Since complex statements can be fragmented, programs can be modified easily in the event of error.

BASIC is good for use with home computers. It is the simplest language to learn and can be used for a wide variety of applications. BASIC programs have been written for purposes of accounting, business, science, education, games, engineering, etc.; it can be used with 4K or 8K memory (K = 1,024). (EXTENDED BASIC can be used with 12K memory. 4K BASIC has a set of 16 statements, 4 commands, and 6 functions. 8K BASIC has a set of 20 statements, 4 commands, and 6 functions.)

BASIC is used via a compiler, and debugging can be done from a keyboard.

COBOL (Common Business Oriented Language)

COBOL is a procedure-oriented, problem-oriented business language. It uses English-language statements in its source program. It was developed for commercial problem-solving and is used with a computer via a compiler.

PL/1 (Programming Language 1)

PL/1 is designed for instances when scientific and business problems are handled together. It has features that integrate FORTRAN and COBOL functions.

APL

APL was developed by Kenneth Iverson in 1962 for computer application in mathematics. Today, it is used for business and economic problems. APL is easy to use because time for developing the program is cut and therefore debugging is easier. One character in APL can be equivalent to an entire statement in another language because of the way symbols are used. Improvements in APL, APL-PLUS, apply to its use in interactive systems (time-sharing systems).

ALGOL

ALGOL resembles FORTRAN and PL/1. It is designed for arithmetic and logical processes.

SNOBOL

SNOBOL comes from two other languages: IPL-V and COMIT. It is designed for list processing and consists of statements which aid in the processing of strings of characters. SNOBOL is based on pattern recognition/matching as is designated by the programmer.

LISP (List Processing)

LISP is an interpretative language. It is used to handle symbolic lists, and with mathematical and arithmetic logic.

SLIP

SLIP is another list-processing language.

SIMSCRIPT, GPSS (General-Purpose Simulation System—IBM)

These are simulation languages. They allow for more detection of mistakes in the program than general-purpose languages such as FORTRAN. They are often used with linear programming and other modelling processes.

ASCII Codes

CCC_2 (columns) / $RRRR_2$ (rows)

	000	001	010	011	100	101	110	111
0000	NUL	DLE	SP	0	@	P	`	p
0001	SOH	DC1	!	1	A	Q	a	q
0010	STX	DC2	"	2	B	R	b	r
0011	ETX	DC3	#	3	C	S	c	s
0100	EOT	DC4	$	4	D	T	d	t
0101	ENQ	NAK	%	5	E	U	e	u
0110	ACK	SYN	&	6	F	V	f	v
0111	BEL	ETB	'	7	G	W	g	w
1000	BS	CAN	(	8	H	X	h	x
1001	HT	EM	)	9	I	Y	i	y
1010	LF	SUB	*	:	J	Z	j	z
1011	VT	ESC	+	;	K	[	k	{
1100	FF	FS	,	<	L	\	l	|
1101	CR	GS	−	=	M	]	m	}
1110	SO	RS	.	>	N	∧	n	~
1111	SI	US	/	?	O	___	o	DEL

Control Characters

NUL	Null (All Zeros)	DC1	Device Control 1
SOH	Start of Heading	DC2	Device Control 2
STX	Start of Text	DC3	Device Control 3
ETX	End of Text	DC4	Device Control 4
EOT	End of Transmission	NAK	Negative Acknowledgement
ENQ	Enquiry	SYN	Synchronous/Idle
ACK	Acknowledgement	ETB	End of Transmitted Block
BEL	Bell, or Attention Signal	CAN	Cancel (Error in Data)
BS	Backspace	EM	End of Medium
HT	Horizontal Tabulation	SUB	Start of Special Sequence
LF	Line Feed	ESC	Escape
VT	Vertical Tabulation	FS	File Separator
FF	Form Feed	GS	Group Separator
CR	Carriage Return	RS	Record Separator
SO	Shift Out	US	Unit Separator
SI	Shift In	SP	Space
DLE	Data Link Escape	DEL	Delete

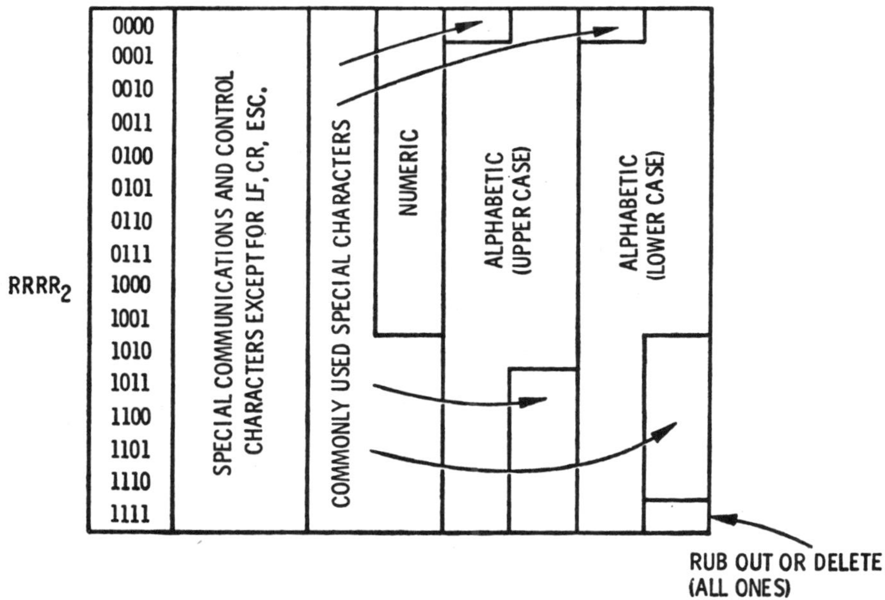

To find the character equivalent of a 7-bit binary number, divide the number into CCC RRRR$_2$ and look under the respective row RRRR and column CCC.

EBCDIC Codes

Bit Positions 1, 2, 3, 4 (columns); Bit Positions 5, 6, 7, 8 (rows)

	0000	0001	0010	0011	0100	0101	0110	0111	1000	1001	1010	1011	1100	1101	1110	1111
0000	NUL	DLE	DS		SP	&	-						{	}	\	0
0001	SOH	DC1	SOS				/		a	j	~		A	J		1
0010	STX	DC2	FS	SYN					b	k	s		B	K	S	2
0011	ETX	TM							c	l	t		C	L	T	3
0100	PF	RES	BYP	PN					d	m	u		D	M	U	4
0101	HT	NL	LF	RS					e	n	v		E	N	V	5
0110	LC	BS	ETB	UC					f	o	w		F	O	W	6
0111	DEL	IL	ESC	EOT					g	p	x		G	P	X	7
1000		CAN							h	q	y		H	Q	Y	8
1001		EM						`	i	r	z		I	R	Z	9
1010	SMM	CC	SM		¢	!	¦	:								|
1011	VT	CU1	CU2	CU3	.	$	,	#								
1100	FF	IFS		DC4	<	*	%	@					⑁		⑀	
1101	CR	IGS	ENQ	NAK	(	)	_	'								
1110	SO	IRS	ACK		+	;	>	=					⑂			
1111	SI	IUS	BEL	SUB	|	¬	?	"								

Bit Positions

1	2	3	4	5	6	7	8

Special Graphic Characters

<table>
<tr><td>¢</td><td>Cent Sign</td><td>_</td><td>Underscore</td></tr>
<tr><td>.</td><td>Period, Decimal Point</td><td>></td><td>Greater-Than Sign</td></tr>
<tr><td><</td><td>Less-Than Sign</td><td>?</td><td>Question Mark</td></tr>
<tr><td>(</td><td>Left Parenthesis</td><td>`</td><td>Accent Mark</td></tr>
<tr><td>+</td><td>Plus Sign</td><td>:</td><td>Colon</td></tr>
<tr><td>|</td><td>Logical OR, Absolute</td><td>#</td><td>Number Sign</td></tr>
<tr><td>&</td><td>Ampersand</td><td>@</td><td>At Sign</td></tr>
<tr><td>!</td><td>Exclamation Point</td><td>'</td><td>Prime, Apostrophe</td></tr>
<tr><td>$</td><td>Dollar Sign</td><td>=</td><td>Equal Sign</td></tr>
<tr><td>*</td><td>Asterisk</td><td>"</td><td>Quotation Mark</td></tr>
<tr><td>)</td><td>Right Parenthesis</td><td>~</td><td>Tilde</td></tr>
<tr><td>;</td><td>Semicoln</td><td>{</td><td>Left Brace</td></tr>
<tr><td>¬</td><td>Logical NOT</td><td>}</td><td>Right Brace</td></tr>
<tr><td>-</td><td>Minus Sign, Hyphen</td><td>\</td><td>Backslash</td></tr>
<tr><td>/</td><td>Slash</td><td>|</td><td>Logical OR, Absolute</td></tr>
<tr><td>¦</td><td>Logical OR, Absolute</td><td>⑀</td><td>Hook</td></tr>
<tr><td>,</td><td>Comma</td><td>⑂</td><td>Fork</td></tr>
<tr><td>%</td><td>Percent</td><td>⑁</td><td>Chair</td></tr>
</table>

Control Characters

NUL	Null (All Zeros)	IFS	Interchange File Separator
SOH	Start of Heading	IGS	Interchange Group Separator
STX	Start of Text	IRS	Interchange Record Separator
ETX	End of Text	IUS	Interchange Unit Separator
PF	Punch Off	DS	Digit Select
HT	Horizontal Tabulation	SOS	Start of Significance
LC	Lower Case	FS	Field Separator
DEL	Delete	BYP	Bypass
SMM	Start of Manual Message	LF	Line Feed
VT	Vertical Tabulation	ETB	End of Transmission Block
FF	Form Feed	ESC	Escape
CR	Carriage Return	SM	Set Mode
SO	Shift Out	CU2	Customer Use 2
SI	Shift In	ENQ	Enquiry
DLE	Data Link Escape	ACK	Acknowledgment
DC1	Device Control 1	BEL	Bell, or Attention Signal
DC2	Device Control 2	SYN	Synchronous/Idle
TM	Tape Mark	PN	Punch On
RES	Restore	RS	Reader Stop
NL	New Line	UC	Upper case
BS	Backspace	EOT	End of Transmission
IL	Idle	CU3	Customer Use 3
CAN	Cancel (Error in Data)	DC4	Device Control 4
EM	End of Medium	NAK	Negative Acknowledgement
CC	Cursor Control	SUB	Substitute
CU1	Customer Use 1	SP	Space

FLOW CHART SYMBOLS

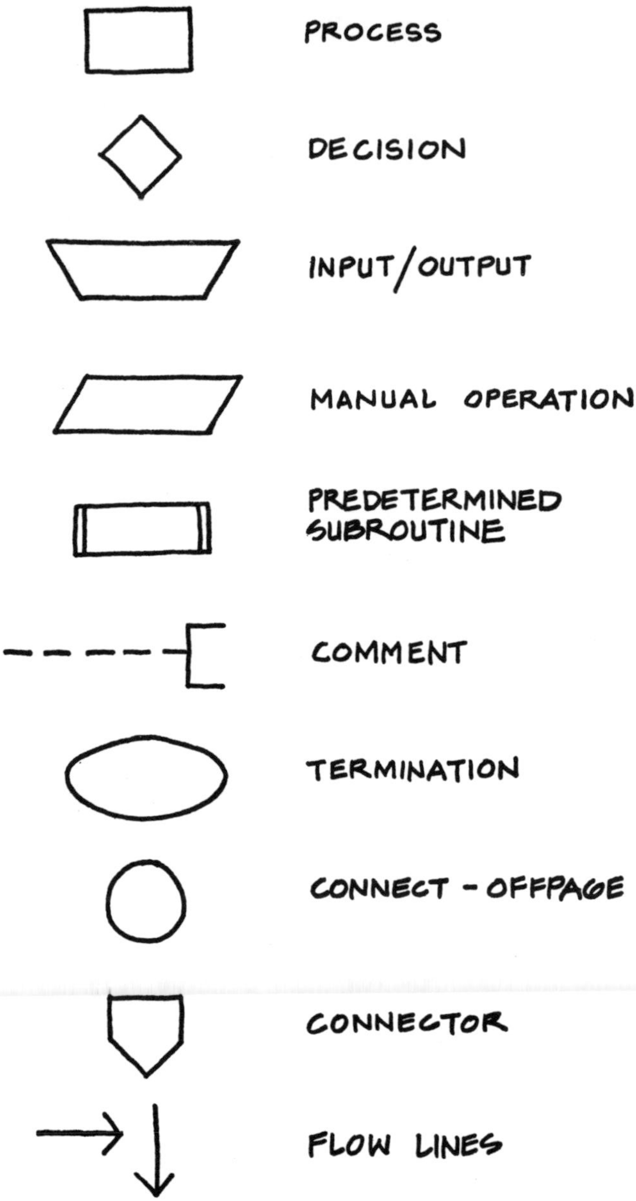

FLOW CHART OF LOGIC OF PROGRAM

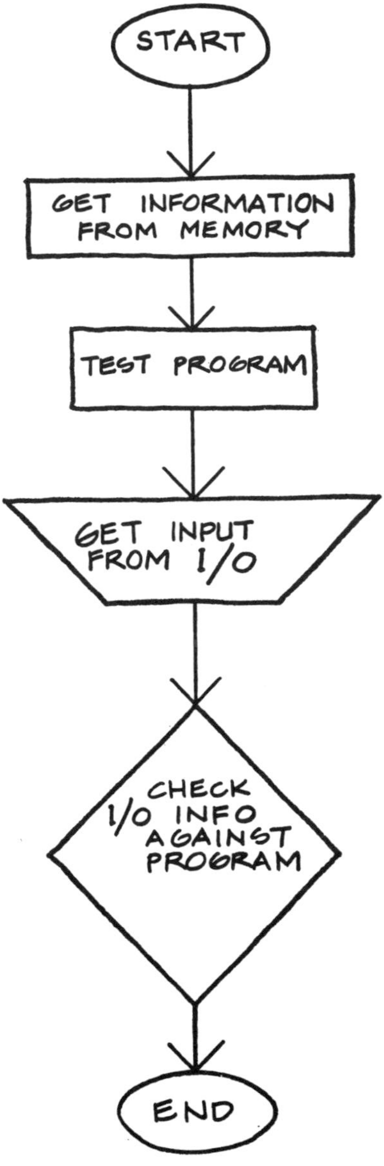

7

The Binary System and Its Use in Computers

Understanding the binary number system and its relationship to how information is stored and retrieved in the computer is basic to an understanding of computers.

How does the binary system work?

The binary system, like the decimal system, is a place-value system. The difference between them is that the binary system uses 2 as a basis for filling in places rather than 10. When counting in binary, you count in 1's, 2's, 4's, 8's, 16's, etc. The binary number 1001 means

$$\underbrace{(1 \times 2 \times 2 \times 2)}_{\text{eights}} + \underbrace{(0 \times 2 \times 2)}_{\text{fours}} + \underbrace{(0 \times 2)}_{\text{twos}} + \underbrace{1}_{\text{ones}}$$

or the decimal digit 9. When you add two binary numbers, you are doing the same thing that you do when adding decimal numbers. The difference is that one place value in the binary system cannot exceed 1, as one place value in the decimal system cannot exceed 9. So a 1 has to be carried to the next place. Example:

$$\begin{array}{rr} 1001 & (9) \\ +111 & +(7) \\ \hline 10000 & (16) \end{array}$$

Why are 1's and 0's of machine language more "understandable" to computers than other numbers represented by the digits 2,3,4,5,6,7,8,9?

The digits 0–9 represent the decimal number system. The decimal number system grew out of the fact that humans have 10 fingers. When humans needed a way to represent and record quantities that exceeded 10, they needed a system of numbers. The abacus aided in counting, but there was no way to record what the abacus counted other than by scratching on some kind of tablet, and much later by using Roman numerals, which were difficult to handle. When Arabic numerals came into use, humans could record digits easily and numbers could be made of a tremendous variety of combinations of the digits 0–9. Quantities were still represented using the same kind of placement arrangement as in the abacus. The decimal number system is a place-value system. This means that you can count in ones, tens, hundreds, thousands, etc. When you write the number 8268, what is being represented is:

$$\underbrace{(8 \times 10 \times 10 \times 10)}_{\text{thousands}} + \underbrace{(2 \times 10 \times 10)}_{\text{hundreds}} + \underbrace{(6 \times 10)}_{\text{tens}} + \underbrace{(8)}_{\text{ones}}$$

If you were to add 8268 + 732, you would be exceeding the amount in each place, by 1 in this case, since each place can only hold single digits up to 9. So, you would have to carry the one over to the necessary places:

$$\begin{array}{r} {\scriptstyle 1\,1\,1} \\ 8\,2\,6\,8 \\ +\;7\,3\,2 \\ \hline 9\,0\,0\,0 \end{array}$$

The decimal system was used with early calculating devices. These mechanical systems could accommodate 0–9 on wheels put in columns which represented the places. Yet, with the advent of electronics, where slow mechanical operations were replaced with faster electronic operations, computer technology required the use of a different number system. Since electronic operations happen faster than mechanical ones, there also had to be an adequate way of designing an electronic calculating system to work effectively and do the same kinds of operations early computing machines could do and more, because at the time computers were really needed, more sophisticated problems had to be solved. Thus, the designing of electronic circuitry demanded that a simpler number system be used not only for calculating but also for the logical solution of problems.

In 1938, Claude Shannon of MIT observed that Boolean algebra could be applied to the design of electronic circuitry. Boolean algebra was developed by the English logician George Boole in the 19th century. In 1854, he published "An Investigation of the Laws of Thought, on Which are Founded the Mathematical Theories of Logic and Probabilities."

Boolean algebra is an algebra of logic. Logic is a kind of mathematics that deals with how abstract quantities are related, given certain conditions. Algebra of logic is an algebra because it follows certain laws of algebra, i.e., the commutative, distributive, and associative laws. Boole developed two kinds of algebras of logic. The algebra of classes deals with the relations of groups of things and is governed by a set of rules. The algebra of propositions is governed by the same set of rules and deals principally with the same relations. The difference is that the algebra of propositions can deal with meaning. Propositions are statements that can be either true or false. In the algebra of propositions, then, there are two variables. They can be related in three ways: AND, OR & EXCLUSIVE OR, and NOT. The truth or falsehood of two variables as related in one of three ways can be seen in a *truth table*.

Given the above two-valued Boolean algebra and the three relations of the two values, computer circuits or logic gates can be designed into a computer in a way that corresponds to the way in which the algebra functions. The 1's and 0's can correspond with the possible two variables and, therefore, to any number of input signals given to a circuit which cause it to be on (for 1) or off (for 0). The logical relations of 1 and 0 can correspond to how the actual circuits are laid out, so that complex circuitry can be designed by combining the circuitry for each kind of relation.

Example: for two signals of input p and q
to produce one signal of output which
is the result of their relation p AND q:

LOGIC GATE CIRCUIT

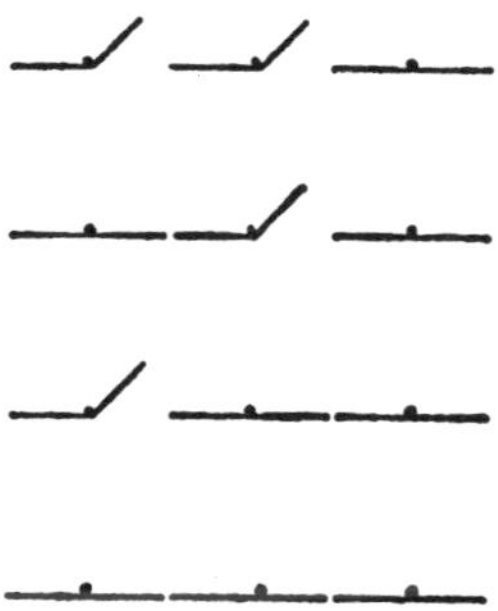

STATUS	P	Q	P+Q
BOTH GATES OPEN; NO CURRENT FLOW	0	0	0
ONE GATE CLOSED; ONE GATE OPEN; NO CURRENT FLOW	1	0	0
ONE GATE OPEN; ONE GATE CLOSED; NO CURRENT FLOW	0	1	0
BOTH GATES CLOSED CURRENT FLOW	1	1	1

(TRUTH TABLE)

Circuitry can become complex. Simplifying it has been a matter of corresponding De Morgan's Theorem to circuitry design. This theorem states that combinations of Boolean operations can be put in terms of AND and NOT logic operations. What this means to circuitry design is that a computer need only have combinations of AND circuits and NOT circuits (called inverters) in order to do everything it has to do to work effectively.

The values 1 and 0 are digits in the binary number system. This is the system that constitutes the code that computers directly translate into electronic operations.

How do you convert a decimal number to a binary number?

There are two ways to do this:

Using one method, divide the decimal number by 2, divide that quotient by 2, divide that quotient by 2, and so on, until you cannot divide the resulting quotients by 2 any more. In this process, you must keep track of the remainders. The remainders will constitute the binary number.

Example: $13_{10} = 1101_2$

$13 \div 2 = 6$ remainder 1 → 1

$6 \div 2 = 3$ remainder 0 → 0

$3 \div 2 = 1$ remainder 1 → 1

1 cannot be divided by 2 remainder 1 → 1

Using another method, figure out what powers of 2, when added together, equal the decimal number.

Example: $13_{10} = 1101_2$

$13 = 1 \times 2 \times 2 \times 2$ (8)

$+ 1 \times 2 \times 2$ (4)

$+ 0 \times 2$ (0)

$+ 1$ (1)

↓ 1 1 0 1_2 13_{10}

Are there any other number systems used in computing?

Because binary numbers can become extremely long, other number systems are used in program design to represent binary numbers.

The octal number system groups binary digits in groups of three. Its base for counting is 8. The digits from which other numbers can be made are 0,1,2,3,4, 5,6,7.

Binary to octal conversion: $111001110101_2 = 7165_8$

111 =	001 =	110 =	101 =
7	1	6	5

In the octal system, bits are taken in groups of three because a total in one binary group will not exceed 7 in octal.

The hexadecimal number system groups bits in groups of four. Its base for counting is 16. The digits from which other numbers can be made are 0,1,2,3,4, 5,6,7,8,9,A,B,C,D,E,F.

Binary to hexadecimal conversion: $111001110101_2 = E75_{16}$

1110 =	0111 =	0101 =
E	7	5

Bits are taken in groups of four because the total in one binary group will not exceed F in hexadecimal.

It is not always necessary to figure the conversions from scratch. There are tables that correspond to all the number-system values used in computing.

Can letters of the alphabet be represented by bits?

Combinations of bits can represent combinations of letters and numbers and special characters, such as punctuation. These combinations are described as *alphanumeric*. In data communications, standard coding systems have been developed in which letters of the alphabet and the decimal-system characters, as well as special characters, have been assigned a binary code. These codes are called EBCDIC code and ASCII code. The EBCDIC code (Extended Binary Coded Decimal Interchange Code) represents each character in groups of 8 bits; these groupings can be broken down into the hexadecimal system by putting the 8 bits in two groups of 4 bits. The ASCII code (American Standard Code for Information Interchange) represents each character (A–Z, 0–9) in hexadecimal code. This code is used for communications between different kinds of computers over telephone lines.

Since a computer can know what it is being told to do only by how signals are sent to it, and since bits are the signaling medium, bits must be arranged in specific ways to indicate specific kinds of signals. The basic unit into which bits are grouped is the *memory word.* It is called the memory word because in order to operate, a computer must be programmed and the program stored in the computer memory. The most common home computer word size is 8 bits in length. This is in contrast to a minicomputer's word size of 16 bits and the largest computer's word size of 64 bits. Word length can determine the accuracy of a computer but an increase in word size can also increase the complexity of computer operations. An 8-bit memory word is also called a memory byte. The byte is the most common means to describe data units.

A memory word is the smallest unit of information that can be retrieved (accessed) from computer memory. A memory word can represent a quantity or an instruction. In the home computer memory words are dealt with in pairs of two bytes by the computer. The arrangement of bits in the bytes and the order in which the bytes are used determines the status of the words. This means that words could specify quantities, instruction codes, or character codes.

A series of bits can indicate a variety of input signals to a computer. Depending upon how they are strung together, bits can mean instructions, numbers, memory locations, conditional statements, etc. Bits constitute the machine language of the computer. Any language that is used to write a computer program must always be translated into binary machine language in order for the computer to operate. This translation is done by assemblers, compilers, or interpreter programs, as mentioned before. These programs will produce object programs out of an original source program. The object program is the program that will be loaded into the computer memory so that you may use the computer as you have chosen to.

Programs must be precise in order for the logical sequence of events to occur correctly. The reason for this is that in order for a computer to operate without error as it is expected to, bits must be strung together in the proper sequence and proper lengths to convey any information to the computer. The bits will only signal to the computer which circuits are to have current flowing. If bits are not strung together properly, this means that you have not written the program properly and therefore the program has not been put into proper machine code. The computer, therefore, is being told to do what it cannot do. To put the machine code in the right order, you will have to go through the process called *debugging* to discover and correct the error. Bits are the final step to computer operation.

8

Your Own Home Computer System

Perhaps by now you have become excited by the prospect of owning a home computer, and have decided to invest in a system. You are in for a series of adventures not unlike those of a customer for the automobile around the turn of the century. The whole personal computing "industry" is still disorderly and fragmented, and your own activities will influence it during the next few pioneering years. While you can purchase the elements of a high-fidelity system by dropping into a store within a few minutes of your home almost anywhere you live in the United States, computer stores are unlikely to be that widespread for some time. Shopping for a suitable system is not so easy.

By the end of 1977, some 300 legitimate computer specialty stores were operating in the United States. Most of these stores are clustered in the major metropolitan areas like San Francisco, Los Angeles, New York, Chicago, and Boston, where the diligent would-be computer customer can not only play with a demonstration system, but can do genuine comparison shopping, trying out alternative computers and peripherals.

Such "stores" are listed in Appendix H of this book and in computer magazines. When home computers boomed, many individuals and small groups sensed an opportunity to get in on the ground floor of a new field without much capital. They applied for dealerships to companies that were delighted with the surge of interest and business and were willing to give "dealer" status to anybody who ordered as much as $10,000 worth of equipment. This encouraged the formation of small groups of customers who pooled their orders to reach the minimums and then obtained "dealer" discounts. When you begin your search for a suitable dealer, you may visit "store" addresses that turn out to be private homes or hole-in-the-wall shops that are open only in the evening. This is not to disparage the performance or intent of such small operations, but to point out that you can't always tell from the listings what the nature of the dealership will be. You'll want to make some inquiries before giving substantial sums of money to strangers.

Even a modest, reasonably stocked computer store represents a $100,000 investment to its proprietor these days, so the people with whom you deal are likely to be seriously dedicated to their work.

Don't look for computers in your local chain outlet just yet. If you want to get into home computing, go ahead and do it, by whatever channel is available to you. Sure, everything will be different in a couple of years, but it will all be different again two years after *that.*

If you can't comfortably deal with a computer store nearby (is that hi-fi shop carrying computers now?), you can buy computers by mail. That approach has its hazards, perhaps, but a great deal of computer business is done by mail to the satisfaction of most customers.

Selecting a Home Computer System

To refer to the pioneering automobile days again: an old gag speaks of a sign at the end of a dirt road that snakes off to the horizon. The sign says to the entering motorist: "Choose your ruts carefully; you'll be in them for the next 30 miles." Much the same caution applies to the purchase of a computer. The first item you purchase largely determines what you'll be buying in the future, unless you have the desire and the money to go back and start over at some later date.

As you will see in the Buyer's Guide (Appendix B),

every imaginable device for every purpose is available. There is a catch, though. These things cannot be randomly intermixed in systems, at least not without a lot of technical expertise provided by the customer himself. Almost any hi-fi turntable works with any amplifier and any speaker, but computer system elements are not widely compatible. You will want to choose your system very carefully.

To begin with, a computer by itself is not good for much except entertaining technicians. If you buy a computer in a box, that's what you'll get. It probably has a handsome front panel loaded with switches and lights that blink at you alluringly and mysteriously. If you're a real computer buff, all primed with enthusiasm for programming in machine language, you can throw those switches in patterns that feed the computer octal code (machine-language code). Following the code listings that are provided in the machine literature, you can actually put a program and some data into the machine and see the lights flicker while it thinks about what you said. At length, the computer stops blinking and you can decode the final pattern, learning what your program accomplished. Technicians may be pleased with this activity, but the casual user of computers needs more. This means more equipment.

One necessity is a keyboard that will type ordinary letters and numbers into the machine. Another is a display to see what has been typed and what the computer has done in response. That calls for a television monitor with the appropriate circuitry that lets the computer tell it what to show, or an automatic electric typewriter of some kind with appropriate circuitry that lets the computer tell it what to type.

That circuitry for control of the peripheral devices may be available in the form of circuit boards that plug into the computer itself, that is, into the box that houses the computer.

So far, then, the system outlined includes:

—a computer
—a keyboard

—a TV monitor or a computer-controlled typewriter
—a video control card.

What else do you want? Chances are that the random-access memory (RAM) built into the computer is minimal and that you'd like more. Add another memory card of some size to your system list.

You know you will get tired of typing long program listings into the computer (complete with the tedious task of proofreading and correcting complex material), so you probably want a tape cassette recorder that lets you read recorded program material and data directly into the computer. The same device lets you record programs and data from the computer for storage and later use. That cassette recorder (almost any cheap recorder will do) needs appropriate control circuitry—so add another card to your list.

Floppy-disc recorders are very convenient, because they operate so rapidly, with quick access to any record on the disc. Moreover, you'd like to be able to read from one disc, let the computer operate on the information, and record the altered material on a second disc. (Maybe you are updating a report or mailing list.) In fact, you may want three floppy-disc recorders so that you can merge old and new information from two discs into a third composite record.

Floppy-disc systems are not just independent pieces of hardware that require a hardware interface to a computer. The *software* for disc systems is special and the computer must be equipped with its own disc operating system (DOS) to make use of the devices.

And here is the real point of this discussion: the peripherals and related software do not work with just *any* computer; even computers using the same microprocessors are not necessarily all compatible with a given peripheral. The computer you choose has built-in "ruts." You will be stuck in those ruts when you want to buy attractive but incompatible peripherals.

Everybody in the home computing field cries aloud for standards, and a sort of *de facto* standard was established when MITS first offered its Altair computer with a 100-pin bus or S-100 Bus. This is deserving of some discussion to aid the computer customer.

Every subcircuit in a computer needs electrical power at some voltage. Usually, two or three different voltages are required at different places in a single system.

Every computer takes information from outside and puts information back out.

Certain matters like these are of universal interest to computer designers. It's possible for the designer to build from scratch every time, running power into each subsystem as necessary, creating new input and output channels wherever they seem to fit. However, the thoughtful designer plans ahead, so the overall system is consistent and doesn't just grow like Topsy.

The MITS Altair was designed around a single electronics circuit card plug that has two rows of 50 pins. Power at a particular voltage was run to a particular pin in that plug. Power at another voltage went to another pin. Input data was assigned to a particular pin . . . and so on. Circuit cards with 50 pins on a side fit into that plug and can tap power at particular, known points.

In fact, any manufacturer knowing the layout of the Altair bus—for that is what this organization of functions is called—could design a circuit card that could be plugged into the Altair and would work. A number of manufacturers did begin to make memory boards, video control boards, and the like for the Altair shortly after it was introduced, providing more variety in the computer system than the one company could produce alone. Inevitably, other companies began to produce full computers employing the same bus structure, and the Altair bus became a useful standard.

Other manufacturers hated to name MITS or use competitive computer brand names in their own ads while explaining their bus structure, so they decided informally to establish a neutral name for the standard they shared. They called it the S-100 Bus. You will see that name a great deal. MITS, of course, believes that "Altair bus" is the only proper name. It has proved difficult for them to force this view on others.

As a computer customer, do you want a system based on the S-100 Bus? There is a lot of equipment compatible with it now, but some other manufacturers scorn it and are moving in other directions, believing that the S-100 is technically awkward and unsuitable for mass-production techniques.

Choose your ruts carefully.

Unless you are already a computer technician, you will need help in figuring out what you want to buy. The storekeeper may be helpful to you. However, many such retailers are technical addicts who went into the computer-store business because of a love of engaging in technical gossip with other addicts. That sort of storekeeper may be more confusing than helpful.

Find somebody—friend, storekeeper, hired adviser, but *somebody*—to help you match your budget and your applications to the real marketplace, both present and future. (One manufacturer, just cranking up full production on a new non-S-100 system, commented: "I wish we could persuade people that the rest of our system really is coming, the printers, the floppies, and all the rest. They've been burned so often that they don't believe what we say.") What is coming? When? At what price? There's no way to anticipate the specifics of the future market more than a few months ahead of time, but you can, with help, get a sense of the important trends.

The home computer industry started with computer kits, which were far less expensive to the consumer than any computer system being manufactured at that time. The kit was a boon to the home computer enthusiast not because it was the best way to go, but because it was the only economical way to go. The first suppliers of computer kits did not so much manufacture a product as give skilled electronics hobbyists a collection of parts and a general idea of how to build a computer. In a few cases, the kits were assembled by naive builders and, miraculously, worked at once. For the most part, the assembled systems required extensive testing and debugging—including alteration of the manufacturer's faulty plans and documentation. In effect, hobbyist technicians built computers with a little help from manufacturers.

The trend has been away from kits, for various reasons. Some of the manufacturers have found that the correspondence and repair work necessary to help a customer get his system working is about as expensive as sending the customer an assembled, tested system that works when he plugs it in. More nontechnician customers are trying to buy computers. Mass-manufacturing techniques are being applied to computers for the first time, so that their cost is being reduced gradually to that of record players and television sets.

It's true that Heathkits for computers are on the market and that such well-designed, very well-documented kits will be generally available for a long time. You can build a kit if you want to, but you don't *have* to. You can build a marvelous Heathkit television set, and some people do, but they don't save appreciable money on it and most buyers choose the ready-made product.

If you do get a kit, the effort of building the computer and checking it out will give you a far better grasp of how the system works and what it can do, and you may enjoy the work. But you now have a choice between kit and ready-made at no great cost penalty.

As in most undertakings, the key to picking a satisfactory computer system is in figuring out what you want to do. Then choose hardware to serve the function, compromising where you must to fit a limited budget, but not in ignorance.

For example, you may be enchanted by the word-processing capabilities of home computers, for which you'll need a rather full system. (Many writers have observed that writing is not too difficult, but *typing* is a horrible labor. A word-processing system with its endless capacity for correction and improvement in a video display, even before any ink is put to paper, removes much of the drudgery of preparing typed documents.) Those of us who cannot type a clean-looking letter on the first or second pass are dazzled at the prospect of using a word-processing system.

However, it's almost no use fooling with the system unless the printer employed is a good one. Note that an ordinary typewriter strikes a key with a raised letter against the ribbon to imprint a character on paper backed by a platen. A good, clean typewriter with a fresh ribbon produces crisp text on the paper. If you are applying for a job, soliciting funds, dressing down bureaucrats, or recommending deserving acquaintances for honors, then clean, crisp text is what you want. Don't assume that you'll get it from any old printer.

For decades the standard computer printer has been the Teletype machine. Most Teletypes print only capital letters in a ragged row on rolls of newsprintlike paper. It's hard to crank out a good-looking letter on such a machine.

The printers designed to go with computers these days are much classier machines that work at satisfactorily high speeds, so they don't unduly waste the time of quick-as-lightning computers. The DECwriter is a prime example of such an elegant and desirable machine. However, like most new printers, the DECwriter is a *matrix printer,* at least in the standard models.

A matrix printer doesn't strike the ribbon and paper with standard typewriter keys. Instead, it punches the ends of a cluster of wires against the ribbon, imprinting the paper with a pattern of dots. Not all of the wires are pushed in for every key, so the pattern is controllable and can produce alphanumeric symbols.

They are legible, and are excellent for accounting and similar workaday applications, but chances are that you do not want to send important letters typed this way. Magazine editors, for example, hate reading submissions produced on matrix printers and are biased against the pieces even before they can consider the meanings of the symbols on the paper.

Various solutions to the problem are available. Some involve money; some involve patience.

An IBM Selectric typewriter can be adapted to computer control. It costs almost as much for a modified Selectric complete with the special interface for the computer of your choice as it does for a DECwriter. The Selectric does not have special control and command keys for the computer system, just the normal complement of keys for typing. That's a drawback. Furthermore, the Selectric will not type faster than 10 or 15 characters a second—very slow by computer standards. That is where the patience comes in. You grin and bear it, because the Selectric (or some other machine like it) will indeed produce nice, crisp finished copy.

You would probably rather have one of the magnificent "daisy-wheel" printers, like the Qume or Diablo machines now available at high, but not ridiculous, cost. These devices are the stuff that dreams are made of. They use neither wire matrices nor type balls, but constantly whirling discs equipped with "petals" on which raised letters are formed. The printer notices which letter has been requested, either by the computer or your typing finger, then taps the right petal smartly when it comes flying by to make a clean impression on the paper.

The daisy-wheel machines are miracles of timing, and they perform marvelous electronic tricks as well. They operate very fast. Just what you need for word-processing, if you can afford them.

Similar considerations affect every item in the system. If you plan to enter a great many numerical values in your computer applications, you will surely want a 10-key numerical pad (like that on a pocket calculator) on your input keyboard. If you *need* a light pen to manipulate graphics quickly, don't fail to get it out of sheer forgetfulness.

Your own hopes, dreams, fears, and needs are much more important than the convenience of the dealer, who may not be familiar with lines other than his own. If he will not search, you do it.

Chances are that you can buy substantially what you need to serve your purposes if you can define your purposes.

Getting the System Up and Running

The elements of your computer system will probably be packed in boxes when they come to you. You'll get 100,000 plastic-foam packing peanuts in the bargain. As you sort the computer system out from among the peanuts, check carefully for odd little packets of product that might easily be lost.

If you are unpacking a kit, of course, you'll want to count every last little resistor and screw, checking the items off the master list (if any) so that you know what is missing. Something is always missing, either backordered or forgotten. Take nothing for granted. Look for, and at, everything.

Computers don't travel very well. There's not much to break (except switches and the video tubes in displays), but everything tends to come loose. All circuit cards tend to work loose in their sockets. Sheet-metal screws come loose in transit. Nuts and bolts separate. Your best course is to assume that everything has come apart and to go through the whole system, carefully pushing things into place and tightening up whatever seems to be loose. Caution: Do not just go wild with the screwdriver, turning things until they snap off. Be firm, not brutal; and whatever you do, do not arbitrarily tighten things on the circuit boards just because they have slots in them made to receive the screwdriver. Occasionally you'll find potentiometers (variable resistors) with screw adjustments. Do not monkey with them unless you know what you are doing.

Find a place to set up the system where it can stay for a while without antagonizing other members of the family, who ordinarily resent commandeering of useful work surfaces like the kitchen table. You don't want to move the system while you're working on it, because if it has startup problems, you won't know for sure whether you're pulling plugs loose, or what. Check the system in one place.

The literature provided with your system may not be in English, but in technicalese designed for a qualified digital engineer. Your sensible course is to do the best you can to follow the documentation and get the system running if you can without damaging anything. As time passes, and manufacturers deal increasingly with intelligent, nontechnical customers, the odds will improve that any given system will work just fine when it's plugged in and that the naive user will be able to get the software up and running.

If the literature proves to be gibberish, your primary recourse is to go back to the dealer and demand step-by-step assistance. This may solve your problem, and you'll come back to your system with a sheaf of notes on setting the Parity bits, turning on the bootstrap loader, and so on, that will let you whiz through the process. More likely, you'll relieve your feelings a bit by hollering at somebody and writing a good tart letter, but the obscure matters will remain obscure.

This is where your friendship with an experienced computer hand will pay off—or your membership in a computer club. Somebody who knows computers can help you get the system up and show you how to keep it going. This whole field of home computing was made possible not by computer *users* but by computer *hobbyists,* enthusiastic technical tinkerers who were able to make poorly designed and badly documented systems work. Find such a useful citizen if you plan to acquire a complex computer system that is not yet designed for the ham-handed consumer. You will need help.

Once you are running, of course, the electronics systems fail infrequently. Mechanical devices like printers and floppy discs do tend to get out of adjustment and call for tender care, but those problems are not fundamental, merely annoying.

Programming

It is important to understand what you are doing when you program and operate a computer. Here is a simple analogy. Imagine that an extraterrestrial being has landed on earth. You want to show the being how to do something, such as ride a bike. Many things have to be explained.

First, you have to understand how the being processes information; i.e., what its language is, how it goes from one thought to another, and how it organizes and tests the information that it gathers in order to know what to do. You then have to test the being to know its logic. This is what you do with a computer. You must know how it deals with the information that you give it. This is revealed in the way it assembles, sorts, integrates, and then uses data and refers to its memory.

So, if you want to describe riding a bike, you have to understand in what sequence you say and/or show instructions to the being. For example, you have to explain why one rides a bike in the first place; why gravity helps to balance the bike; why pressing on the pedals makes the chain turn the wheels; and so on. The order in which you tell the being about this depends on how it processes information. If it needs general information first, you begin with an explanation of gravity. If it needs specific information, you explain the way the chain is linked to the wheel. If your information is out of order, the being will not be able to ride the bike.

Once the fundamental ideas have been explained, the being has to explore the variable data. This is similar to the data you feed into the computer once the rules of operation have been fed in and organized. Thus, if the being understands the rules of gravity, $F = MA$ (see page 229), how the bike is constructed to meet those rules, you then feed in the slope of the hill on which the being is to ride, the size of the tires, the strength of the being's legs, the surface on which it will ride, the ratio of gears on the bike, etc.

Perhaps in describing the bike you are so eager to explain it in motion that you forget to explain how the brakes work. If so, the being will get started only to crash at the first obstacle. This is the same as if you program a computer to do some set or problem and never terminate the program: the computer operates forever, or it does not begin at all because it has a built-in logic that never starts unless it knows how to stop. The being perhaps operates in a similar way, and you may have lost its confidence by not including the brakes in your explanation.

Thus, when you program a computer, you do the following: (1) learn the logic and order of a description of a process; (2) enter this logic into the computer in a way that matches its own logical setup, providing the cycles of operations; (3) feed in the variables and let the computer run; (4) learn by repeating this process.

If you are not a disciplined computer enthusiast, but merely a computer user who wants to use the system as a tool for accomplishing certain tasks, then you probably want to use a high-level language for programming the system. In its most primitive state, a computer requires its operator to throw switches in certain patterns to enter data and set up programs. These patterns can be stated in strings of binary numbers. At a slightly higher level of development, the computer can be addressed with more compact octal or hexadecimal codes that the computer recognizes as commands. It uses these commands to set all those switches in the proper binary configuration without nearly so much detailed work on the operator's part. At a still higher level, the computer recognizes words, ordinary numbers, and sentences written in the tightly stylized syntax of some "computer language" like BASIC, FORTRAN, COBOL, APL, or a hundred others.

These high-level languages approach "natural human language" more and more closely, making it increasingly easy for the operator to instruct the computer without knowing much about the machine. If it's easier for the operator, it's harder for the machine, of course, and the higher-level languages are less efficient in their use of the computer. In general, programs well written in machine language run faster and require less RAM for operation than do programs in higher-level languages. (Indeed, this may affect your choice of computers for purchase. If you are a capable machine-language programmer, you can squeeze more performance out of a small system than the casual user finds practical.)

All manufacturers of home computer systems have found it necessary to provide some higher-level language to their customers. Ordinarily, that language is BASIC, which is regarded widely as the easiest approach to making a computer do something in particular. Other languages are increasingly available as programmers adapt them from the big systems for which they were originally developed to the more limited microcomputers used personally. FORTRAN, for example, is now generally available.

The virtue of adapting languages like BASIC and FORTRAN to home computers is that a vast body of program literature already exists in these languages. Ideally, for a number of years, we can tap the great reservoir of programs developed in business and government over the years. Presumably, smart people who have learned a great deal from experience could write a whole new set of better languages, but the price of conversion is painfully high. Home computers are communicating in the languages of their parents.

On the other hand, the virtue of the tradition is largely an illusion. You will discover this when you bring your own system up. Home computers using BASIC do not simply speak a pure mother tongue of BASIC or ALGOL or what-have-you. They speak dialects of the mother tongue, and computers are terrible linguists. Each understands *only* its own dialect and regards other dialects as gibberish.

The particular dialect of the computer you purchase will be determined largely by the microprocessor on which it's based. When MITS first produced the Altair for personal use, one of the smartest moves the company made was to acquire rights to a BASIC dialect written specifically for the 8080 microprocessor at the heart of the Altair. This became Altair BASIC, and by all reports, it is extremely well written, running in 8K of RAM very efficiently. Enthusiastic users have freely stolen Altair BASIC, which was written by Microsoft, Inc., for use in other 8080 systems.

All users of Altair BASIC can exchange programs freely. On the other hand, programs written in Altair

BASIC do not run on 6502-microprocessor based machines like the Apple, OSI, or Commodore products, and vice versa. Microsoft has written BASIC for Commodore and OSI, so it is not lack of knowledge or differing philosophy that makes the dialects mutually unintelligible. It is the fact that the hardware is slightly different from case to case. Yes, any real programmer can interpret from one dialect to another readily, but the casual user of computers cannot be sure that just any program is going to work.

This is all by way of explaining that every home computer is a special case. No general trial programs are available for use on new systems, and no set of instructions is generally applicable. You will want to discuss this all very carefully with your dealer or other consultant before taking the plunge. Some nonspecific comments here may be useful.

Virtually all home computers these days are equipped with circuit boards containing "bootstrap" programs in read-only memory (ROM). These boards enormously ease the operator's task in setting up the computer for use. BASIC does not live in the RAM of the computer when the machine comes from the factory. If you want BASIC in your computer, you have to put it there, either by switching the codes into the computer through its front panel switches or reading in the codes automatically from punched paper tape or magnetic recordings on tape or disc.

Even the automatic systems need some help. That is where the bootstrap comes in. There's just enough information in permanent memory so that the computer knows what to do with BASIC when it begins to come in. It knows where to put everything. That is a big help. Even at that, it may take anywhere from 5 to 30 minutes to load BASIC into the machine, and if the tape is bad or some hiccup occurs in the electrical system, you will have to go back to start over. (Imagine your frustration if you must switch in BASIC by hand and the dog stumbles over the power cord and the computer forgets what it knows.)

Better by far is the scheme of putting BASIC (or some other language of your choice) into read-only memory, *complete,* so that when you give the command, BASIC is dumped into RAM in a second or two and you can get on about your business. As memory prices have dropped spectacularly, it has become practical to dedicate 12K of ROM to this purpose. Ordinarily, the ROM contains an operating system in addition to the language so the computer is always set up to operate with peripherals.

Once again, price controls the use of ROM for many other applications. You should be able to buy ROM boards with alternate languages so you can switch from one to another promptly. You should be able to buy full libraries of useful subroutines in ROM, say the makings of an accounting system that you adapt to your particular needs, or an inventory control system, or sets of statistical routines. Software in this form will proliferate grandly with growth of the market.

To get your system up and running, the manufacturer usually provides a test program or two that will let you debug your system, checking to see that certain functions are actually working and that information is where it should be. The manufacturer usually provides a game or two on tape cassette (Star Trek, typically) so that you can both check the system and do something real with it, even if you're a complete novice.

You may spend the rest of your life playing Star Trek or press on to becoming a real programmer. It is up to you.

Service and Repair

One computer retailer who has opened stores in many communities has commented on the "up-front phenomenon." An hour before the store is scheduled to open on its first day, a long line forms out front. Its members are all carrying hardware that they've built at home and are hoping to have repaired.

Service is still a difficult problem. IBM, of course, has solved the problem in its usual fashion. The company makes a truly fine home computer system, the 5100, complete with a video display and a tape memory in a single tidy package with the computer itself. The introductory price was about $9,000—high, but not outrageous for a good system with the capability of the 5100. One can buy a service contract for the 5100, just as one can buy one for an IBM Selectric typewriter. The low version of that contract was priced at $85 per month, with higher charges for more complex versions of the system. Service is excellent.

At this writing, IBM has not committed itself to fixed-price service contracts. No "typical" service-contract price has been established, though many computer stores have made a point of giving good service. Skilled technicians in those service departments charge $15 to $25 an hour for work on home computers. With their oscilloscopes and an array of other equipment, their work is really a bargain at those prices . . . but will you need much of their help? Probably not.

Recall that computers have never been manufactured in true mass-production style by anyone, anywhere in the world. If color television sets were still made the way computers are made, they would still cost $2,000 apiece and could be serviced only at the factory. Consider an example of this:

A party was visiting the manufacturing plant of a Midwestern manufacturer of record players. The host pointed to one of his production lines and commented that he could produce 11,000 record players a day on that one line. One of the guests, who happened to work for General Electric, admired the line, commenting: "That's a handsome setup, just right for what you're doing. Of course, if you ever get up to real mass production of a product like that, you need somebody like us or RCA or Zenith to handle it." The other guests, who had been frantically calculating in their heads, were astounded. This one line could produce

2.5 million record players in a year, but that didn't count as mass production.

Nobody is set up to produce 100,000 computers in a year now. Things are changing very rapidly, but the disciplines of quality control in large production have not yet been visited on computers. As those disciplines are brought to bear, computers will become as reliable as television sets and typewriters.

In the meantime, remember that warm friendship you have worked up with a technically competent friend. Troubleshooting and maintenance help can be extremely valuable to him or her. There's just no substitute for somebody who enjoys fooling with the equipment.

The dealer who sells you the equipment is honor-bound to make the system sold to you work somehow, even if it's a kit that you have mangled yourself. The dealer wants to be on good terms with you so that you'll be a long-term customer. He will probably cast an interested eye on your problems and help with diagnosis. But without going broke, the dealer cannot indefinitely treat your equipment and fix it gratis.

Again, the electronics seldom fail, once they are up, but mechanical systems are fussier. Your car needs attention more often than your television set. You will probably find more problems with your peripherals than with the computer itself, and more problems in the interfaces than in either computer or peripherals. If the timing changes in a peripheral, the computer may not be able to understand what it is doing. If plugs and connectors get tarnished or dirty, intermittent problems will develop in the system. These are not big problems, just annoying. You will find that simple maintenance procedures will keep your system in good shape for years.

If you are a technician, none of this is news to you. If you are not, you will want to pick your system with an eye to reliability and your dealer with an eye to his competence as a service center.

In Summary

You must be able to make hard decisions about yourself, your interests, your capabilities, and your personality in order to make sensible decisions about the computer system you might like to own and use.

The market already has something for everyone, and you can confidently expect to put exciting computer power to work for your purposes if you study yourself and the market with equal care.

9

The Home Computer Software Scene

How do you get a home computer to work? What do you do once the system is sitting in your home, plugged in and humming? What are the first steps?

First of all, do you want to learn to program? If you do, you must learn the language necessary to tell your computer what to do with information. It is detailed, time-consuming work. You do not have to know how to program in order to run your home computer system. Cassette tapes are available which allow you to enter (1) assembler information; (2) program language; and (3) program information into the computer's CPU and its memory. Floppy discs may also be used as storage mechanisms or as a method for entering data. But compared to cassette tapes, they cost more and are generally less available.

The following steps are necessary in order to begin to operate your home computer:

Step 1

First, you need an assembler cassette. This will instruct your CPU as to how it should operate. The CPU needs this information to know how it is going to receive information, how it is going to display it, etc. The assembler cassette is placed into the cassette tape deck. Using your keyboard, you instruct your computer what to do by following the instructions that come with your system and the assembler cassette. These instructions will direct the home computer CPU to take the information from the cassette and enter it into the assembler, thereby activating the proper machine codes and instructions. The results of feeding this tape into the CPU will be displayed on your CRT.

Step 2

Now you need a language tape. Most home computers offer BASIC as a standard language. This is a standard language, since most of the instructions are in English and not computerese. For example, you can load a program into the computer from a cassette simply by typing the word LOAD on the keyboard. If you use a BASIC cassette, this will be the language used to enter information through your keyboard and to display information on the CRT. BASIC usually comes in either 4K or 8K. The choice between the two depends on the size of the programs you will enter and use once the language is in your machine.

Step 3

Your home computer is now ready to accept a program. If you are a computer programmer you can do it yourself. Chances are you will want to purchase program cassettes instead. Such programs range in application from home accounting to solving mathematical problems to playing games. (See discussion later in this chapter.) Once you decide which program to buy, you place the cassette in the tape deck. Following the instructions that came with your BASIC cassette, you use your keyboard to instruct the computer to read the program from the cassette deck. Now the program is in your home computer. If, for example, you are using a home accounting program, your CRT will display "Enter your monthly expense categories." You then enter "rent, automobile, utilities," etc., following the instructions for the program and the BASIC cassette. Next, other questions appear and you follow the course of the program. The CRT displays the results as you enter necessary information on your keyboard. You can use a floppy disc to store both the program and your use of it. This makes possible access to and retrieval of information.

Most software, including assembler, program language, and programs, include detailed instruction manuals to tell you how to operate the keyboard once you have entered the program through the cassette. You can begin to operate your home computer (without knowing how to program) once you have a keyboard, a CRT, a CPU (of course), and a cassette tape deck. Without the cassette tape deck, you will have to program the entire process yourself and enter the assembler, program languages, and programs through your keyboard.

Once you develop familiarity with your home computer, you may want to learn programming. This will enable you to create your own tapes, or modify existing languages to suit your purposes. It will also allow you to use the extensive software available in written form. This kind of software involves meticulous step-by-step entry on your keyboard.

Available Programs

What programs are available in cassette form? A brief sampler from several home computer companies follows:

Polymorphic Systems Inc.

Among software programs offered in BASIC by Polymorphic Systems are:

Cashflow, a program which is a personal financial package used to write budgets, record transactions and reconcile checking accounts.

Lander, a game program which tests your skill as a lunar astronaut. You must use your retrorocket skillfully and efficiently to land softly on the moon. This involves selecting and varying the rocket thrust, and keeping your eye on altitude, speed, and fuel consumption. Each game is slightly different. Miss the platform and you crash. The computer will then provide a critique of your flying skills.

Other Polymorphic Systems games and problems include Backgammon, Hangman, Craps, Horse, Biocycle, and The Manhattan Indian Problem.

Cromemco

Software (punched paper tape) programs available from Cromemco and priced at $15 each include: Spacewar (two persons); Life, in full color; Dazzle-Writer, for alphanumeric displays in color; Dazzle-mation; Tic-Tac-Toe (you play the computer); Dazzle-Doodle (1 person; you draw pictures in four colors); Track (1 person; move the dot to the center of spiral); and Kaleidoscope, in full color.

Compucolor

Compucolor Corporation designs programs priced at $11.95 to take full advantage of the graphics and color capability of the Compucolor 8001. Programs include: Acey Deucey; Biorhythms; Blackjack; Bluff; Checkbook; Christmas/Space Ship; Lunar Lander; Master Bagel; Math/Dice; Math Tutor; One-Armed Bandit; Star Trek #1; Two-to-Ten; Checkers; Chess; Risk #2; Risk #6; and Star Trek #2.

Digital Group Systems Inc.

Software systems available from the Digital Group Software Systems Inc. include Super Clock, a program that allows you to turn your home computer into a very expensive clock. It can be set as a 24-hour or 12-1 hour clock and gives hours, minutes, and seconds. Includes source listing and operating instructions.

Maxi-Basic Game Set 1.

Magic-Square: computer vs. human in an attempt to complete a Magic-Square while blocking the opponent.

Depth-Charge: Sink the submarine before it sinks you, a three-dimensional search game.

Reverse: A Maxi version of the popular solitaire game of number manipulation.

Bagels: Try to guess the computer's number based on such clues as PICO FERMI and BAGELS.

Birthday: Learn some interesting and important facts about what has transpired since your natal day.

Maxi-Basic Game Set 2.

Word: A word guessing game which includes 102 five-letter words.

Gunnery: A challenging artillery game which includes windage and shot variations.

Wombat: A grid-search game to find the wombat.

Sunsign: Given certain factors which are different for every individual, this program produces unique signs.

Compound-Interest: If you put $10 out of each paycheck in the bank at 6%, how much would you have in 10 years?

Maxi-Basic Game Set 3.

Awari: Modeled after an ancient African game of skill and strategy—you against the computer.

Target: space war in three dimensions using circular coordinates.

Bulcow: a numbers guessing game with clues as to the relationship of your guess to the number.

Loan-Payments: This program computes the payment schedule for a loan.

Button: a guessing game where you try to guess which one of seven "people" has the button; they give you clues.

Maxi-Basic Game Set 4.

Hurkle: Find the shy Hurkle in the grid, using computer-supplied clues.

ICBM: You are the controller for an antimissile base —get the ICBM before it gets you.

Change: Computes change in bills and coins given the price and amount tendered.

Radiz Arith: In the duodecimal system (base 12), how much is 3A + B7?

Letter: Guess a letter given clues relative to your last guess.

Number: Find the secret number in the minimum number of tries.

Maxi-Basic Game Set 5.

Fipfop: Change a row of X's to O's with a new set of rules for each game.

NIM: Modeled after an ancient Chinese game.

Hangman: Beautiful graphics make this word-guessing game great fun to play.

Taxman: Learn factoring while trying to outfox the Taxman.

Checkbook: This program can help you balance your checkbook.

Maxi-Basic Game Set 6.

Lunar Landing: a somewhat out-of-the-ordinary Lunar Lander which can be beaten.

23 Matches: Develop a strategy so that you don't have to take the last match.

Radix Conv: Converts any number up to 262143 decimal to octal and vice versa.

Pizza: a "screwball" game where you have to figure out where the pizzas go.

Biorhythm: A very comprehensive version of Biorhythm which flags "critical" days and computes the composite.

Maxi-Basic Game Set 7.

Bridge-Dealer: generates and deals bridge hands all sorted and arranged.

War-Cards: This popular card game pits you against the computer for control of the deck.

Acey-Deucy: a game designed to drive sane people nuts when they match the pot on a King-Three.

Horserace: They're off and running at "Wherever Racetrack." Good odds, several horses, and unlimited bets.

Blackjack: A casino-level version of this game; plays by Vegas rules for a dealer.

Kingdom-Life 1 & 2: Kingdom lets you be "King" of land/bushels/acres and population of your "Kingdom." Object is to accumulate 1 million acres and/or bushels, which can only be done by buying and selling land. Life 1 is standard Life which takes a pattern and, with simple Life rules, iterates until a stable situation is reached. Life 2 is a bisymmetrical pattern generator but a stable situation is never reached. It will continue to run and never repeat a pattern for approximately 10^{31} years.

Galaxy: A true *Star Trek* game complete in every respect. Your mission: to destroy some number of Klingons in a specified number of star dates. Seven commands permit three levels of scanning, movement in 16 different directions at 64 different speeds. Phasers and Photon Torpedoes as weapons and energy transfers to the shields in battle. Star Bases are available for reprovisioning between battles.

Tiny Basic Extended Games:

Chomp, Checkers, 20-Questions, Chief for Z-80 Systems:

Assembler, disassembler, text editor.

MITS, Inc.

The available software packages from MITS include:

Altair Business System: floppy disc packages for keeping general ledgers concerning business transactions, for keeping track of receivable, payable, and payroll accounts, for processing texts, and for managing inventory;

Altair 4K, 8K, and Extended BASIC: in cassette form for handling numerical and alphanumeric data.

National Semiconductor

Software from National Semiconductor includes:

Paper tape coded in NIBL (National Industrial Basic Language) for use with the 8-bit SC/MP microprocessor.

Southwest Technical Products

SWTP software includes:

4K BASIC software packages available in both cassette tape and paper tape form;

8K BASIC software packages also available in cassette tape and paper tape form.

iCOM Microperipherals

This peripheral company provides software including:

iCOM BASIC-M: floppy disc packages for programming microcomputers to handle accounting, inventory, and mailing list data.

HAL Communications

HAL Communications' software includes:

8K Floating Point BASIC in cassette form for use with HAL EIGHT THOUSAND System.

Ohio Scientific Instruments

OSI software comes on their Auto-Load™ cassettes and includes:

4K and 8K Tiny BASIC, 6502 Resident Assembler, Extended Monitor, "Life," Graphics editor, 6502 8K BASIC, and games.

Microcomputer Associates

Microcomputer Associates software includes:

RAP/Tiny BASIC ROM packages;

RAP/Tiny BASIC on seven 1702A PROMs;

Tiny BASIC on paper tape;

Tiny BASIC on nine 1702A PROMs.

Appendix A:

Glossary of Home Computer Terms

accumulator (AC): an area of circuitry contained in the CPU for temporarily storing data words accessed out of memory, arithmetic and logical operands, and results of CPU operations.

address: a code that specifies the location of memory words in memory.

algorithm: a well-defined set of rules pertaining to the solution of a problem in a definite number of steps.

alphanumeric: a term describing information that consists of both letters and numbers.

analog computer: a computer in which quantities are represented by physical entities (e.g., angle of gear) and one continuous signal (discrete signals are used in digital computers).

AND: a Boolean logic operator.

arithmetic logic unit (ALU): the logic components contained in the CPU which are responsible for carrying out arithmetic and Boolean logic operations on binary data.

artificial intelligence: the mode of programming which allows a computer to operate on its own, for example to learn, adapt, reason, or correct and improve itself.

ASCII: American Standard Code for Information Interchange.

assembler: a program which translates an assembly-language source program into a machine-language object program that can be loaded immediately into the computer.

assembly language: a language used for writing source programs; it uses a symbolic form to represent instructions and must be translated by assembler program into machine code before being used by computer.

assembly program: a source program written in symbolic language which will be translated into machine language by assembler.

asynchronous operation: describes machine operations which are triggered successively not by a clock but by the completion of an operation.

base number: that number which is the basis for counting in a particular number system; e.g., 10 is the base number for the decimal number system.

baud: signifies the measure of serial data transmission in bits per second.

benchmark program: a program that aids in the evaluation and comparison of computers.

binary-coded decimal (BCD): a mode of representing decimal numbers in patterns of 1's and 0's.

binary data: data which is written in binary, octal, or hexadecimal form and which can indicate various codes to be used for computer operation.

binary digit (bit): In the binary system, a bit can represent either 1 or 0; to a computer, a bit will indicate an off or on signal. Bits are the units of information which, when combined in certain configurations, will signal to the computer what it is to do.

bistable: describes that which is able to assume one of two stable states; e.g., a flip-flop circuit is bistable.

Boolean Algebra: a system of logic expressed in mathematical terms developed by George Boole (1815–64) on which computer logic operations have been based.

bootstrap loader: a technique or device used to lead a routine into computer memory.

branch (jump): a means of departing from the sequence of the main program to another routine or sequence of operations as indicated by a branch instruction whose execution is dependent on the conditions of the results of computer operations.

breadboard: describes the rough model for constructing another device, usually referring to a circuit board which has a specific configuration on it.

breakpoint: a point in a computer program specified by the computer user when the program is to stop running so that the user can check it for error and change it if necessary.

buffer: A temporary storage device connected to a storage device for holding data so that inequalities in speeds of peripheral operations, for example, can be compensated for.

bug: an error in program or defect in computer hardware causing a malfunction in computer operation.

bus: a circuit path over which data and/or instructions are transferred throughout the computer. Buses allow for the transmission of information among memory, CPU, and I/O devices. Different bus lines have specific purposes; e.g., data bus, address bus, control bus, etc. S–100 Bus is becoming an industry standard—it means there are 100 connections to circuits.

byte: a unit of information composed of 8 bits, which is treated by the computer as a single unit.

card punch: a peripheral device for punching holes in cards in specific arrays for the purpose of storing information.

Carry bit: a conditional status flag bit contained in a CPU accumulator.

cassette: a medium for the electronic storage of data similar to magnetic tape.

cathode ray tube (CRT): a display unit output device resembling a TV tube.

central processing unit (CPU): the part of computer hardware that is responsible for interpreting data and executing instructions. The CPU contains the ALU, accumulators, program counter, data counter, instruction register, control unit, etc.

characters: describes units of data arranged in order to express information; characters can represent the digits 0–9, the letters A–Z, punctuation marks, and other symbols which are coded in bits for computer use.

chip: describes the semiconductor material on which integrated circuits are imprinted. A rectangular or square silicon chip is cut from a circular silicon wafer in mass production; the chip can range in size from less than 1/10 inch on a side to more than 1/4 inch.

clock: a device that initiates pulses for the synchronization of computer operations.

code: a means to represent information conforming to a set of rules. A code can represent discrete signals which can specify numbers, letters, and other symbols.

compiler: a program which translates a high-level language source program into a machine-language object program to be loaded into the computer.

computer: an electronic calculating device which is programmable and which processes, operates on, and outputs information according to its stored program upon receipt of signals through an I/O device.

computer language: a language that is used for programming a computer.

computer science: the area of science that concentrates on the development and application of computers. It is derived from mathematics, logic, language and programming development, computer hardware design, and engineering of computer systems.

control unit (CU): the hardware contained in the CPU which controls the sequencing of operations, interpretation of codes, and the allocation of signals to their proper place.

cross assembler: a program that works in one kind of computer to translate source programs into object programs to be loaded into another kind of computer.

cybernetics: the science of control and communications among systems.

cycle: the time interval for completing a set of machine operations.

cycle stealing: the process of controlling the CPU during direct memory access.

data: the information (or set of signals) that is processed by a computer.

data processing: the computer activity of receiving information, operating on it, and producing a desired result.

data word: a unit of data to be operated on by a computer.

debug: to find and correct a malfunction in computer operation or in a program.

decode: in machine operation, to translate data and/or instructions to determine exactly how and where signals are to be sent.

De Morgan's Theorem: allows Boolean operations to be stated in terms of AND and NOT.

digital computer: a computer that processes information in response to discrete signals (an analog computer uses a continuous signal).

digital to analog converter (DAC): a device that changes digital signals into one continuous signal.

diode: an electronic device having two terminals which allows current to flow in one direction.

direct memory access (DMA): a procedure used to access data stored in a high-speed storage device (e.g., magnetic tape) without involving the CPU.

disc (disk): a device resembling a phonograph record on which data can be magnetically stored.

display device: an output device that stores results from computer operation and translates them into graphic, numerical, or literal symbols to be seen by the computer user.

driver: a control unit for peripheral device; e.g., a floppy disc drive.

dual in-line package (DIP): a device on which a microprocessor chip is mounted to connect it with the rest of the computer.

EBCDIC: Extended Binary Coded Decimal Interchange Code.

editor: a program used in the preparation of text material for assembly-language source programs.

EDP: electronic data processing.

EXCLUSIVE OR: a Boolean logic operator.

execute: in machine operation, to interpret instructions and carry out designated operations.

feedback (loop): the information which is output to a system to inform it of its present condition so that the desired activity of the system is reached; e.g., a thermostat.

fetch: in machine operation, to access data and/or instructions from memory and bring it to the CPU to be operated on.

firmware: fixed software (microprogram) by hardware manufacturer that is put into ROM and is not changeable.

flag bit: a bit which specifically indicates a condition or status to be met by arithmetic operations; e.g., Carry, Overflow, Zero, Sign, Parity.

flip-flop circuit: a type of circuitry configuration which can assume one of two states and which will not change until a signal is given it to do so.

floppy disc: a device for storing data external to the computer mainframe. It is a thin plastic square which looks like a record but is thinner and so called "floppy."

flow chart: the representation of a computer program procedure which aids a programmer in determining the exact sequence of instructions which will be stated in the program as well as the data that is to be manipulated.

gate: a circuitry configuration which has several input channels and one output channel.

hardware: the physical equipment which makes up a computer system.

hexadecimal: describes the number system whose base number is 16 and which uses the digits 0–9, A,B,C,D,E,F.

high-level language: a problem-oriented computer programming language—e.g., FORTRAN, APL, and COBOL—which requires the use of a compiler program before any program written in the language can be understood by a computer.

Hollerith code: an alphanumeric code punched on cards, developed by Hans Hollerith in 1889.

input: describes the signals that are given to a computer for processing.

input device: hardware used for putting data into a computer for processing; e.g., a keyboard.

input/output device (I/O device): the hardware used for communication with a computer.

input/output port: connection between the CPU and an external I/O device.

instruction: the coded set of bits which specifies the operation a computer is to carry out.

instruction register (IR): the register contained in the CPU which retains the currently-being-executed instruction.

instruction set: the specific group of instructions that a particular computer is capable of executing because of the configuration of its machinery.

integrated circuit (IC): describes a number of interconnected circuits imprinted on semiconductor material.

integration: describes the complexity of gates contained on a single chip; e.g., MSI, medium-scale integration

(100–1,000 gates per chip), or LSI, large-scale integration (over 1,000 gates per chip).

interface: the connection between two systems.

interpreter: a program which translates an interpretive-language source program into machine code and operates on it immediately rather than producing an object program.

interrupt: a stop in computer operation due to machine malfunction or error in program.

interrupt service routine: a routine implemented in case of interrupt signal to save presently-being-operated-on information in the stack, to take care of cause for interrupt, and return the computer to previous operation before interrupt occurred.

inverter: a circuit that converts a signal into the opposite signal.

K: symbol meaning 1,024, used to describe the number of information units (bits, bytes, or words) that can be stored in a computer system.

keyboard: an I/O device that encodes data by the pressing of keys.

LCD: liquid-crystal display.

LED: light-emitting diode.

line printer: a peripheral device that prints data in lines or columns.

loader: a program which transfers a program from an input device into random-access memory.

logic: an area of mathematics that deals with the relationship among events.

logical circuit: interconnected logic elements; a switching circuit.

logic element: a circuit configuration such as an AND gate or a flip-flop circuit.

loop: a series of instructions which is self-contained and whose last instruction specifies a repetition of the entire series until a preset condition is reached to stop the repetition.

machine cycle: the amount of time it takes for the CPU to carry out an operation.

machine language: the binary language or machine code that is immediately understood by the computer. All programs not in machine language must be translated into machine language before being loaded into computer memory.

macroprogram (see microprogram): a group of procedural statements which consist of macroinstructions which are sequences of microinstructions, the instructions which are the microprogram.

mainframe: the main part of the computer containing the processing unit.

medium, I/O: the means to carry data and instructions in and out of the computer.

memory: the area in the computer for storage of data and instructions.

memory address: a coded designation for the location of a memory word.

memory addressing modes: the ways in which the memory can be addressed; the mode can be indirect, direct, immediate, relative, or indexed.

memory word: the smallest unit of information that can be accessed out of memory.

microcomputer: a digital computer whose processing unit is a microprocessor, whose common word length is 8 bits, and whose cost is less than $500 (a minicomputer has a word length up to 36 bits and can cost up to $25,000).

microprocessing unit (MPU): microcomputer hardware composed of a group of separate elements including read-only memory and random-access memory, microprocessor, interface logic for I/O, timing circuitry, and circuitry for transmitting signals from one element to another.

microprocessor: the LSI central processing unit of a microcomputer.

microprogram: the set of computer instructions in read-only memory.

mnemonic: symbolic name assigned to an instruction, a particular register, a certain memory location, etc.

MODEM: (Modulation/Demodulation) describes the device that is used for hooking up a computer with a remote terminal over telephone lines.

MOS: metal-oxide semiconductor.

p-channel MOS (PMOS): type of semiconductor where current can pass through holes rather than through silicon crystals;

n-channel MOS (NMOS): a semiconductor where current can pass through silicon crystals; faster than PMOS;

VMOS: a semiconductor where material is inscribed with V-shaped grooves in addition to having NMOS capability; faster than NMOS;

CMOS (complementary MOS): type of semiconductor that uses both p- and n-channel MOS technology.

NAND: a Boolean logic operator combining NOT and AND.

NANO: 10^{-9} times a unit; e.g., a nanosecond is 10^{-9} second, or 1,000,000,000th of a second.

nesting: describes the way subroutines, which can be called into action by other subroutines, are packed together.

NOR: a Boolean logic operator combining logical operations **NOT** and **OR.**

NOT: a Boolean logic operator specifying negation.

object program: the machine-language program which can be loaded into computer; a result of assembler or compiler program execution on an assembly-language or high-level-language source program.

octal: describes a number system whose base number is 8.

on-line: describes the direct interaction of devices with a computer processor.

operand: a quantity on which an operation is performed.

operator: a symbol representing the operations to be performed on an operand.

OR: a Boolean logic operator.

output: the results of computer operations on input.

output device: the hardware that receives processed input signals and puts them into a form understandable to computer user; e.g., a line printer.

Overflow flag bit: A condition flag bit which is set to signal if results of CPU operation exceed the number of bits that will fit into a register.

page: describes a way in which memory locations are grouped in terms of high-order address bits.

paper tape: a storage medium also usable as an input medium.

parallel I/O: describes information that is transferred simultaneously unlike serial I/O.

Parity bit: a flag bit that checks for the accurate transfer of data from memory to processor.

PCM: plug-compatible manufacturers.

peripheral device: a piece of equipment that works outside the computer mainframe.

program: a set of instructions arranged in a specific sequence for directing the execution of a specific task or the solution of a problem by a computer.

program counter: a register in the CPU that retains the instruction address to be fetched and executed.

programmable read-only memory (PROM): a ROM device which is programmable by computer user and functions like ROM cf. (EPROM can be erased and reprogrammed by the computer user).

punched card: a card on which information is recorded in the form of holes; a storage medium also usable as an input medium.

random-access memory (RAM): a storage device, consisting of a number of chips, which can be read from and written into and is, therefore, changeable in computer operation.

read-only memory (ROM): a storage device that cannot be changed in computer operation and can only be read from. It is used mainly for storage of the microprogram.

register: One or more registers are contained in the CPU and are used for temporary storage of information for the facilitation of the efficiency of CPU operation.

routine/subroutine: a small program used to guide a more specific task than is to be performed through the execution of the main program.

scratchpad memory: a temporary storage device such as register or accumulator.

semiconductor: a material such as silicon on which integrated circuits are imprinted.

serial I/O: describes information that is transferred sequentially, unlike parallel I/O.

signal: an electronic pulse that conveys information.

Sign bit: a flag bit which specifies the algebraic sign of the result of an arithmetic operation.

software: the term used to describe the information that a computer handles; e.g., program, language.

source program: the original program that is written in assembly or high-level language and is translated into a machine-language object program for use in the computer by an assembler or compiler program (respectively).

stack (register): a temporary storage device used especially in the case of interruption in computer operation because of machine malfunction or program error.

switching: causing connection or breaking connection in a circuit.

synchronous: describes the use of a clock to synchronize data transfer operations.

terminal: the I/O hardware that can link up to a computer.

time-sharing: a means by which one or more terminals can be connected to and work with one central computer system.

truth table: a mathematical table demonstrating the relationships among variables according to Boolean logic operations.

TTY: Teletype.

UART: Universal Asynchronous Receiver Transmitter.

word (memory or computer): the smallest unit of information dealt with by a computer. Words can specify data or instructions.

word length: the number of bits contained in a computer or memory word. The size of word length determines the flexibility and accuracy of the computer.

zero flag bit: A condition flag bit that is set to show if the results of CPU operation is zero or not.

Appendix B:

Buyer's Guide

Before you buy a home computer you can go through this list of questions and answers. This list will help you to see both some of the things you should look for in your home computer and some things to look out for:

Where can I buy a home computer?

See the list of manufacturers and clubs in the Appendices for references. You also can look at the ads in the computer magazines or in the yellow pages under electronics stores or computer stores.

How am I going to use my home computer?

For accounting: to do your checks and income taxes. For games: as a chess opponent. For learning: to teach yourself a language. For security: to program turning on and off lights, radios, etc. in your home, etc.

In what form will my home computer be?

Closed console with front panel switches; semi-console with front panel switches and inner hardware exposed; PC board; PC board with I/O; intelligent terminal. Console with I/O interfaces, etc.

Is the unit I select available as a kit or an assembled unit?

If it is a kit, you must ask yourself, do you want to build it and do you have the time and the tools. Ask the computer store owner what kind of guarantee is available if the set is built from a kit. The extra cost may be small enough to make it worth buying an assembled unit.

What microprocessor is used in my home computer?

There is a wide range of MOS (metal oxide-semiconductor) microprocessor types. Two have become standard for the industry: the Intel 8080 and the Motorola MC6800. These microprocessors have a convenient logic which adapts well to BASIC language. Other models of MOS microprocessors are the MCS 6502, the Fairchild F-8, the National Semiconductor PACE SC/HP, the Signetics 2650, and the Intersil IM 6100.

In what language will my programs be written?

You will choose. Some options are BASIC, APL, and FORTRAN which are the most popular and accessible, and have the widest variety of uses and libraries of programs, etc.

What software is provided by the manufacturer?

If none, you should definitely think about buying from another dealer and/or buying another set.

Are there manuals available for guiding the programming of my particular home computer?

Make sure that a debugging program and an initial trial testing program are provided. In addition look for a way of selecting the right types of complementary programs.

How large do I want to make my program?

Your first program will perhaps have ten steps. As your familiarity with it increases, you will be able to add to the number of steps and the range of variables. The size of the program you want will affect your choice of a system.

What memory devices are possible?

The memory that is required will be included in your home computer. Usually, it consists of a small ROM and a small RAM. Any additions to it will require more expense, but check to see if your system will adapt to other memories.

Will I need to program these memory devices?

You will need to program the microcomputer to access to the memory, but not program the memory itself.

What tools do I need for the above?

If you are not buying a kit you will only need a pencil and paper to write out your programs, or a book of software and an outlet to plug in the home computer.

What and how many external storage devices do I need?

This will depend on your usage. In the beginning, a small amount of memory is needed. As you increase your demands, you will see what you need. For example, if you want to eventually have a 300 stage program and include 5000 points of variation, you will need an extensive memory capacity. Certainly 8K is adequate for beginning.

What I/O devices will I need?

You will need the I/O devices that allow you to program and run your set. Your home computer may come with a series of lights and switches on the front through which you can enter data so all you need is some output device. Or you might want to immediately get a home computer with a video display and a keyboard teletype which gives you a wide range of access and response. The need is developed by the user.

Can I use my TV set for display?

Yes. But you may find that you will want a CRT since it may have finer display controls and a built-in memory.

What peripherals do I need? For programming, loading and writing? For storage implementation? For hard-copy output?

For programming, you need whatever is supplied with the home computer as the input device which can be supplemented by keyboard, teletype, light pencil, etc. For loading, you need the same. For writing, you need a pencil and paper and perhaps a small programmable pocket calculator to test out some of your steps and thoughts. You need some sort of memory device for storage if it goes beyond the capability that comes with your home computer. Floppy disc, magnetic tape, and many other units are available for this. For hard-copy printing, you need a line printer like the DEC writer, or a very fast and sophisticated printer.

What other accessories do I need?

Your accessories will build as you develop an understanding of the machine. If you buy a system that has a direct input device, CPU, memory, and output, you have all you need to start.

What tools do I need to set up my system?

You won't need any tools if you buy a preassembled set. If you buy a kit, you will need a complete set of electrician's tools as well as testing equipment.

What power is needed to run my system?

Normal home voltage will drive the majority of home computers.

Do I need extra power supplies?

No, unless you are not going to turn off your set, or you live in an area that is subject to blackouts.

Can I expand my system later if I want to?

Find out if your set is expandable before you buy it. Some sets are expandable, some are not. If you think that you will want to expand, be sure to ask for a set that adapts to expanding needs.

What about repair service?

Repairs are common. Pay attention to the dealer from whom you buy your set. Electronics are delicate tools (especially with the new user). There may be instances where the set is improperly used. Your repair access is crucial. Find a dealer who can provide expert repair service.

Does my home computer have a warranty?

Most home computers do have a warranty. Don't buy one without it.

What about extra parts and their availability?

This is an issue for kit builders, but not so much for preassembled home computers. If you buy from a reliable store, you won't have problems.

How much will I spend?

At first you will spend anywhere from $500 to $1000. As you expand your interest, your costs will go where you direct them.

Where can I find out about other home computer owners and users and clubs?

See Appendix "Clubs." Visit your local computer store, or use as a reference the home computer magazines listed in the Appendix.

When buying a home computer, you will want to compare the specifications of the available machines. The following list will help you to do so. However, because the home computer scene is constantly changing, you may want to verify the information at the computer store or with the manufacturer. Manufacturers are continually upgrading and altering specifications.

In specification comparisons, please note the following information:

Model name.

Microproccssor used: tells you which of the various microprocessors are in the system.

S-100 Bus: tells you if the system uses the Altair 100 bus as the connection between the CPU and the other peripherals. It is the one most widely used and is an asset to any system.

Switches & lights: tells you if the input for your home computer goes directly into the microprocessor through switches and lights rather than keyboards or other means. Switches and lights require you to understand machine language and binary presentation of information.

Keyboard and/or interface: indicates whether the home computer is equipped with a keyboard or just an interface, or neither.

Video display and/or interface: indicates whether the home computer is equipped with a CRT video display, or simply the interface for it, or neither.

Cassette and/or interface: indicates whether the home computer is equipped with a cassette memory device, or simply with the interface for it, or neither.

Floppy disc and/or interface: indicates whether the home computer is equipped with a floppy disc, or only with the interface for it, or neither.

ROM monitor or bootstrap: indicates whether the home computer is equipped with a read-only memory, (a monitor for memory) or a programmable feed-in memory device called a bootstrap, or neither.

RAM: indicates the memory capacity of the RAM of the home computer and its size. If nothing is indicated, a RAM is not included in the system. The capacity is noted in bytes.

Kit; Assembled: indicates whether the system is available in kit form, assembled form, or both.

The addresses of most of the home computer companies mentioned here are listed in Appendix F.

Apple Computer Company

Computer system: Apple II
Microprocessor used: 6502
S–100 Bus:

Mainframe
Switches & lights:
Keyboard and/or interface: interface

Video display and/or interface: video display
Cassette and/or interface: interface

Memory
Floppy disc and/or interface: interface
ROM monitor or bootstrap: bootstrap
RAM capacity: 4K bytes

Kit:
Assembled: yes

Apple Computer Company

Computer system: Apple I
Microprocessor used: 6502
S–100 Bus:

Mainframe
Switches & lights:
Keyboard and/or interface: interface
Video display and/or interface: video/interface
Cassette and/or interface: interface

Memory
Floppy disc and/or interface: interface
ROM monitor or bootstrap: bootstrap
RAM capacity: 4K bytes

Kit:
Assembled: yes

Applied Microtechnology

Computer system: AMT 2650
Microprocessor used: 2650
S–100 Bus:

Mainframe
Switches & lights:
Keyboard and/or interface: interface
Video display and/or interface: LED's
Cassette and/or interface: interface

Memory
Floppy disc and/or interface: interface

ROM monitor or bootstrap: monitor
RAM capacity: 256 bytes

Kit:
Assembled: yes

Bitech, Inc.

Computer system: Micro 2000
Microprocessor used: 8080
S–100 Bus:

Mainframe
Switches & lights:
Keyboard and/or interface: keyboard
Video display and/or interface: video display
Cassette and/or interface: interface

Memory
Floppy disc and/or interface: floppy disc
ROM monitor or bootstrap: monitor
RAM capacity: 16K bytes

Kit:
Assembled: yes

packaged by BYTE Shops

Computer system: BYT–8
Microprocessor used: 8080A
S–100 Bus: yes

Mainframe
Switches & lights: optional
Keyboard and/or interface: interface
Video display and/or interface: interface
Cassette and/or interface: interface

Memory
Floppy disc and/or interface: interface
ROM monitor or bootstrap: optional
RAM capacity: 4K bytes

Kit: yes
Assembled: yes

CGRS Microtech

Computer system: Microputer 6000 Series
Microprocessor used: MOS TECHNOLOGY 6502
S–100 Bus: yes

Mainframe
Switches and lights: switches
Keyboard and/or interface:
Video display and/or interface: LED's
Cassette and/or interface:

Memory
Floppy disc and/or interface:
ROM monitor or bootstrap: EPROM
RAM capacity: 2K bytes

Kit:
Assembled: yes

Commodore

Computer system: Commodore PET
Microprocessor used: 6502
S–100 Bus: yes

Mainframe
Switches and lights:
Keyboard and/or interface: keyboard
Video display and/or interface: video display
Cassette and/or interface: interface

Memory
Floppy disc and/or interface: interface
ROM monitor or bootstrap: bootstrap
RAM capacity: 4K bytes

Kit:
Assembled: yes

Compucolor Corp.

Computer system: Compucolor 8001
Microprocessor used: 8080
S–100 Bus:

Mainframe
Switches & lights:
Keyboard and/or interface: keyboard
Video display and/or interface: video display
Cassette and/or interface: interface

Memory
Floppy disc and/or interface: floppy disc
ROM monitor or bootstrap: bootstrap
RAM capacity: 11K bytes

Kit:
Assembled: yes

Computer Data Systems

Computer system: Desktop Video Computer
Microprocessor used: 8080
S–100 Bus: yes

Mainframe
Switches & lights:
Keyboard and/or interface: keyboard
Video display and/or interface: video display
Cassette and/or interface: interface

Memory
Floppy disc and/or interface: interface
ROM monitor or bootstrap: monitor
RAM capacity: 4K bytes

Kit:
Assembled: yes

packaged by Computer Power & Light

Computer system: COMPAL 80
Microprocessor used: 8080A
S–100 Bus: yes

Mainframe
Switches & lights:
Keyboard and/or interface: keyboard and interface
Video display and/or interface: video and interface
Cassette and/or interface: cassette and interface

Memory
Floppy disc and/or interface: interface
ROM monitor or bootstrap: bootstrap
RAM capacity: 14K bytes

Kit:
Assembled: yes

Cramer Electronics

Computer system: 8080 Cramerkit
Microprocessor used: TI 8080
S–100 Bus: yes

Mainframe
Switches & lights: yes
Keyboard and/or interface: interface
Video display and/or interface:
Cassette and/or interface: interface

Memory
Floppy disc and/or interface:
ROM monitor or bootstrap: bootstrap
RAM capacity: 1K bytes

Kit: yes
Assembled:

Cramer Electronics

Computer system: 8080A Cramerkit
Microprocessor used: Intel 8080A
S–100 Bus: yes

Mainframe
Switches & lights: yes
Keyboard and/or interface: interface
Video display and/or interface:
Cassette and/or interface: cassette

Memory
Floppy disc and/or interface:
ROM monitor or bootstrap: bootstrap
RAM capacity: 1K bytes

Kit: yes
Assembled:

Cramer Electronics

Computer system: 6800 Cramerkit
Microprocessor used: 6800
S–100 Bus: yes

Mainframe
Switches & lights: yes
Keyboard and/or interface: keyboard
Video display and/or interface:
Cassette and/or interface: cassette

Memory
Floppy disc and/or interface:
ROM monitor or bootstrap: bootstrap
RAM capacity: 1K bytes

Kit: Yes
Assembled:

Cramer Electronics

Computer system: F8 Cramerkit
Microprocessor used: Mostek 8
S–100 Bus: yes

Mainframe
Switches & lights: yes
Keyboard and/or interface: keyboard
Video display and/or interface:
Cassette and/or interface: cassette

Memory
Floppy disc and/or interface:
ROM monitor or bootstrap: bootstrap
RAM capacity: 1K bytes

Kit: yes
Assembled:

Cramer Electronics

Computer system: Cosmac Cramerkit
Microprocessor used: RCA Cosmac
S–100 Bus: yes

Mainframe
Switches & lights: yes
Keyboard and/or interface: keyboard
Video display and/or interface:
Cassette and/or interface: cassette

Memory
Floppy disc and/or interface:
ROM monitor or bootstrap: bootstrap
RAM capacity: 1K bytes

Kit: yes
Assembled:

Cramer Electronics

Computer system: 16 bit microcomputer kit
Microprocessor used: Texas Instrument TMS–9900
S–100 Bus: yes

Mainframe
Switches and lights:
Keyboard and/or interface: interface
Video display and/or interface: interface
Cassette and/or interface: interface

Memory
Floppy disc and/or interface: interface
ROM monitor or bootstrap: monitor
RAM capacity: 16K bytes

Kit: yes
Assembled:

CROMEMCO

Computer system: Z–1
Microprocessor used: Z–80
S–100 Bus: yes

Mainframe
Switches & lights: yes
Keyboard and/or interface: interface
Video display and/or interface:
Cassette and/or interface:

Memory
Floppy disc and/or interface:
ROM monitor or bootstrap: bootstrap
RAM capacity: 8K bytes

Kit:
Assembled: yes

Cybersystem, Inc.

Computer system: Microcyber 1000
Microprocessor used: 8080
S–100 Bus: yes

Mainframe
Switches & lights: yes
Keyboard and/or interface: keyboard
Video display and/or interface: video display
Cassette and/or interface: interface

Memory
Floppy disc and/or interface:
ROM monitor or bootstrap: bootstrap
RAM capacity: 8K bytes

Kit:
Assembled: yes

Data General Corp.

Computer system: Micro Nova
Microprocessor used: Data General
S–100 Bus: yes

Mainframe
Switches & lights:
Keyboard and/or interface: interface
Video display and/or interface: interface
Cassette and/or interface: cassette

Memory
Floppy disc and/or interface: floppy disc
ROM monitor or bootstrap: bootstrap
RAM capacity: 8K bytes

Kit:
Assembled: yes

Digital Electronics Corp.

Computer system: DE–68 Briefcase Computer
Microprocessor used: 6800
S–100 Bus: yes

Mainframe
Switches & lights:
Keyboard and/or interface: keyboard
Video display and/or interface:
Cassette and/or interface:

Memory
Floppy disc and/or interface:
ROM monitor or bootstrap: monitor
RAM capacity: 1K bytes

Kit:
Assembled: yes

Digital Electronics Corp.

Computer system: DE68DT Microcomputer
Microprocessor used: 6800
S–100 Bus: yes

Mainframe
Switches and lights:
Keyboard and/or interface: keyboard
Video display and/or interface: LED's and Video Display interface
Cassette and/or interface: interface

Memory
Floppy disc and/or interface: floppy disc
ROM monitor or bootstrap: monitor
RAM capacity: 65K bytes

Kit:
Assembled: yes

Digital Equipment Corp.

Computer system: LSI–11
Microprocessor used: MCP 1600
S–100 Bus: yes

Mainframe
Switches & lights:
Keyboard and/or interface: interface
Video display and/or interface: interface
Cassette and/or interface:

Memory
Floppy disc and/or interface:
ROM monitor or bootstrap: bootstrap
RAM capacity: 4K bytes

Kit:
Assembled: yes

The Digital Group

Computer system: Digital Group Systems
Microprocessor used: Z–80; 8080A; MOSTEK 6800; MOS 6502
S–100 Bus:

Mainframe
Switches & lights:
Keyboard and/or interface:
Video display and/or interface: interface
Cassette and/or interface: interface

Memory
Floppy disc and/or interface:
ROM monitor or bootstrap: bootstrap
RAM capacity: 8K bytes

Kit:
Assembled: yes

E & L Instruments

Computer system: Mini-Micro Designer (MMD–1)
Microprocessor used: 8080A
S–100 Bus: yes

Mainframe
Switches & lights:
Keyboard and/or interface: interface
Video Display and/or interface: LED's
Cassette and/or interface:

Memory
Floppy disc and/or interface:
ROM monitor or bootstrap: monitor
RAM capacity: .5K bytes

Kit: yes
Assembled: yes

EBKA

Computer system: 6502 Familiarizor
Microprocessor used: Mostek 6502
S–100 Bus:

Mainframe
Switches & lights:
Keyboard and/or interface: keyboard
Video display and/or interface: video display
Cassette and/or interface:

Memory
Floppy disc and/or interface:
ROM monitor or bootstrap: bootstrap
RAM capacity: 1K bytes

Kit: yes
Assembled: yes

EBNEK, Inc.

Computer system: EBNEK 77
Microprocessor used: Texas Instruments TMS9900
S–100 Bus: yes

Mainframe
Switches & lights:
Keyboard and/or interface: keyboard
Video display and/or interface: video display
Cassette and/or interface: cassette

Memory
Floppy disc and/or interface: interface
ROM monitor or bootstrap: bootstrap
RAM capacity: 16K bytes

Kit:
Assembled: yes

ECD Corp.

Computer system: Micromind 1
Microprocessor used: 6512 A
S–100 Bus:

Mainframe
Switches & lights:
Keyboard and/or interface: keyboard
Video display and/or interface: interface
Cassette and/or interface: interface

Memory
Floppy disc and/or interface:
ROM monitor or bootstrap: bootstrap
RAM capacity: 8K bytes

Kit:
Assembled: yes

Electronic Control Technology

Computer system: ECT–100
Microprocessor used: 8080A
S–100 Bus: yes

Mainframe
Switches & lights:
Keyboard and/or interface:
Video display and/or interface:
Cassette and/or interface:

Memory
Floppy disc and/or interface:
ROM monitor or bootstrap: bootstrap optional
RAM capacity:

Kit: yes
Assembled: yes

Electronic Products Assoc.

Computer system: Expanded – 68
Microprocessor used: AMI 6800
S–100 Bus:

Mainframe
Switches & lights: yes
Keyboard and/or interface: keyboard
Video display and/or interface: interface
Cassette and/or interface: interface

Memory
Floppy disc and/or interface: interface
ROM monitor or bootstrap:
RAM capacity: 8K bytes

Kit:
Assembled: yes

Electronic Tool Co.

Computer system: Micro 1000 Systems
Microprocessor used: 6502
S–100 Bus:

Mainframe
Switches & lights:
Keyboard and/or interface: keyboard
Video display and/or interface: LED 8-digit
Cassette and/or interface: interface

Memory
Floppy disc and/or interface: interface
ROM monitor or bootstrap:
RAM capacity: 4K bytes

Kit:
Assembled: yes

Fairchild

Computer system: Mini Formulator
Microprocessor used: F8
S–100 Bus: yes

Mainframe
Switches & lights:
Keyboard and/or interface: keyboard
Video display and/or interface: video display
Cassette and/or interface: cassette

Memory
Floppy disc and/or interface: interface
ROM monitor or bootstrap: bootstrap
RAM capacity: 16K bytes

Kit:
Assembled: yes

HAL Communications

Computer system: MCEM—8080
Microprocessor used: 8080
S–100 Bus:

Mainframe
Switches & lights:
Keyboard and/or interface: keyboard
Video display and/or interface: video display
Cassette and/or interface: interface

Memory
Floppy disc and/or interface:
ROM monitor or bootstrap: bootstrap
RAM capacity: 9K bytes

Kit:
Assembled: yes

HAL Communications

Computer system: Hal Eight Thousand
Microprocessor used: 8080A
S–100 Bus: yes

Mainframe
Switches and lights:
Keyboard and/or interface: keyboard
Video display and/or interface: interface
Cassette and/or interface: interface

Memory
Floppy disc and/or interface: interface
ROM monitor or bootstrap: monitor
RAM capacity: 2K bytes

Kit:
Assembled: yes

Heath Company

Computer system: System One—H8
Microprocessor used: 8080A
S–100 Bus:

Mainframe
Switches and lights:
Keyboard and/or interface: keyboard
Video display and/or interface: video display
Cassette and/or interface: cassette

Memory
Floppy disc and/or interface: interface
ROM monitor or bootstrap: monitor
RAM capacity:

Kit: yes
Assembled:

Heath Company

Computer system: System Two—H11
Microprocessor used: LSI–11
S–100 Bus:

Mainframe
Switches and lights:
Keyboard and/or interface: keyboard
Video display and/or interface: video display
Cassette and/or interface: cassette

Memory
Floppy disc and/or interface: interface
ROM monitor or bootstrap: monitor
RAM capacity: 8K bytes

Kit: yes
Assembled:

Heath Company

Computer system: System Three—H11
Microprocessor used: LSI–11
S–100 Bus:

Mainframe
Switches and lights:
Keyboard and/or interface: keyboard
Video display and/or interface: video display
Cassette and/or interface: interface

Memory
Floppy disc and/or interface: interface
ROM monitor or bootstrap: monitor
RAM capacity: 4K bytes

Kit: yes
Assembled:

Hewlett-Packard

Computer system: HP9831A desk top computer
Microprocessor used: HP9831
S–100 Bus:

Mainframe
Switches and lights:
Keyboard and/or interface: keyboard
Video display and/or interface: LED's
Cassette and/or interface: cassette

Memory
Floppy disc and/or interface: interface
ROM monitor or bootstrap: bootstrap
RAM capacity: 8K bytes

Kit:
Assembled: yes

IMS Associates

Computer system: IMSAI 8080
Microprocessor used: 8080A
S–100 Bus: yes

Mainframe
Switches & lights: yes
Keyboard and/or interface: interface
Video display and/or interface:
Cassette and/or interface: interface

Memory
Floppy disc and/or interface: interface
ROM monitor or bootstrap:
RAM capacity:

Kit: yes
Assembled: yes

IMS Associates

Computer system: IMSAI 8084
Microprocessor used: Intel 8084
S–100 Bus:

Mainframe
Switches & lights:
Keyboard and/or interface: keyboard
Video display and/or interface:
Cassette and/or interface:

Memory
Floppy disc and/or interface:
ROM monitor or bootstrap: monitor
RAM capacity: 1K bytes

Kit: yes
Assembled: yes

IMS Associates

Computer system: PCS–80
Microprocessor used: 8085
S–100 Bus: yes

Mainframe
Switches and lights:
Keyboard and/or interface: keyboard
Video display and/or interface: video display
Cassette and/or interface: interface

Memory
Floppy disc and/or interface: floppy disc
ROM monitor or bootstrap: monitor
RAM capacity: 16K bytes

Kit:
Assembled: yes

IMS Associates

Computer system: VDP–80
Microprocessor used: 8080
S–100 Bus: yes

Mainframe
Switches and lights:
Keyboard and/or interface: keyboard
Video display and/or interface: video display
Cassette and/or interface: interface

Memory
Floppy disc and/or interface: floppy disc
ROM monitor or bootstrap: monitor
RAM capacity: 32K bytes

Kit:
Assembled: yes

Infinite

Computer system: UC 1800
Microprocessor used:
S–100 Bus: yes

Mainframe
Switches & lights:
Keyboard and/or interface: keyboard
Video display and/or interface: LED display
Cassette and/or interface:

Memory
Floppy disc and/or interface:
ROM monitor or bootstrap:
RAM capacity: 256 bytes

Kit: yes
Assembled: yes

Intelligent Systems Corp.

Computer system: Intecolor 8001
Microprocessor used: 8080A
S–100 Bus:

Mainframe
Switches & lights:
Keyboard and/or interface: keyboard
Video display and/or interface: video display
Cassette and/or interface:

Memory
Floppy disc and/or interface: interface
ROM monitor or bootstrap: bootstrap
RAM capacity: 4K bytes

Kit:
Assembled: yes

Intelligent Systems Corp.

Computer system: Intecolor 8051 Desk Top Computer
Microprocessor used: 8080
S–100 Bus: yes

Mainframe
Switches and lights:
Keyboard and/or interface: keyboard
Video display and/or interface: video display
Cassette and/or interface: interface

Memory
Floppy disc and/or interface: floppy disc
ROM monitor or bootstrap: bootstrap
RAM capacity: 27K bytes

Kit:
Assembled: yes

M&R Enterprises

Computer system: Astral 2000
Microprocessor used: 6800
S–100 Bus:

Mainframe
Switches & lights:
Keyboard and/or interface: interface
Video display and/or interface: interface
Cassette and/or interface: interface

Memory
Floppy disc and/or interface:
ROM monitor or bootstrap: monitor
RAM capacity: 8K bytes

Kit: yes
Assembled:

Martin Research

Computer system: Mike III
Microprocessor used: 8080
S–100 Bus: yes

Mainframe
Switches & lights:
Keyboard and/or interface: interface
Video display and/or interface: LED's and interface
Cassette and/or interface: interface

Memory
Floppy disc and/or interface:
ROM monitor or bootstrap: bootstrap
RAM capacity: 4K bytes

Kit:
Assembled: yes

Martin Research

Computer system: Mike-VIII Model 882
Microprocessor used: Z–80
S–100 Bus:

Mainframe
Switches and lights:
Keyboard and/or interface: keyboard
Video display and/or interface: LED's
Cassette and/or interface:

Memory
Floppy disc and/or interface:
ROM monitor or bootstrap: monitor
RAM capacity: 4K bytes

Kit:
Assembled: yes

Microcomputer Assoc.

Computer system: Jolt
Microprocessor used: Mostek 6502
S–100 Bus:

Mainframe
Switches & lights:
Keyboard and/or interface: keyboard
Video display and/or interface:
Cassette and/or interface:

Memory
Floppy disc and/or interface:
ROM monitor or bootstrap: bootstrap
RAM capacity: 512 bytes

Kit:
Assembled: yes

Microdata Systems

Computer system: F800 Computer
Microprocessor used: Mostek F8
S–100 Bus: yes

Mainframe
Switches and lights:
Keyboard and/or interface: interface
Video display and/or interface: interface
Cassette and/or interface: interface

Memory
Floppy disc and/or interface: interface
ROM monitor or bootstrap: monitor
RAM capacity: 8K bytes

Kit: yes
Assembled: yes

Microkit

Computer system: Microkit 8/16
Microprocessor used: 8080
S–100 Bus:

Mainframe
Switches & lights:
Keyboard and/or interface: keyboard
Video display and/or interface: video display
Cassette and/or interface: cassette

Memory
Floppy disc and/or interface: floppy disc
ROM monitor or bootstrap: bootstrap
RAM capacity: 8K bytes

Kit:
Assembled: yes

Microkit

Computer system: Microkit 8/16
Microprocessor used: AMI 6800
S–100 Bus:

Mainframe
Switches & lights:
Keyboard and/or interface: keyboard
Video display and/or interface: video display
Cassette and/or interface: cassette

Memory
Floppy disc and/or interface: floppy disc
ROM monitor or bootstrap: bootstrap
RAM capacity: 8K bytes

Kit:
Assembled: yes

Midwest Scientific Instruments

Computer system: MSI 6800
Microprocessor used: 6800
S–100 Bus: yes

Mainframe
Switches and lights:
Keyboard and/or interface: interface
Video display and/or interface: interface
Cassette and/or interface: interface

Memory
Floppy disc and/or interface: interface
ROM monitor or bootstrap: bootstrap
RAM capacity: 8K bytes

Kit: yes
Assembled: yes

MITS, Inc.

Computer system: ALTAIR 8800B
Microprocessor used: 8080A
S–100 Bus: yes

Mainframe
Switches & lights:
Keyboard and/or interface:
Video display and/or interface:
Cassette and/or interface: interface

Memory
Floppy disc and/or interface: interface
ROM monitor or bootstrap:
RAM capacity:

Kit: yes
Assembled: yes

MITS, Inc.

Computer system: ALTAIR 6800B
Microprocessor used: 6800
S–100 Bus:

Mainframe
Switches & lights: yes
Keyboard and/or interface: interface
Video display and/or interface: interface
Cassette and/or interface: interface

Memory
Floppy disc and/or interface:
ROM monitor or bootstrap: bootstrap
RAM capacity: 1K bytes

Kit: yes
Assembled: yes

Monolithic Systems

Computer system: MCS 8080
Microprocessor used: 8080A
S–100 Bus: yes

Mainframe
Switches & lights: yes
Keyboard and/or interface: keyboard
Video display and/or interface: interface
Cassette and/or interface: interface

Memory
Floppy disc and/or interface: interface
ROM monitor or bootstrap: bootstrap
RAM capacity: 4K bytes

Kit: yes
Assembled:

Monolithic Systems

Computer system: MCS 8080
Microprocessor used: 8080A
S–100 Bus: yes

Mainframe
Switches & lights: yes
Keyboard and/or interface: keyboard
Video display and/or interface: interface
Cassette and/or interface: interface

Memory
Floppy disc and/or interface: interface
ROM monitor or bootstrap: bootstrap
RAM capacity: 4K bytes

Kit:
Assembled: yes

MOS Technology

Computer system: KIM–1
Microprocessor used: Mostek 6502
S–100 Bus:

Mainframe
Switches & lights:
Keyboard and/or interface: keyboard
Video display and/or interface: video display
Cassette and/or interface: cassette

Memory
Floppy disc and/or interface:
ROM monitor or bootstrap: monitor
RAM capacity: 1K bytes

Kit:
Assembled: yes

Multisonics, Inc.

Computer system: 8080A Microcomputer
Microprocessor used: 8080A
S–100 Bus:

Mainframe
Switches & lights:
Keyboard and/or interface: keyboard
Video display and/or interface: video display
Cassette and/or interface:

Memory
Floppy disc and/or interface: floppy disc
ROM monitor or bootstrap: bootstrap
RAM capacity: 64K bytes

Kit:
Assembled: yes

National Semiconductor

Computer system: PACE
Microprocessor used: PACE
S–100 Bus:

Mainframe
Switches & lights:
Keyboard and/or interface: interface
Video display and/or interface:
Cassette and/or interface:

Memory
Floppy disc and/or interface:
ROM monitor or bootstrap: bootstrap
RAM capacity: 1K bytes

Kit:
Assembled: yes

National Semiconductor

Computer system: IMP–16L Microcomputer
Microprocessor used: IMP–16
S–100 Bus:

Mainframe
Switches and lights: yes
Keyboard and/or interface: interface
Video display and/or interface: interface
Cassette and/or interface: interface

Memory
Floppy disc and/or interface: interface
ROM monitor or bootstrap: monitor
RAM capacity: 4K x 16 bytes

Kit:
Assembled: yes

Noval Inc.

Computer system: Noval
Microprocessor used: 8080
S–100 Bus:

Mainframe
Switches & lights:
Keyboard and/or interface: keyboard
Video display and/or interface: video display
Cassette and/or interface: cassette

Memory
Floppy disc and/or interface: floppy disc
ROM monitor or bootstrap: bootstrap
RAM capacity: 16K bytes

Kit:
Assembled: yes

Ohio Scientific Instruments

Computer system: Systems Package 1
Microprocessor used: 6502A
S–100 Bus:

Mainframe
Switches & lights:
Keyboard and/or interface: keyboard
Video display and/or interface: video display
Cassette and/or interface:

Memory
Floppy disc and/or interface: floppy disc
ROM monitor or bootstrap: bootstrap
RAM capacity: 16K bytes

Kit:
Assembled: yes

Pacific Cyber/Metrix, Inc.

Computer system: PCM–12
Microprocessor used: IM 6100
S–100 Bus: yes

Mainframe
Switches & lights:
Keyboard and/or interface: interface
Video display and/or interface: interface
Cassette and/or interface: interface

Memory
Floppy disc and/or interface: interface
ROM monitor or bootstrap: monitor
RAM capacity: 1K bytes

Kit: yes
Assembled:

Pacific Cyber/Metrix, Inc.

Computer system: PCM–12A
Microprocessor used: Intersil IM 6100
S–100 Bus: yes

Mainframe
Switches and lights:
Keyboard and/or interface: interface
Video display and/or interface: interface
Cassette and/or interface: interface

Memory
Floppy disc and/or interface: interface
ROM monitor or bootstrap: bootstrap
RAM capacity: 1K bytes

Kit: yes
Assembled: yes

Plessey Microsystems

Computer system: Miproc–16
Microprocessor used: Schottky Bipolar
S–100 Bus:

Mainframe
Switches & lights:
Keyboard and/or interface: interface
Video display and/or interface: interface
Cassette and/or interface: interface

Memory
Floppy disc and/or interface: interface
ROM monitor or bootstrap: monitor
RAM capacity: 16K bytes

Kit:
Assembled: yes

Polymorphic Systems

Computer system: POLY–88 System 16
Microprocessor used: 8080A
S–100 Bus: yes

Mainframe
Switches & lights:
Keyboard and/or interface: keyboard
Video display and/or interface: video display
Cassette and/or interface: cassette

Memory
Floppy disc and/or interface:
ROM monitor or bootstrap: bootstrap
RAM capacity: 16K bytes

Kit:
Assembled: yes

Processor Technology

Computer system: SOL–20
Microprocessor used: 8080A
S–100 Bus: yes

Mainframe
Switches & lights:
Keyboard and/or interface: keyboard
Video display and/or interface: interface
Cassette and/or interface: interface

Memory
Floppy disc and/or interface:
ROM monitor or bootstrap: bootstrap
RAM capacity: 4K bytes

Kit:
Assembled: yes

Realistic Controls Corp.

Computer system: Z/100 Series
Microprocessor used: 8080
S–100 Bus:

Mainframe
Switches & lights:
Keyboard and/or interface: interface
Video display and/or interface: interface
Cassette and/or interface: interface

Memory
Floppy disc and/or interface: floppy disc
ROM monitor or bootstrap: monitor
RAM capacity: 33K bytes

Kit:
Assembled: yes

Southwest Technical Products

Computer system: SWTP 6800
Microprocessor used: 6800
S–100 Bus:

Mainframe
Switches & lights:
Keyboard and/or interface: interface
Video display and/or interface: interface
Cassette and/or interface: interface

Memory
Floppy disc and/or interface:
ROM monitor or bootstrap: bootstrap
RAM capacity: 4K bytes

Kit: yes
Assembled:

Sphere Corp.

Computer system: Sphere 310
Microprocessor used: 6800
S–100 Bus:

Mainframe
Switches & lights:
Keyboard and/or interface: keyboard
Video display and/or interface: video display
Cassette and/or interface: cassette

Memory
Floppy disc and/or interface: floppy disc
ROM monitor or bootstrap: monitor
RAM capacity:

Kit: yes
Assembled:

Sphere Corp.

Computer system: Sphere Series 500
Microprocessor used: 6800
S–100 Bus: yes

Mainframe
Switches & lights:
Keyboard and/or interface: keyboard
Video display and/or interface: video display
Cassette and/or interface: interface

Memory
Floppy disc and/or interface: floppy disc
ROM monitor or bootstrap: bootstrap
RAM capacity: 4K bytes

Kit:
Assembled: yes

Sphere Corp.

Computer system: Micro-Sphere 200
Microprocessor used: 6800
S–100 Bus:

Mainframe
Switches & lights:
Keyboard and/or interface: keyboard
Video display and/or interface: interface
Cassette and/or interface: interface

Memory
Floppy disc and/or interface:
ROM monitor or bootstrap: monitor
RAM capacity: 4K bytes

Kit:
Assembled: yes

STS Systems

Computer system: BABY! 1 Briefcase Computer
Microprocessor used: 6502
S–100 Bus:

Mainframe
Switches & lights:
Keyboard and/or interface: keyboard
Video display and/or interface: video display
Cassette and/or interface: cassette

Memory
Floppy disc and/or interface:
ROM monitor or bootstrap: monitor
RAM capacity: 4K bytes

Kit:
Assembled: yes

Systems Research

Computer system: SR 1–500 Series
Microprocessor used: Fairchild F8
S–100 Bus: yes

Mainframe
Switches & lights:
Keyboard and/or interface: keyboard
Video display and/or interface: interface
Cassette and/or interface: interface

Memory
Floppy disc and/or interface:
ROM monitor or bootstrap: monitor
RAM capacity: 1K bytes

Kit:
Assembled: yes

Tandy Corporation/Radio Shack

Computer system: TRS–80
Microprocessor used: Z 80
S–100 Bus:

Mainframe
Switches and lights:
Keyboard and/or interface: keyboard
Video display and/or interface: video display
Cassette and/or interface: interface

Memory
Floppy disc and/or interface: interface
ROM monitor or bootstrap: bootstrap
RAM capacity: 4K bytes

Kit:
Assembled: yes

Technical Design Labs

Computer system: XITAN Alpha 2
Microprocessor used: Z–80
S–100 Bus:

Mainframe
Switches & lights:
Keyboard and/or interface: interface
Video display and/or interface: interface
Cassette and/or interface: interface

Memory
Floppy disc and/or interface: interface
ROM monitor or bootstrap: monitor
RAM capacity: 18K bytes

Kit: yes
Assembled: yes

Terak Corporation

Computer system: Terak 8510
Microprocessor used: MCP 1600
S–100 Bus:

Mainframe
Switches & lights:
Keyboard and/or interface: interface
Video display and/or interface: interface
Cassette and/or interface:

Memory
Floppy disc and/or interface: floppy disc
ROM monitor or bootstrap:
RAM capacity:

Kit:
Assembled: yes

TLF

Computer system: Data 12
Microprocessor used: IM 6100
S–100 Bus:

Mainframe
Switches & lights:
Keyboard and/or interface: interface
Video display and/or interface: interface
Cassette and/or interface: cassette

Memory
Floppy disc and/or interface: floppy disc
ROM monitor or bootstrap:
RAM capacity:

Kit:
Assembled: yes

Tranti Systems

Computer system: MuScope Model 8000
Microprocessor used: 8080
S–100 Bus:

Mainframe
Switches & lights:
Keyboard and/or interface: keyboard
Video display and/or interface: video display
Cassette and/or interface: cassette

Memory
Floppy disc and/or interface:
ROM monitor or bootstrap: monitor
RAM capacity:

Kit:
Assembled: yes

Vector Graphic

Computer system: Vector 1
Microprocessor used: 8080
S–100 Bus: yes

Mainframe
Switches & lights:
Keyboard and/or interface:
Video display and/or interface: interface
Cassette and/or interface: interface

Memory
Floppy disc and/or interface: interface
ROM monitor or bootstrap: monitor
RAM capacity: 1K bytes

Kit: yes
Assembled: yes

Veras Systems

Computer system: F8
Microprocessor used: F8
S–100 Bus:

Mainframe
Switches & lights:
Keyboard and/or interface: interface
Video display and/or interface: interface
Cassette and/or interface: interface

Memory
Floppy disc and/or interface:
ROM monitor or bootstrap: bootstrap
RAM capacity: 1,000 bytes

Kit: yes
Assembled: yes

Warner & Swasey Co.

Computer system: Micral
Microprocessor used: AMD 9080 A4
S–100 Bus:

Mainframe
Switches & lights:
Keyboard and/or interface: keyboard
Video display and/or interface: video display
Cassette and/or interface: cassette

Memory
Floppy disc and/or interface: floppy disc
ROM monitor or bootstrap: monitor
RAM capacity: 64K bytes

Kit:
Assembled: yes

Wave Mate

Computer system: Jupiter II C
Microprocessor used: 6800
S–100 Bus:

Mainframe
Switches & lights:
Keyboard and/or interface: keyboard
Video display and/or interface: video display
Cassette and/or interface: cassette

Memory
Floppy disc and/or interface: interface
ROM monitor or bootstrap: bootstrap
RAM capacity: 8K bytes

Kit: yes
Assembled: yes

Wave Mate

Computer system: Jupiter III C
Microprocessor used: Z–80
S–100 Bus:

Mainframe
Switches & lights:
Keyboard and/or interface: keyboard
Video display and/or interface: video display
Cassette and/or interface: cassette

Memory
Floppy disc and/or interface: interface
ROM monitor or bootstrap: bootstrap
RAM capacity: 8K bytes

Kit: yes
Assembled: yes

Western Data Systems

Computer system: DATA Handler
Microprocessor used: MOS 6502
S–100 Bus: yes

Mainframe
Switches & lights: yes
Keyboard and/or interface:
Video display and/or interface:
Cassette and/or interface:

Memory
Floppy disc and/or interface:
ROM monitor or bootstrap: monitor
RAM capacity: 1K bytes

Kit:
Assembled: yes

Wyle Computer Products

Computer system: mu-P Series Microcomputers
Microprocessor used: 8080A
S–100 Bus:

Mainframe
Switches & lights: yes
Keyboard and/or interface: interface
Video display and/or interface: interface
Cassette and/or interface: interface

Memory
Floppy disc and/or interface:
ROM monitor or bootstrap: bootstrap
RAM capacity: 256 bytes

Kit:
Assembled: yes

Appendix C:

Peripherals

Type 1—intelligent terminal: a terminal I/O device that is controlled by a microprocessor and program, and has capacity for further storage; usually contains keyboard and display.

Type 2—dumb terminal: a terminal I/O device not controlled by a microprocessor. It is capable of operating in a location that is remote from a main computer, and it usually has a keyboard and/or some type of display or print device.

Type 3—keyboard: an I/O device, resembling a typewriter keyboard, that encodes data into a binary code upon depression of keys.

Type 4—PROM/EPROM programmer: a device that actively stores information in a PROM or EPROM memory module.

Type 5—printer: a device that automatically prints computer output in hard-copy form. It can be an alphanumeric, character, line, matrix, or graphic printer.

Type 6—floppy disc: hardware resembling a phonograph record that is used for storage of information outside the computer mainframe.

Type 6a—floppy disc drive: a device that reads from or writes into a floppy disc.

Type 6b—floppy disc system: a combination of disc, drive, and complete operating system.

Type 7—video display (CRT): a device resembling a TV through which I/O is displayed on a screen.

Type 8—analog-to-digital converter (ADC) or digital-to-analog converter: a device that converts incoming analog

DIAGRAM OF USES OF MULTI-CHANNEL MICROCOMPUTER ANALOG INTERFACE
by Cromemco

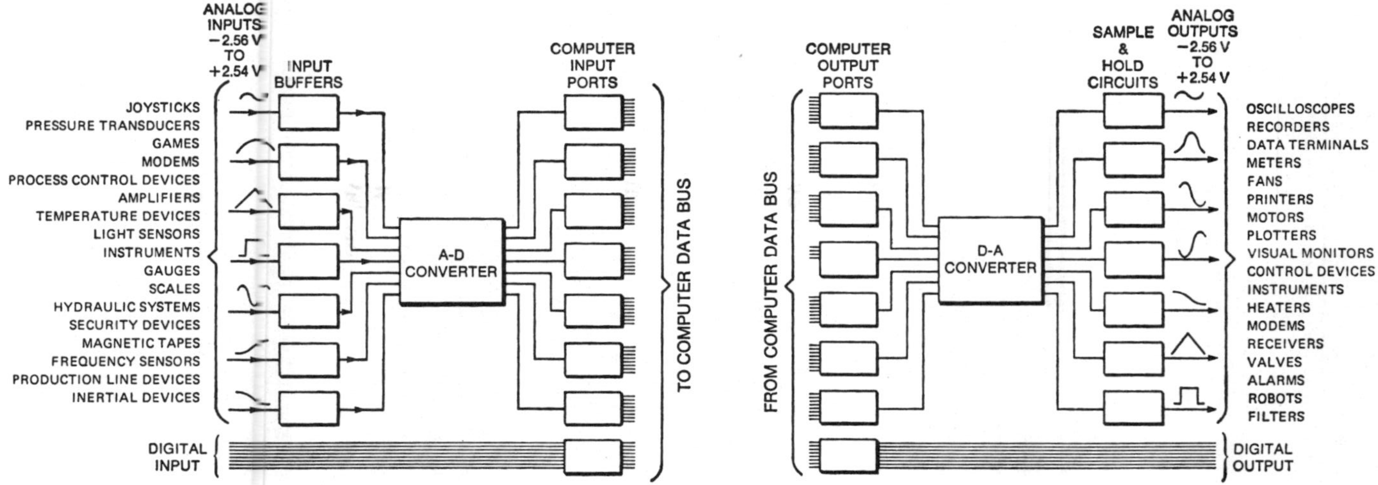

or continuous signal data into digital discrete signal data for input to a computer, or vice versa.

Type 9—cassette tape transport/data recorder: a device that passes magnetic cassette tape over sensing and recording heads.

Type 10—cassette storage system: the system which includes magnetic tape cassette for the purpose of storage of programmed information that can be input directly to the computer.

Type 11—paper tape reader: a device over which encoded paper tape is passed and decoded.

Type 12—joystick/data loader: a device to speed up data entry and to be used in interactive programs.

Type 13—TV interface module: a device used to enhance information display for usage with CRT.

Peripheral Companies and Products

Abacus Computer Systems
- Abacus Computer Systems Terminals—type 2
- Model 800 portable hard-copy Computer terminal—type 2

Addmaster Corp.
- Model 640 Data Loader—type 12
- Model 601 Paper Tape Reader—type 11

Alanthus Data Communications
- Model T-300 Data Terminal—type 2

American Microsystems
- Hard-copy-oriented microcomputer terminal—type 2
- AMI6800 intelligent terminal—type 1

Amilon Corp.
- A7 cassette transport—type 9
- A9 cassette transport—type 9

Anderson Jacobsen
- AJ841 typewriter terminal—type 2

Applied Computing Technology
- Series 900 interactive Medium Speed Matrix Printer—type 5

Associated Electronics
1702A manual EPROM programmer—type 4

Axiom Corp.
EX–800 line printer—type 5

B&M Communications
Model 33 Data terminals—type 2

Bargain Electronics Enterprises
BEE microdisc kit—type 6b

Beehive International
B100 terminal—type 2

Bowmar Instrument Corp.
TP–3120 thermal printer—type 5

Braemar Devices
CS–400 Digital Cassette tape transport—type 9

Burr-Brown
MP8600 analog I/O system—type 8
DAC 82 Digital to Analog converter—type 8

Burroughs
Model D8565 computer display terminal—type 2

CalComp (California Computer Products)
Floppy disc systems—type 6b

Central Data
3320 RTTY/Computer Display System—type 7

Centronics
306–C printers—type 5
MICRO–1 MICROPRINTER—type 5

CMC Marketing Corp.
Model MCS—PT Processor terminal—type 1

Collimation, Inc.
D50.53F Desk top keyboard—type 3

Computer Components, Inc.
Terminals—type 2

Computer Conversion Corp.
CONVERSOR 4000 Display terminal interfaced with telephone—type 2
CONVERSOR 8000—type 2

Computer Data Systems
CRT terminals—type 2

Computer Electronics, Inc.
CEI Custom keyboards—type 3

Computer Kits, Inc.
INTELLITERM$_{TM}$—type 1

Computer Labs, Inc.
Series M3000 Disk Memory systems—type 6b

Computer Transceiver Systems, Inc.
EXECUPORT 3000 portable terminal—type 1

Computerwise, Inc.
Transactor I Data Terminal—type 2

Control Data Corp.
751–10 intelligent terminal and display—type 1
753–10 nonimpact printer—type 5

Cromemco
Joystick JS–1K—type 12
Joystick JS–1W—type 12
BYTESAVER$_{TM}$ PROM programmer—type 4
TV DAZZLER$_{TM}$ computer/TV interface—type 13
D + 7A$_{TM}$ digital-to-analog converter—type 8

Data I/O Corp.
Model 9 PROM programmer—type 4

Datamedia Corp.
ELITE 1500 A CRT terminal—type 2

Datapoint Corp.
3300–200 thermal printer—type 5

Data Products Corp.
Models B–180, B–300 line printers—type 5
Model M–200 impact matrix printer—type 5
Model T–80 thermal matrix printer—type 5

Data Sync
DS–100 "Educated" terminal—type 1
DS Stand-alone keyboard—type 3

Datel Systems Inc.
12-bit Digital to Analog Converter—type 8

Digital Electronics Corp.
DE/200 Random Access MicroDisplay—type 7

Digital Equipment Corp.
PRS01 paper tape reader—type 11
DECwriters—type 5

Digital Group
Character printer—type 5
Line width matrix impact printer—type 5
Cassette storage system—type 10
Keyboard—type 3
Javelin TV monitor—type 7

Digital Laboratories
ACT–1200 storage unit—type 10

Digital Research
CP/M Disk Operating System—type 6b

Digital Systems
Floppy-disc systems—type 6b

EBNEK, Inc.
Keyboard—type 3
CRT—type 7

Economy Co.
Phi-Deck cassette transport—type 9

Economy Terminals
ET1 CRT terminals—type 2

EECO
Model 2001–4 Reader/Spooler—type 11
Model 2001–5 Reader/Spooler—type 11
Model 2001–2 Reader—type 11

Electronic Products Associates, Inc.
IMP1–A printer—type 5
Diablo HYTYPE 30 CPS printer—type 5
Floppy Disk Dual Drive Systems—type 6a
ADC–1 analog-to-digital converter—type 8
Model 40C Dot Matrix Impact printer—type 5
MICRO–68 floppy disc system—type 6b

Engineering Resources
Model 8700 PROM programmer (kit)—type 4

Expandor, Inc.
Hobbyist printer—type 5

General Electric Data Communications Products
GETerminet 30 Matrix Teleprinter—type 5

Genisco
GCT–3071 tabletop mount ASCII code keyboard—type 3

GNAT
MC–200 Data Storage systems—type 10

HAL Communications
MCEM KB/VDU keyboard/visual display unit—type 2

Heathkit
H10 paper tape reader/punch—type 11
H9 video terminal—type 2

Hewlett–Packard
HP2648A microprocessor controlled graphic CRT terminal—type 1

Honeywell
MICROSWITCH keyboards—type 3

ICOM Microperipherals
$MICROFLOPPY_{TM}$—type 6b
FRUGAL $FLOPPY_{TM}$ Model FF–36—type 6b
$MINIFLOPPY_{TM}$ floppy-disc system—type 6b
FDOS and FD 360 floppy disc—type 6b and 6

IMS Associates, Inc.
Model 30A Character Printer—type 5
Model 30A–TF Character Printer—type 5

Model 300A Line Printer—type 5
AP–32 Alphanumeric Printer—type 5
FDD floppy diskette—type 6
FDC floppy-disc drive and power—type 6a
DISK–50; –8–; –200—type 6
Keyboard 53-key ASCII code—type 3
Video Display—type 7

Information Terminals
ITC Floppy Disks—type 6
ITC Flippy$_{TM}$ Disks—type 6
ITC MI–50 Mini-diskettes—type 6

Information Terminals Corp.
VERBATIM Minidisk—type 6
VERBATIM ITC MD 525 flexible disc cartridge—type 6

Info-Tech, Inc.
Model 66c terminal—type 2
KSR-type terminal—type 2

Innovex Corp.
Series 400 Floppy Disk—type 6b

Integral Data Systems
Integral Impact printer—type 5

Interactive Systems
CDU–3216 Video display unit—type 7
CDU–6416 Video display unit—type 7

International Data Systems, Inc.
DAC 8-bit digital-to-analog converter—type 8

Intersil
6970 IFDOS floppy-disc operating system—type 6b

C. Itoh Electronics, Inc.
C1 Model 7040 line printer—type 5
C1 Model 7080 alphanumeric dot matrix printer—type 5

Kennedy Co.
Series 5300 Disk Drive—type 6a

Lear Siegler
ADM–3A Video Display Terminal—type 2

Leasco Data Communications Corp.
Model 33 Data Terminal—type 2
Model L–30 Data Terminal—type 2
Model 1200 Data Terminal—type 2

LRC, Inc.
Model 140 stand-alone printer—type 5

Master Digital Corp. (available from)
388 Series PRECISA printers—type 5

Matrox Electronic Systems of Canada
MYX–2480 Video Display—type 7
ALT–256 **2 TV Interface—type 13
MTX–1632L Video Display—type 7

MECA
Alpha–1/2 cassette storage system—type 10

Memodyne Corp.
Digital cassette transport—type 9
Model 764 servocontrolled cassette transport—type 9

MEMOREX
550 Flexible Disk File—type 6b

MFE Corp.
Model 5000 Buffered Tape Cassette transport—type 9
Model 250 Tape Cassette Transport system—type 9
Model 5000 Buffered Data Terminal—type 1

Micon Industries
KDM/1 portable display—type 7

Microcomputer Associates
VT100 video terminal—type 2

Microcomputer Techniques/Cramer Electronics
2708 EROM programmer Cramerkit—type 4
2704 EROM programmer Cramerkit—type 4

Microdata Corp.
$\text{SCRIBE}_{\text{TM}}$ matrix printer—type 5
$\text{LODESTAR}_{\text{TM}}$ tape cartridge drive—type 9

Micro-Designs
Model 200 cassette storage system—type 10
Model 100 cassette storage system—type 10

Microkit, Inc.
MICRODISK Disk Operating System—type 6b
MICROPRINT/65 line printer—type 5
MICROEMULATOR 8080 EPROM programmer—type 4

Micromation
MACRODISC dual disc system—type 6b

Micro-Networks Corp.
Analog to Digital Converter—type 8

Microperipherals/Microprocessor Systems & Peripherals
MP–40 printer—type 5
SSP–40 printer—type 5
KP–40 printer—type 5
Series B82 Flexible Disc Drives—type 6a

Micropolis
1024 Mod I single-drive floppy disc—type 6 and 6a
1043 Mod II single-drive disc storage subsystem—type 6b
1053 Mod II dual-drive disc storage subsystem—type 6b
METAFLOPPY$_{TM}$ floppy-disc system—type 6b

Microprocessor Marketing
Model 800P alphanumeric impact printer—type 5

Micro-Term, Inc.
ACT I, ACT II, ACT III, ACT IV CRT terminals—type 2

Microtonics
THE BYTE READER$_{TM}$ paper tape reader—type 11

Midwest Scientific Instruments
FD–8 floppy-disc system—type 6b
PR 1 PROM programmer—type 4
PR–2 PROM programmer—type 4

Mikra-D Inc.
1702 PROM programmer—type 4
8223 PROM programmer—type 4
VT–1920 CRT terminal—type 2

BASIC–8 intelligent terminal—type 1
MTS–8 intelligent terminal—type 1

Miniterm Assoc., Inc.
MERLIN intelligent video interface/monitor—types 13 and 7
Dual Minifloppy* System 80/2—type 6b
MERLIN Super Dense add-on kit—type 13

MITS, Inc.
ALTAIR 7000 graphic printer—type 5
MITS 88–ADC analog-to-digital converter—type 8
ALTAIR Floppy Disk Operating System—type 6b
ALTAIR 110 line printer—type 5
ALTAIR C700 high-speed serial character printer—type 5
ALTAIR Minidisk—type 6b

Multiterm Corp.
T–3000 Data Terminal—type 1

National Computer Systems
Model 5200 Megabyte Storage system—type 10

National Multiplex
COMPUTER AID Digital Data Recorder Models CC–7, CC–8, 3M1, 3M3—type 9

National Semiconductor
KIT KB portable terminal—type 2

North Star Computer, Inc.
MICRO-DISK $\text{SYSTEM}_{\text{TM}}$—type 6b

Ohio Scientific Instruments
OSI 470 floppy disc—type 6 and 6a
OSI 470B floppy disc—type 6 and 6a

Okidata
Model 110 line printer—type 5

Oliver Audio Engineering
Model OP–80A TTY paper tape reader—type 11
OAE PP–2708/16 PROM programmer—type 4

PAIA
8780 Digital to Analog Converter—type 8

Percom Data Co.
CIS–30+ cassette and I/O device—type 10
Floppy-disc drive and diskettes—types 6a and 6

Peripheral Vision, Inc.
Impact printer—type 5
S–100 Bus floppy disc—type 6b

PERSCI
Model 70 Diskette Drive—type 6
Model 270 Dual Diskette Drive—type 6a

Pertec, Peripheral Equipment Division
FD4000 disc drives—type 6a

Pinnacle Products
4-channel Digital to Analog Converter—type 8

Practical Automation, Inc.
DMTP–6 Series alphanumeric data printers—type 5

Processor Applications
PAL FDC–1016 floppy disc—type 6 and 6a

Processor Technology
VDM–1 video display module—type 7
HELIOS II disc system—type 6b

Proko Electronics
PTR–11 paper tape reader—type 11

Qantex Division of North Atlantic Industries
$\text{MINIDRIVE}_{\text{TM}}$—type 9

Radio Shack
Archer ASCII Keyboard Encoder kit—type 3

Raeco
TPR–1 paper tape reader—type 11

Ramtek Corp.
"Micrographic" Terminal—type 1

Realistic Controls
Z125 FORTRAN IV Mini Floppy—type 6b

George Risk Industries
Model 753 keyboard—type 3

Charles River Data Systems, Inc.
FD–11 Floppy disc add-on system—type 6b

Shepardson Microsystems, Inc.
PROM programmer—type 4

Shugart Associates
SA400 minifloppy$_{TM}$ disc drive—type 6a
SA104/105 minidiskette$_{TM}$—type 6
SA 850/851 double-sided floppy disc drive—type 6a

Smoke Signal Broadcasting
BFD–68 floppy disc system—type 6b
(with dual or triple drive)

Soroc Technology, Inc.
IQ120 CRT terminal—type 2

Southwest Technical Products
PR–40 alphanumeric printer—type 5
GT–6144 display—type 7
CT–1024 terminal system (kit)—type 2
GT–61 graphic terminal (kit)—type 2
CT–64 terminal kit—type 2
MF–68 dual mini-floppy disc system—type 6b

Sphere Corp.
Disc Operating System—type 6b
Videographics System—type 7
Dual Floppy Disc Drive—type 6a

Suntronix Co.
Mode KBDIV keyboard—type 3

Sylvanhills Lab
TR–4 photoelectric punched paper tape reader—type 11

Synetic Designs
FDS–2 floppy-disc system—type 6b

TEI Special Systems Group
PROCESSOR TERMINAL—type 1

Tektronix
619 storage display monitor—type 7

Teleterminal Corp.
Paper tape reader for KIM–1—type 11

Teletype Corp.
- Model 33 keyboard ASCII ASR—type 3
- Model 43 keyboard ASCII KSR—type 3

Tenney Engineering, Inc.
- DIGITERM microprocessor programmer—type 4

Terminal Data Corp.
- Model 954 programmer—type 4

Texas Instruments
- Model 810 multi-copy printer—type 5
- Silent 700—Model 645 portable hard-copy printer—type 5

3M Co./Minicom Division
- Wollensak models 9575, 9576, 9577 cassette transports—type 9

3 Readiness Society
- Simplified keyboard—type 3

Verada 214
- VIATRON 2111 microprocessor terminal—type 1
- VIATRON cassette deck—type 9

Video Terminal
- VT–4000 Video Computer Terminal—type 2

Volker-Craig, Ltd. of Canada
- VC 303A Character Display Terminal—type 2

VTT, Inc.
- VT–4800 Video Computer Terminal—type 2

Wave Mate
- Jupiter Dual Disk System—type 6b

Wintek
- BRB video terminal—type 2

Wyle Computer Products
- CRT terminals—type 2

XYBEK
- PRAMMER EROM programmer—type 4
- PRAMSYS EROM programmer—type 4

Appendix D:

Home Computer Books

General

Adler, Irving. *Thinking Machines: A Layman's Introduction to Logic, Boolean Algebra & Computers.* New York: John Day Co., 1961.

Atwood, Jerry T. *The Systems Analyst; How to Design Computer-Based Systems,* Rochelle Park, N.J.: Hayden Book Co., 1976.

Avebury, Lord, Ron Converson, John Humphries, and Brian Meek, eds. *Computers and the Year 2000.* Rochelle Park, N.J.: Hayden Book Co., Inc. 1973.

Bell, Daniel. *The Coming of the Post-Industrial Society.* New York: Basic Books, 1973.

Bemer, Richard. *Computers and Crisis.* New York: Association for Computing Machinery, 1972.

Benrey, Ronald. *Understanding Digital Computers.* Rochelle Park, N.J.: Hayden Book Co., Inc. 1964.

Bernice, Daniel D. *Introduction to Computers and Data Processing.* Englewood Cliffs, N.J.: Prentice-Hall, 1970.

Brown, John A., and Robert S. Workman. *How a Computer System Works.* New York: Arco Pub. Co., 1975.

Crowley, Thomas. *Understanding Computers.* New York: McGraw-Hill Book Co., 1967.

Curtis, Richard F., and Maynard L. Erickson. *Primer in Computer Utilization.* Morristown, N.J.: General Learning Press, 1974.

Davenport, William P. *Modern Data Communication: Concepts, Language and Media.* Rochelle Park, N.J.: Hayden Book Co., 1971.

Desmond, William H. *Computers & Their Uses*, Englewood Cliffs, N.J.: Prentice-Hall, 1975.

Eames, Charles and Ray. *A Computer Perspective*. Cambridge, Mass.: Harvard University Press, 1973.

Eilenberg, Samuel. *Automata, Language and Machines*. New York: Academic Press, 1976.

Feigenbaum, Edward A., and Julian Feldman, eds. *Computers and Thought*. New York: McGraw Hill, 1963.

Fink, Donald G. *Computers and the Human Mind*. Garden City, N.J.: Doubleday, 1966.

Gildersleeve, Thomas R. *Organizing and Documenting Data Processing Information*, Rochelle Park, N.J.: Hayden Book Co., 1976.

Hanson, Peggy. *Operating Data Entry Systems*, Englewood Cliffs, N.J.: Prentice-Hall, 1976.

Hawkes, Nigel. *The Computer Revolution*. New York: E.P. Dutton, 1972.

Kemeny, J.G. *Man and the Computer*. New York: Charles Scribner's Sons, 1972.

King, Dennis A. *The Underground Buying Guide for Hams, CBERS, Experimenters and Computer Hobbyists*. PMS Publishing Co., 1977.

Lytel, Allen, and Lawrence Buckmaster. *ABC's of Computers*. Indianapolis: Howard W. Sams and Co., 1974.

Martin, James, and Adrian R.D. Norman. *The Computerized Society*. Englewood Cliffs, N.J.: Prentice-Hall, 1970.

Moshowitz, Abbe. *The Conquest of Will: Information Processing in Human Affairs*. Reading, Mass.: Addison-Wesley, 1976.

Mumford, Enid, and Harold Sackman, eds. *Human Choice and Computers*. Amsterdam, North-Holland, New York: Elsevier, 1975.

Nelson, Theodor H. *Computer Lib/Dream Machines*. Chicago: Theodor H. Nelson, 1974.

Porter, Kent. *Computers Made Really Simple*. New York: Crowell, 1976.

Price, Wilson T. *Introduction to Computer Data Processing*, New York: Dryden Press, 1977.

Raphael, Bertram. *The Thinking Computer*. San Francisco: W.H. Freeman & Co., 1976.

Ryan, Ray. *Basic Digital Electronics—Understanding Number Systems, Boolean Algebra & Logic Circuits*, Blue Ridge Summit, Pa.: Tab Books, 1976.

Schaefler, G.F. *Introducing Computers.* Sydney, Australia: John Wiley and Sons Australasia Pty, Ltd., 1975

Schon, Donald A. *Technology and Change.* New York: Delacorte Press, 1967.

Spencer, Donald D. *Computers in Society: The Wheres, Whys, and Hows of Computer Use.* Rochelle Park, N.J.: Hayden Book Co., 1974.

———. *Computers in Action: How Computers Work.* Rochelle Park, N.J.: Hayden Book Co., 1974.

———. *What Computers Can Do.* Baldwin Park, Cal.: Camelot Pub. Co., 1977.

Stehling, Kurt A. *Computers and You.* New York: Mentor, 1973.

Streeter, Donald A. *The Scientific Process and the Computer.* New York: John Wiley and Sons, 1974.

Thomas, Shirley. *Computers: Their History, Present Applications, and Future.* New York: Holt, Rinehart and Winston, 1965.

Turn, Rein. *Computers in the 1980's.* New York and London: Columbia University Press, 1974.

Van Tassel, Dennie L. *The Compleat Computer.* Chicago: Science Research Associates, 1976.

Ward, Brice. *Boolean Algebra.* Indianapolis: Howard W. Sams & Co., 1971.

———. *Computer Technicians Handbook.* Blue Ridge Summit, Pa.: Tab Books, 1971.

Weizenbaum, Joseph. *Computer Power and Human Reason: From Judgment to Calculation.* San Francisco: W.H. Freeman & Co., 1976.

Winston, Patrick Henry, ed. *The Psychology of Computer Vision.* New York: McGraw-Hill, 1975.

History of Calculating Machines and Computers

Babbage, Charles. *Passages from the Life of a Philosopher.* Longmans, Green, 1964.

Bernstein, Jeremy. *The Analytical Engine.* New York: Random House, 1964.

Eckert, W.J., and Rebecca Jones. *Faster, Faster: A Simple Description of a Giant Electronic Calculator and the Problems It Solves.* New York: McGraw-Hill, 1955.

Goldstine, Herman. *The Computer from Pascal to Von Neumann.* Princeton: Princeton University Press, 1972.

Halacy, Dan. *Charles Babbage, Father of the Computer.* New York: Macmillan, 1970.

Harmon, Margaret. *Stretching Man's Mind: A History of Data Processing.* New York: Mason/Charter, 1975.

Morrison, Philip, and Emily Morrison, eds. *Charles Babbage and His Calculating Engines: Selected Writings by Babbage and Others.* New York: Dover, 1964.

Mosley, Maboth. *Irascible Genius: The Life of Charles Babbage.* Chicago: Henry Regnery Co., 1964.

Pfeiffer, John. *The Thinking Machine.* Philadelphia and New York: J.B. Lippincott Co., 1962.

Randall, Brian. *The Origins of Digital Computing.* New York: Springer-Verlag, 1975.

Rosenberg, Jerry M. *The Computer Prophets.* London: Collier Macmillan Ltd., 1969.

Turck, J.A.V. *Origin of Modern Calculating Machines.* Chicago: 1921 (published under the auspices of the Western Society for Engineers).

Turing, Alan M. "Can a Machine Think?" in James Newman, ed., *The World of Mathematics*, vol. 3. New York: Simon and Schuster, 1956.

Turing, Sara. *Alan M. Turing.* Cambridge, England: W. Heffner and Sons, 1959.

UNIVAC Corp. *The Origins and Evolution of UNIVAC Computer Systems.*

von Neumann, John. "The General and Logical Theory of Automata," in James Newman, ed., *The World of Mathematics*, vol. 3. New York: Simon and Schuster, 1956.

Cybernetics and Artificial Intelligence

Amosov, N.M. *Modeling of Thinking and the Mind.* Rochelle Park, N.J.: Hayden Book Co., 1967.

Brand, Stewart. *II Cybernetic Frontiers.* New York: Random House, 1974.

Dewan, Edmond M., ed. *Cybernetics and the Management of Large Systems: Second Annual Symposium of the American Society for Cybernetics.* Rochelle Park, N.J.: Hayden Book Co., 1969.

George, F.H., and J.D. Humphries. *The Robots Are Coming: The Implications of Artificial Intelligence De-*

velopments. Rochelle Park, N.J.: Hayden Book Co., 1974.

Michie, David. *On Machine Intelligence.* Edinburgh, Scotland: Edinburgh University Press, n.d.; Halstead Press, 1974.

Pask, Gordon. *An Approach to Cybernetics.* New York: Harper & Row, 1961, 1962.

Porter, Arthur. *Cybernetics Symplified.* New York: Barnes & Noble, 1969.

Robinson, Herbert W., ed. *Cybernetics, Artificial Intelligence and Ecology, Fourth Annual Symposium of the American Society for Cybernetics.* Rochelle Park, N.J.: Hayden Book Co., 1971.

Schank, Roger C., and Kenneth Mark Colby, eds. *Computer Models of Thought and Language.* San Francisco: W.H. Freeman, 1973.

Trask, Maurice. *The Story of Cybernetics.* London: Institute of Contemporary Arts, Studio Vista/Dutton Pictureback, 1971.

von Foerster, Heinz, John D. White, Larry J. Peterston, and John K. Russell, eds. *Purposive Systems: Proceedings of the 1967 Conference of the American Society for Cybernetics.* Rochelle Park, N.J.: Hayden Book Co., 1969.

von Neumann, John. *Computers and the Brain.* New Haven: Yale University Press, 1958.

Weiner, Norbert. *The Human Use of Human Beings.* New York: Avon Books, 1967.

———. *Cybernetics; or Control & Communication in the Animal and the Machine*, 2nd edition. Cambridge, Mass.: MIT Press, 1961.

Computer Science, Technology, and Design

Abd-alla, Abd-Elfataah M., and Arnold C. Meltzer. *Principles of Digital Computer Design.* Englewood Cliffs, N.J.: Prentice-Hall, 1976.

Banks, P.M., and J.R. Doupnik. *Introduction to Computer Science.* New York: John Wiley and Sons, 1976.

Barna, A., and D.L. Pornat. *Integrated Circuits in Digital Electronics.* New York: Wiley-Interscience, 1973.

Becher, William D. *Logical Design Using Integrated Circuits*, Rochelle Park, N.J.: Hayden Book Co., 1976.

Becvar, J., ed. *Mathematic Foundations of Computer Science.* New York: Springer-Verlag, 1975.

Bell, C., and A. Newell. *Computer Structures.* New York: McGraw-Hill, 1970.

Belzer, Jack, Albert Holtzman, and Allen Kent. *Encyclopedia of Computer Science and Technology.* New York: Dekker, 1975, 1976.

Boyce, Jefferson. *Digital Computer Fundamentals.* Englewood Cliffs, N.J.: Prentice-Hall, 1976.

Chirlian, Paul W. *Analysis and Design of Digital Circuits and Computer Systems.* Champaign, Ill.: Matrix, 1977.

Chu, Y. *Digital Computer Design Fundamentals.* New York: McGraw-Hill, 1962.

Conrad, Clifford L., Nancy T. Conrad, and Harry B. Higley. *Computer Mathematics.* Rochelle Park, N.J.: Hayden Book Co., 1975.

Dodd, K.N. *Logical Design for Computers and Control.* Philadelphia: Auerbach Publishers, Inc., 1972.

Embinder, J., ed. *Semiconductor Memories.* New York: Wiley-Interscience, 1971.

Gasperini, Richard E. *Digital Trouble Shooting: Practical Digital Theory & Troubleshooting Tips*, Rochelle Park, N.J.: Hayden Book Co., 1975.

———. *Digital Experiments: Workbook of IC Experiments*, Rochelle Park, N.J.: Hayden Book Co., 1974.

Kohonen, T. *Digital Circuits and Devices.* Englewood Cliffs, N.J.: Prentice-Hall, 1972.

Lee, Samuel C. *Digital Circuits and Logical Design.* Englewood Cliffs, N.J.: Prentice-Hall, 1976.

Libes, Sol. *Fundamentals and Applications of Digital Logic Circuits.* Rochelle Park, N.J.: Hayden, 1975.

Malvino, A., and D. Leach, *Digital Principles and Applications*, 2nd ed., New York: McGraw-Hill, 1976.

Murphy, John S. *Basics of Digital Computers*, 2nd ed., 3 vols. Rochelle Park, N.J.: Hayden Book Co., 1970.

Noll, Edward M. *Linear IC Principles, Experiments, and Projects*, Indianapolis, Indiana: Howard W. Sams, 1976.

Orlicky, J. *The Successful Computer System.* New York: McGraw-Hill, 1969.

Perlis, Allan J. *Introduction to Computer Science.* New York: Harper & Row, 1975.

Potten, A. *Introduction to Digital Logic.* Rochelle Park, N.J.: Hayden Book Co., 1975.

Ralston, Anthony. *Introduction to Programming and Computer Science.* New York: McGraw-Hill, 1971.

———, and Chester Meek, eds. *Encyclopedia of Computer Science.* New York: Petrocelli/Charter, 1977.

Sessions, Kendall W., ed. *Master Handbook of 1001 Practical Electronic Circuits,* Blue Ridge Summit, Pa.: Tab Books, 1976.

Smith, John I. *Modern Operational Circuit Design.* New York: Wiley-Interscience, 1971.

Spencer, Donald D. *Computer Science Mathematics.* Columbus, Ohio: Charles E. Merrill Pub. Co., 1976.

Stearns, Samuel D. *Digital Signal Analysis,* Rochelle Park, N.J.: Hayden Books Co., 1976.

———. *Digital/Logic Electronics Handbook,* Blue Ridge Summit, Pa.: Tab Books, 1976.

Stone, H.S. *Introduction to Computer Organization and Data Structures.* New York: McGraw-Hill, 1972.

Texas Instruments Learning Center Library, *The Interface Circuits Data Book for Design Engineers,* Dallas, Texas: Texas Instruments, 1977.

Towers, T.D., and Sol Libes, *Semiconductor Circuit Elements,* Rochelle Park, N.J.: Hayden Book Co., 1976.

Tracton, Ken. *Display Electronics,* Blue Ridge Summit, Pa.: Tab Books, 1977.

Microprocessors and Microcomputers

Alan, George. *The Shoestring, Start-at-Home, Computer Business Handbook: From the Garage, Basement, Bedroom, or Closet for the Aspiring Computrepreneur,* Deerfield, Ill.: DataSearch, Inc., 1977.

American Micro-Systems. *MOS Integrated Circuits.* New York: Van Nostrand Reinhold, 1972.

Barden, William, Jr. *How to Buy and Use Minicomputers and Microcomputers.* Indianapolis: Howard W. Sams & Co., 1976.

Barna, Arpad, and Dan L. Porat. *Introduction to Microcomputers and Microprocessors.* New York: Wiley-Interscience, 1976.

Blakeslee, Thomas L. *Digital Design with Standard MSI and LSI.* New York: John Wiley and Sons, 1975.

Boyet, Howard. *8080 Microcomputer Experiments,* Forest Grove, Ore.: Dilithium Press, 1977.

Compiled by the BYTE SHOP, *BYTE Shopper, The Affordable Computer Catalog*, Tempe, Ariz.: Byte Shop, 1977.

Camenzend, H.R. *Electronic Integrated System Design.* New York: Van Nostrand Reinhold, 1977.

Computer Center Inc., *Microcomputer Recipe Book*, San Francisco, Ca.: Computer Center, Inc., 1977.

Didday, Richard L. *Home Computers: 2^{10} Questions and Answers About Software.* Forest Grove, Ore.: Dilithium Press, 1977.

———. *Home Computers: 2^{10} Questions and Answers About Hardware.* Forest Grove, Ore.: Dilithium Press, 1977.

———. *1024 Questions and Answers About Home Computers.* Champaign, Ill.: Matrix Pub., 1977.

Doty, Keith L. *Fundamental Principles of Microcomputer Architecture*, Champaign, Ill.: Matrix, 1977.

EDN Staff. *EDN Microprocessor Design Series*, vols. 1 and 2. Boston: Cahners Pub. Co., 1975.

Elphick, Michael. *Microprocessor Basics*, Rochelle Park, N.J.: Hayden Book Co., 1977.

Flynn, George. *MOS Digital IC's* Indianapolis: Howard W. Sams & Co., 1976.

Grove, A.S. *Physics and Technology of Semiconductor Devices.* New York: John Wiley & Sons, 1967.

Heiserman, David. *Building Your Own Working Robot.* Blue Ridge Summit, Pa.: Tab Books, 1976.

Hibrun, John L. and Paul M. Julich. *Microcomputers/Microprocessors: Hardware, Software and Applications.* Englewood Cliffs, N.J.: Prentice-Hall, 1976.

Holiday, Ensor. *Altair Design.* New York: Pantheon, 1973.

———. *More Altair Design.* New York: Pantheon, 1974.

———. *Altair Design 3.* New York: Pantheon, 1976.

Jung, Walter J. *IC OP-AMP Cookbook.* Indianapolis: Howard W. Sams, 1977.

Klingman, Edwin E. *Microprocessor Systems Design*, Englewood Cliffs, N.J.: Prentice-Hall, 1977.

Lancaster, Don. *CMOS Cookbook.* Indianapolis: Howard W. Sams, 1977.

———. *TTL Cookbook.* Indianapolis: Howard W. Sams, 1977.

———. *RTL Cookbook.* Indianapolis: Howard W. Sams, 1977.

———. *Active-Filter Cookbook.* Indianapolis: Howard W. Sams, 1977.

McGlynn, Daniel L. *Microprocessors: Technology, Architecture and Applications.* New York: Wiley-Interscience, 1976.

Martin, D.P. *Microcomputer Design.* Chicago: Martin Research, Ltd., 1974.

Melsa, James, and David Cohn. *Your Introduction to Home Computers.* Forest Grove, Ore.: Dilithium Press, 1977.

———. *Step by Step Introduction to 8080 Microprocessor Systems,* Forest Grove, Ore.: Dilithium Press, 1977.

Miller, Merl, and David Irwin. *Home Computer Digital Electronics.* Forest Grove, Ore.: Dilithium Press, 1977.

Osborne, Adam. *An Introduction to Microcomputers.* Berkeley, Cal.: Adam Osborne and Assoc., Inc., 1975.

———. *An Introduction to Microcomputers: Volume One: Basic Concepts; Volume Two: Some Real Products; Volume Three: 8080 Programming for Logic Design.* Berkeley, Cal.: Adam Osborne and Assoc., Inc., 1976.

PCC. *PCC's Reference Book of Personal and Home Computing.* Menlo Park, Cal.: PCC, 1977.

73 Magazine staff. *The New Hobby Computers.* Peterborough, N.H.: 73 Inc., 1977.

Scelbi Computer Consulting Inc., *Understanding Microcomputers and Small Computer Systems,* Milford, Conn.: Scelbi Computer Consulting, Inc., 1976.

Sippl, Charles J. *Microcomputer Handbook,* New York: Van Nostrand Reinhold, 1977.

Sippl, Charles J. and Merl Miller. *The Home Computer Primer and Glossary.* Forest Grove, Ore.: Dilithium Press, 1977.

Solomon, Leslie, and Stanley Viet, *Getting Involved with Your Own Computer: A Guide for Beginners,* Short Hills, N.J.: Ridley Enslow Press, 1977.

Soucek, Branko. *Microprocessors and Microcomputers.* New York: Wiley-Interscience, 1976.

Texas Instruments, Engineering Staff, *Bipolar Microcomputer Components Data Book for Design Engineers,* Dallas, Texas; Texas Instruments, Inc., 1977.

Torrero, Edward A., ed. *Microprocessors: New Directions*

for Designers. Rochelle Park, N.J.: Hayden Book Co., 1975.

Waite, Mitchell, and Michael Pardee. *Microcomputer Primer*. Indianapolis: Howard W. Sams, Inc., 1977.

Software/Programming

Agrawala, Ashok K., Tomlinson, and G. Rauscher. *Foundations of Microprogramming: Architecture, Software and Applications*. New York: Academic Press, 1976.

Andree, Richard. *Computer Programming and Related Mathematics*. New York: John Wiley and Sons, 1967.

Bauer, F.L., ed. *Software Engineering: An Advanced Course*. New York: Springer-Verlag, 1973.

Brown, R.W. *Basic Software Library*, 4 vols. Crofton, Md.: Scientific Research, 1977.

Dijkstra, Edsger W. *A Discipline of Programming*. Englewood Cliffs, N.J.: Prentice-Hall, 1976.

Dwyer, Thomas, and Margot Critchfield. *Computer Resource Book—Algebra*. Boston: Houghton Mifflin, 1975.

Findley, Robert. SCELBI *"6800" Software Gourmet Guide and Cookbook*, Milford, Conn.: Scelbi Computer Consulting, Inc., 1976.

———, Scelbi *"8080" Software Gourmet Guide and Cookbook*, Milford, Conn.: Scelbi Computer Consulting, Inc., 1976.

Gries, David. *Compiler Construction for Digital Computers*. New York: John Wiley and Sons, 1971.

Gross, Jonathan L., and Walter S. Brainerd. *22 Fundamentals of Programming Concepts*. New York: Harper & Row, 1972.

Haag, James L. *Comprehensive FORTRAN Programming*. Rochelle Park, N.J.: Hayden Book Co., 1965.

Harrison, Malcolm G. *Data Structures and Programming*. Glenview, Ill.: Scott-Foresman & Co., 1973.

Husson, S.S. *Microprogramming, Principles and Applications*. Englewood Cliffs, N.J.: Prentice-Hall, 1970.

Kernighan, Brian W., and P.J. Planger. *Software Tools*. Reading, Mass.: Addison-Wesley, 1968.

Knuth, Donald W. *Fundamental Algorithms, The Art of Computer Programming*. Reading, Mass.: Addison-Wesley, 1968.

Ledgard, Henry F. *Programming Proverbs.* Rochelle Park, N.J.: Hayden Book Co., 1975.

Levanthal, Lance. *8080A & 8085 Assembly Language Programming*, Berkeley, Calif.: Adam Osborne & Assoc., Inc., 1977.

Maurer, H.A., and M.R. Williams, *A Collection of Programming Problems and Techniques*, Englewood Cliffs, N.J.: Prentice-Hall, 1972.

McGowan, Clement L., and John R. Kelly. *Top Down Structured Programming Techniques.* New York: Petrocelli/Charter, 1975.

McMurran, M.W. *Programming Microprocessors*, Blue Ridge Summit, Pa.: Tab Books, 1976.

Minsky, Marvin, ed. *Semantic Information Processing.* Cambridge, Mass.: MIT Press, 1968.

Murphy, John S. *Basics of Digital Computer Programming*, rev. 2nd ed. Rochelle Park, N.J.: Hayden Book Co., 1972.

Osborne, Adam. *6800 Programming for Logic Design*, Berkeley, Ca.: Adam Osborne & Assoc., Inc., 1977.

Pooch, Udo. *Introduction to PL/1.* Forest Grove, Ore.: Dilithium Press, 1977.

Poole, Lon., and Mary Borchers, *Some Common Basic Programs*, Berkeley, Calif.: Adam Osborne & Assoc., Inc., 1977.

Scelbi Computer Consulting, Inc. *Machine Language Programming for the 8008 and Similar Microprocessors.* Conn.: Scelbi Computer Consulting Inc., 1976.

Schoman, Kenneth E. *The Basic Workbook: Creative Techniques for Beginning Programmers*, Rochelle Park, N.J.: Hayden Book Co., 1976.

Silver, Gerald A., and Joan B. Silver. *Computer Algorithms and Flowcharting.* New York: Gregg-McGraw-Hill, 1975.

Stark, Peter A. *Computer Programming Handbook.* Blue Ridge Summit, Pa.: Tab Books, 1975.

Steinbach, Robert S. *Programming Exercises.* Beverly Hills, Cal.: Glencoe Press, 1969.

Ullman, Jeffrey D. *Fundamental Concepts of Programming Systems.* Reading, Mass.: Addison-Wesley, 1976.

VanTassel, Dennie. *Program Style, Design, Efficiency, Debugging and Testing.* Englewood Cliffs, N.J.: Prentice-Hall, 1974.

———. *The Psychology of Computer Programming.* New York: Van Nostrand Reinhold, 1971.

Wester, John G., and William D. Simpson. *Software Design for Microprocessors.* Dallas, Texas: Texas Instruments, Inc., 1976.

Yourdon, Edward. *Techniques of Program Structure & Design*, Englewood Cliffs, N.J.: Prentice-Hall, 1975.

Languages

Albrecht, Robert. *My Computer Likes Me When I Speak In BASIC.* Menlo Park, Cal.: Dymax, 1972.

———, LeRoy Finkel, and Jerry Brown. *BASIC.* New York: John Wiley and Sons, 1973.

Blakeslee, Thomas R. *Introducing BASIC.* W. Hartford, Conn.: Educomp Corp., 1972.

Coan, James S. *Basic BASIC.* Rochelle Park, N.J.: Hayden Book Co., 1970.

Diehr, George. *Business Programming with BASIC.* New York: John Wiley and Sons, 1972.

Dodes, Irving Allen. *Assembly Language Basics: An Annotated Program Book.* Rochelle Park, N.J.: Hayden Book Co., 1975.

Dwyer, Thomas A., and Michael S. Kaufman. *A Guided Tour of Computer Programming in BASIC.* Boston: Houghton-Mifflin, 1973.

Forsyther, A.I., R.M. Aiken, C.E. Hughes, and E.I. Organick. *Computer Science: Programming in FORTRAN and WATFOR and WATFIV.* New York: John Wiley and Sons, 1975.

Gilman, Leonard, and Allen J. Rose, *APL: An Interactive Approach*, N.Y.: Wiley and Sons, 1976 (revised second edition).

Gruenberger, Fred. *Computing with the BASIC Language.* San Francisco: Canfield Press, 1972.

Harms, Edward, and Michael P. Zabinski, *Introduction to APL and Computer Programming*, N.Y.: Wiley and Sons, 1977.

Iverson, Kenneth. *APL in Exposition*, New York: APL Press, 1976.

———, *Introducing APL to Teachers*, New York: APL Press, 1976.

———, *An Introduction to APL for Scientists and Engineers*, New York: APL Press, 1976.

———, *A Programming Language*. New York: John Wiley and Sons, 1962.

Keller, Dennis P., and Daniel P. Freedman. *Structured Programming with APL*. Cambridge, Mass.: Winthrop, 1976.

Kemeny, J.G., and T.E. Kurtz. *BASIC Programming*. New York: John Wiley and Sons, 1971.

Kennedy, Michael, and Martin B. Solomon, *Ten Statement FORTRAN plus FORTRAN IV*, (second edition), Englewood Cliffs, N.J.: Prentice-Hall, 1976.

Lewis, R., and B.H. Blakeley. *Elements of BASIC*. London: National Computing Center, Ltd., 1972.

Maniotes, John, Harry B. Higley, and James N. Haag. *Beginning FORTRAN: Simplified, 12-Statement Programming*. Rochelle Park, N.J.: Hayden Book Co., 1971.

Newsted, Peter R. *SNOBOL: An Introduction to Programming*. Rochelle Park, N.J.: Hayden Book Co., 1975.

Pakin, Sandra, and the Staff of Computer Innovations, *APL: A Short Course*, Englewood Cliffs, N.J.: Prentice-Hall, 1977.

Pegels, C. Carl. *Basic: A Computer Programming Language with Business and Management Applications*. San Francisco: Halden-Day, 1973.

Peterson, W. Wesley. *Introduction to Programming Languages*. Englewood Cliffs, N.J.: Prentice-Hall, 1974.

Rosenblatt, Lisa and Judah. *Simplified BASIC Programming with Companion Problems*. Reading, Mass.: Addison-Wesley, 1973.

Sack, John R., and Judith L. Meadows. *Entering BASIC*. Chicago: Science Research Assoc., 1972.

Sanderson, Peter. *Interactive Computing in BASIC*. London: Butterworth Group, 1973.

Scelbi Computer Consulting, Inc. *Scelbal: A Higher Level Language for 8008/8080 System*. Milford, Conn.: Scelbi Computer Consulting, Inc., 1976.

Smith, Robert E. *Discovering BASIC: A Problem Solving Approach*. Rochelle Park, N.J.: Hayden Book Co., 1970.

———. *A Visual Approach to BASIC*. Minneapolis, Minn.: ControlData Corp., 1972.

Spencer, Donald. *A Guide to BASIC Programming*. Reading, Mass.: Addison-Wesley, 1975.

Steingrapher, Jack. *FORTRAN Fundamentals: A Short Course*. Rochelle Park, N.J.: Hayden Book Co., 1975.

Weinberg, Gerald. *PL/1 Programming: A Manual of Style*. New York: McGraw-Hill, 1970.

Worth, Thomas. *BASIC for Everyone*. Englewood Cliffs, N.J.: Prentice-Hall, 1976.

———, *COBOL for Beginners*. Englewood Cliffs, N.J.: Prentice-Hall, 1977.

Applications

Abramson, N., and F.F. Kuo. *Computer-Communications Networks*. Englewood Cliffs, N.J.: Prentice-Hall, 1973.

Ahl, David., ed. *101 BASIC Computer Games*. Maynard, Mass.: Digital Equipment Corp., 1973, 1974.

Ahl, David. *The Best of Creative Computing, Vol. 1*. Morristown, N.J.: Creative Computing Press, 1976.

———. *Understanding Mathematics and Logic Using BASIC Computer Games*. Maynard, Mass.: Digital Equipment Corp., 1974.

Albrecht, Robert, Eric Lindberg, and Walter Mara. *Computer Methods in Mathematics*. Menlo Park, Cal.: Addison-Wesley, 1969.

Appleton, Jon H., and Ronald C. Perera. *The Development and Practice of Electronic Music*. Englewood Cliffs, N.J.: Prentice-Hall, 1975.

Arnold, Robert, Harold G. Hill, and Aylmer V. Nichols. *Modern Data Processing*. New York: John Wiley and Sons, 1969.

Bassler, Richard A., and Ed O. Joslin, eds. *Applications of Computer Systems*. Arlington, Va.: College Readings Inc., 1976.

Bates, B., K. Jarvis, and A. van Dwyne. *Advanced Placement Calculus: Exercises with Computer Programs*. Newburyport, Mass.: ENTELEK, 1976.

Cauchon, Paul. *Chemistry with a Computer*. Newburyport, Mass.: ENTELEK, 1976.

Doran, J.E., and F.R. Hodson. *Mathematics and Computers in Archaeology*. Cambridge: Harvard University Press, 1975.

Franke, Herbert W. *Computer Graphics-Computer Art*, trans. Gustav Metzger. London: Phaidon, 1971.

Graham, John. *Making Computers Pay.* New York: Halstead-Wiley, 1976.

Gruenberger, Fred, and M. Jaffray, *Problems for Computer Solution.* New York: John Wiley and Sons, 1965.

Iasis, Inc. *Microcomputer Applications Handbook.* Sunnyvale, Cal.: Iasis, Inc., 1977.

Lancaster, Don. *TV Typewriter Cookbook.* Indianapolis: Howard W. Sams & Co., Inc., 1976.

Leavitt, Ruth, ed. *Artists and Computer.* Morristown, N.J.: Creative Computing Press; New York: Harmony Books, 1976.

Lincoln, Harry B., ed. *The Computer and Music.* Ithaca, N.Y.: Cornell University Press, 1970.

Lourie, Janice. *Textile Graphics/Computer Aided.* New York: Fairchild Publishers, 1973.

Matthews, Max V. *The Technology of Computer Music.* Cambridge, Mass.: MIT Press, 1969.

Newborn, Monroe. *Computer Chess.* New York: Academic Press, 1975.

Newman, Wm. N., and Robert F. Sproull. *Principles of Interactive Computer Graphics.* New York: McGraw-Hill, 1976.

PCC. *What to Do After You Hit Return: PCC's First Book of Computer Games.* Menlo Park, Cal: PCC/Hewlett-Packard, 1975.

Prueitt, Melvin L. *Computer Graphics: 118 Computer-Generated Designs.* New York: Dover, 1975.

Rader, Richard A. *The Entelek Computer-Based Physics Lab.* Newburyport, Mass.: ENTELEK, 1977.

Sage, Edwin R. *Fun and Games with Computers.* Newburyport, Mass.: ENTELEK, 1975.

———. *Problem-Solving with the Computer.* Newburyport, Mass.: ENTELEK, 1969.

Scelbi Computer Consulting, Inc. *Scelbi's Galaxy Game for 8008/8080.* Milford, Conn.: Scelbi Computer Consulting, Inc., 1976.

73 Magazine Staff. *Finite State Fantastic.* Champaign, Ill.: Matrix Publishers, 1976.

Spencer, Donald. *Game Playing with Computers.* Rochelle Park, N.J.: Hayden Book Co., 1975.

Stern, Robert A., and Nancy R. Stern. *Principles of Data Processing.* New York: John Wiley and Sons, 1973.

Stolurow, Lawrence A. *The Entelek Computer-Based Math Lab*. Newburyport, Mass.: ENTELEK, 1977.

Walker, B.S., J.N. Gurd, and E.A. Drawneek. *Interactive Computer Graphics*. New York: Crane and Russak, 1976.

von Foerster, Heinz, and James Beauchamp. *Music by Computer*. New York: John Wiley and Sons, 1969.

Dictionaries

Burton, Philip E. *A Dictionary of Microcomputers*. Garland Library of Science and Technology, 1977.

Meek, Chester L. *Glossary of Computing Terminology*. New York: Macmillan Information, 1972.

Sippl, Charles J., and Charles P. Sippl. *Computer Dictionary and Handbook*. Indianapolis: Howard W. Sams, Inc., 1977.

Sippl, Charles J. *Data Communications Dictionary*. New York: Van Nostrand Reinhold, 1976.

———, and David A. Kidd. *Microcomputer Dictionary and Guide*. Champagne, Ill.: Matrix Publishers, 1976.

Spencer, Donald D. *Computer Acronym Handbook*. Englewood Cliffs, N.J.: Prentice-Hall, 1974.

———. *Computer Dictionary*, Baldwin Park, Cal.: Camelot Publishing Co., 1974.

User's Manuals

4004/4040 Assembly Language Programming Manual. Intel Corp., Santa Clara, Ca., 1974.

8080 User's Manual. Intel Corp., Santa Clara, Cal., 1975.

8080 Assembly Language Programming Manual. Intel Corp., Santa Clara, Cal., 1975.

PL/M High-Level Language Programming Manual. Intel Corp., Santa Clara, Cal., 1975.

M6800 Microprocessor Applications Manual. Motorola Semiconductor Products, Inc., Phoenix, Ariz., 1975.

M6800 Programming Manual. Motorola Semiconductor Products, Inc., Phoenix, Ariz., 1975.

IMP-16C Application Manual. National Semiconductor Corp., Santa Clara, Cal., 1974.

F-8 Microprocessor Application Notes. Fairchild Semiconductor Components Group, Mountain View, Cal., 1975.

F-8 Microprocessor Programming Guide. Fairchild Semiconductor Components Group, Mountain View, Cal., 1975.

CP1600 Microprocessor User's Manual. General Instrument Corp., Hicksville, N.Y., 1975.

Appendix E:

Home Computer Magazines

BYTE
monthly, $1.50/copy; for computer hobbyists
BYTE Publications, Inc.
70 Main St.
Peterborough, N.H. 03458

Computer
monthly, $2.75/copy; for the computer world in general, with some hobbyist material
IEEE Computer Society
Technical Services
345 E. 47th St.
New York, N.Y. 10017

Computer Music Journal
monthly, $2.75/copy; for those interested in the musical applications of digital computers
People's Computer Company
Box E, 1010 Doyle St.
Menlo Park, Cal. 94205

Computer Notes
monthly, $5.00/year; for computer hobbyists
MITS, Inc.
2450 Alamo S.E.
Albuquerque, N.M. 87106

Computerworld
weekly newspaper, $15/year; for the computer world in general
Computerworld, Inc.
797 Washington St.
Newton, Mass. 02160

Creative Computing
bimonthly, $1.50/copy; for computer hobbyists focusing on software
Creative Computing
P.O. Box 789-M
Morristown, N.J. 07960

Datamation
monthly, $24/year; for the computer world in general with some hobbyist material
Technical Publishing Co.
1301 S. Grove Ave.
Barrington, Ill. 60010

Dr. Dobb's Journal of Computer Calisthenics and Orthodontia
monthly, $1.50/copy; for computer hobbyists focusing on software
People's Computer Company
Box 310
Menlo Park, Cal. 94025

Electronic Design
biweekly, $3/copy; for electronic buffs with some hobbyist material
Hayden Publishing Co.
50 Essex St.
Rochelle Park, N.J. 07662

Interface Age
monthly, $1.50/copy; for computer hobbyists
McPheters, Wolfe & Jones
6615 Sunset Blvd.
Hollywood, Cal. 90028

Kilobaud
monthly, $2.00/copy; for computer hobbyists
10001001, Inc.
Peterborough, N.H. 03458

People's Computers
bimonthly, $1.60/copy; for the general home computer audience
People's Computer Company
1263 El Camino Real
Box E
Menlo Park, Cal. 94025

Periodical Guide for Computerists 1976
annual, $2.50; detailed guide to hobbyist publications for computer world in general
E. Berg Publications
1360 S.W. 199th Ct.
Aloha, Ore. 97005

Personal Computing
bimonthly, $2.00/copy; for computer hobbyists
Benwill Publishing Corp.
167 Corey Rd.
Brookline, Mass. 02146

Personal Computing Directory
annual, $4.95; containing *all* personal computing information
Personal Computer Directory
Box 134
Harvard Square
Cambridge, Mass. 02138

Popular Electronics
monthly, $1.00/copy; for electronic buffs with some hobbyist material
Popular Electronics
One Park Ave.
New York, N.Y. 10016

Processor Technology Access
every 6 weeks, newspaper format, 75¢/copy; for computer hobbyists with special emphasis on Processor Technology products
Wible/Rampton Advertising
727-15th Ave.
San Francisco, Cal. 94118

Radio Electronics
monthly, 75¢/copy; for electronic buffs with some hobbyist material
Greensback Publications, Inc.
200 Park Avenue South
New York, N.Y. 10003

ROM
monthly, $2.00/copy; for computer hobbyists
ROM Publications
Route 97
Hampton, Conn. 06247

73 Magazine
monthly, $1.50/copy; for electronic buffs with some hobbyist material
73, Inc.
Peterborough, N.H. 03458

Spectrum
monthly, $4.00/copy; for engineering and electronic buffs with some hobbyist material
IEEE, Inc.
345 East 47th Street
New York, N.Y. 10017

Appendix F:

Home Computer Companies

Apple Computer Company
770 Welch Rd.
Palo Alto, Cal. 94304

Applied Microtechnology
100 N. Winchester Blvd.
Suite 260
Santa Clara, Cal. 95050

Bitech, Inc.
1440 State College Blvd.
Bldg. 6
Anaheim, Cal. 92806

BYTE, Inc.
1261 Birchwood Dr.
Sunnyvale, Cal. 94086

CGRS Microtech
P.O. Box 368
Southampton, Pa. 18966

Commodore
901 California Avenue
Palo Alto, California 94304

Compucolor Corp.
Subsidiary of Intelligent Systems Corp.
5965 Peachtree Corners East
Norcross, Ga. 30071

Computer Data Systems
c/o Robert Boyer
English Village Apts.
Atram Hall #3
Newark, Del. 19711

Computer Power and Light
12321 Ventura Blvd.
Studio City, Cal. 91604

Cramer Electronics
85 Wells Ave.
Newton, Mass. 02159

Cromemco
One First St.
Los Altos, Cal. 94022

Cybersystem, Inc.
4306 Governors Dr.
Huntsville, Ala. 35805

Data General Corp.
Southboro, Mass. 01772

Digital Electronics Corp.
2126 Sixth St.
Berkeley, Cal. 94710

Digital Equipment Corp.
146 Main St.
Maynard, Mass. 01754

The Digital Group
P.O. Box 6528
Denver, Colo. 80206

E&L Instruments
61 First St.
Derby, Conn. 06418

EBKA Industries, Inc.
6920 Melrose Lane
Oklahoma City, Okla. 73127

Ebnek, Inc.
254 N. Washington St.
Wichita, Kansas 67202

ECD Corp.
196 Broadway
Cambridge, Mass. 02139

Electronic Control Technology
P.O. Box 6
Union, N.J. 07083

Electronic Products Associates, Inc.
1157 Vega St.
San Diego, Cal. 92110

Electronic Tool Co.
4736 West El Segundo Blvd.
P.O. Box 1315
Hawthorne, Cal. 90250

Fairchild Microsystems Division
1725 Technology Dr.
San Jose, Cal. 95110

HAL Communications Corp.
Box 365
807 East Green St.
Urbana, Ill. 61801

Heath Company
Benton Harbor, Michigan 49022

Hewlett-Packard Corp.
1501 Page Mill Road
Palo Alto, California 94304

IMS Associates, Inc.
1922 Republic Ave.
San Leandro, Cal. 94577

Infinite, Inc.
1924 Waverly Place
Melborne, Fla. 32901

Intelligent Systems Corp.
5965 Peachtree Corners East
Norcross, Ga. 30071

M&R Enterprises
P.O. Box 61011
Sunnyvale, Cal. 94088

Martin Research
336 Commercial Ave.
Northbrook, Ill. 60062

Microcomputer Associates Inc.
2859 Scott Blvd.
Santa Clara, Cal. 95050

Microdata Systems
2 Mack Road #101
Woburn, Mass. 01801

Microkit Inc.
2180 Colorado Ave.
Santa Monica, Cal. 90490

Midwest Scientific Instruments
220 W. Cedar
Olathe, Kansas 66061

MITS, Inc.
2450 Alamo S.E.
Albuquerque, N.M. 87106

Monolithic Systems Corp.
14 Inverness Dr. East
Englewood, Colo. 80110

MOS Technology Inc.
950 Rittenhouse Rd.
Norristown, Pa. 19401

Multisonics, Inc.
6444 Sierra Court
P.O. Box 2295
Dublin, Cal. 94566

National Semiconductor Corp.
2900 Semiconductor Dr.
Santa Clara, Ca. 95015

Noval Inc.
8401 Aero Dr.
San Diego, Cal. 92123

Ohio Scientific Instruments
11679 Hayden St.
Hiram, Ohio 44234

Pacific Cyber/Metrix, Inc.
180 Thorup Lane
San Ramon, Cal. 94583

Plessey Microsystems
1674 McGaw Ave.
Irvine, Cal. 92714

Polymorphic Systems
737 Kellogg
Goleta, Cal. 93017

Processor Technology
6200-T Hollis St.
Emeryville, Cal. 94608

Radio Shack
2617 West 7th St.
Fort Worth, Texas 76107

Realistic Controls Corp.
3530 Warrensville Center Rd.
Cleveland, Ohio 44122

Southwest Technical Products Corp.
219 W. Rhapsody
San Antonio, Texas 78216

Sphere Group
791 S. 500 W.
Bountiful, Utah 84010

STS Systems
Mount Vernon, N.H. 03057

Systems Research Inc.
1010 Westwood Blvd.
Los Angeles, Cal. 90024

Technical Design Labs
Research Park Bldg. H
1101 State Road
Princeton, N.J.

Terak Corp.
P.O. Box 3078
Scottsdale, Ariz. 85257

TLF
P.O. Box 2298
Littleton, Colo. 80161

Tranti Systems, Inc.
1 Chelmsford Rd.
North Billerica, Mass. 01862

Vector Graphic, Inc.
717 Lakefield Rd., Suite F
Westlake, Cal. 91361

Veras Systems
P.O. Box 74
Somerville, Mass. 02143

Warner & Swasey Co.
30300 Solon Industrial Parkway
Solon, Ohio 44139

Wave Mate
1015 W. 190th Street
Gardena, Cal. 90248

Western Data Systems
3650 Charles St. #2
Santa Clara, Cal. 95050

Wyle Computer Products
3200 Macgruder Blvd.
Hampton, Va. 23666

Appendix G:

Home Computer Clubs

Alabama

North Alabama Computer Club
c/o Jack Crenshaw
1409 Blevins Gap Rd. SE
Huntsville, Ala. 35802

Alaska

Ronald J. Finger
3417 E. 65th Street
Anchorage, Alaska 99502

Arizona

Microprocessors Users Group
c/o Harry C. Stanton
3608 W. Davidson Lane
Phoenix, Ariz. 85020

Scott Jarol/Mark Kailor
3701 E. Shaw Butte Dr.
Phoenix, Ariz. 85028

California

Association for Educational Data Systems
c/o Dr. Jane D. Gawronski
Dept. of Education
6401 Linda Vista Rd.
San Diego, Cal. 92111

Bay Area MicroGroup
4565 Black Ave.
Pleasanton, Cal. 94566

Bay Area Microprocessors Group
c/o Richard Lindberg
1211 Santa Clara Ave.
Alameda, Cal. 94501

Beverly Hills Computer Club
241 Marino Dr.
Beverly Hills, Cal. 90212

California Computer Society
c/o Sheila Clark
Box 9459
N. Hollywood, Cal. 91609

COLA (Computer Organization of Los Angeles)
P.O. Box 43677
Los Angeles, Cal. 90043

Compucolor Users
c/o S.P. Electronics
5250 Van Nuys Blvd.
Van Nuys, Cal. 91401

Computer Guild
P.O. Box 255232
Sacramento, Cal. 95825

Computer Phreaques United
c/o Mac McCormick
2090 Cross Street
Seaside, Cal. 93955

Glendale Community College Computer Club
c/o V.S. Lashleu
1500 N. Verdugo Rd.
Glendale, Cal. 91208

HP-Users Club
2541 W. Camden Place
Santa Ana, Cal. 92704

Homebrew Computer Club
P.O. Box 626
Mountain View, Cal. 94040

Inland Computer Society
c/o Tom Munnecke
P.O. Box 55052
Riverside, Cal. 92517

Jim McCord
330 Vereda Legenda
Goleta, Cal. 93170

Litton Calculator/Computer Club
Litton Guidance and Control Systems
MS 78/31
5500 Canoga Ave.
Woodland Hills, Cal. 91364

LLLRA Hobbyist Group
c/o Charles D. Hoover
35 West Essen St.
Stockton, Cal. 95204

LO*OP Center
8099 La Plaza
Cotati, Cal. 94928

MICRO-8 Computer Club
2497 Lompoc-Casmalia Rd.
Lompoc, Cal. 93436

North Orange County Computer Club (NOCCC)
P.O. Box 3603
Orange, Cal. 92665

29 Palms Area Group
c/o Sgt. Wesley Isgregg
Box 3558, C&E Schools MCB
29 Palms, Cal. 92278
OR
c/o Sgt. Stanley B. Herr
13-C Copper Drive MCB
29 Palms, Cal. 92278

POMONA Group
c/o Al Sutton
4155 Oak Hollow Rd.
Claremont, Cal. 91711

Sacramento Microcomputer Users Group
SMUG
P.O. Box 161513
Sacramento, Cal. 95816

Sacramento Minicomputer Users
P.O. Box 741
Citrus Heights, Cal. 95610

San Diego Computing Society
c/o James W. Farschon
P.O. Box 9988
San Diego, Cal. 92109
OR
c/o Gary Mitchell
Box 35
Chula Vista, Cal. 92012

San Gabriel Chapter—SCCS
c/o Dan Erickson
400 S. Catalina Ave.
Pasadena, Cal. 91106

San Luis Obispo Microcomputer Club
439 Marsh St.
San Luis Obispo, Cal. 93401

Santa Barbara Computer Group
c/o Glenn A. McComb
210 Barrunca #2
Santa Barbara, Cal. 93101

Santa Barbara Nameless Computer Group
c/o Doug Perrod
1445 La Cima Rd.
Santa Barbara, Cal. 93101

Southern California Computer Society
P.O. Box 987
South Pasadena, Cal. 91030
OR
Box 3123
Los Angeles, Cal. 90051
OR
Box 54751
Los Angeles, Cal. 90054

UCLA Computer Club
3514 Boelter Hall
UCLA
Los Angeles, Cal. 90024

Valley Chapter SCCS
c/o R. Stuart Gibbs
5652 Lemona Ave.
Van Nuys, Cal. 91411

Ventura County Club
c/o Eric Strohbehn
4409 Vineyard
Oxnard, Cal. 93030

Ventura County Computer Society
P.O. Box 525
Port Hueneme, Cal. 93041

Colorado

Denver Amateur Computer Society
P.O. Box 6338
Denver, Colo. 80206

Connecticut

Amateur Computer Club
c/o Stephen B. Gray
260 Noroton Ave.
Darien, Conn. 06820

Connecticut Microists
c/o George Ahmuty
60111 Wendy Lane
Westport, Conn. 06881

Southern New England Computer Society
c/o Charles Floto
267 Willow St. "1"
New Haven, Conn. 06511

University of Hartford Microcomputer Club
College of Engineering
Dana Hall
200 Bloomfield Ave.
West Hartford, Conn. 06117

District of Columbia

Washington Amateur Computer Society
c/o Robert J. Jones
4201 Massachusetts Ave. N.W.
#168
Washington, D.C. 20016

Florida

Central Florida Computer Club
c/o Data Entry Engineering
1810 N. Orange Ave.
Orlando, Fla. 32804

Fort Lauderdale Computer Club
c/o Robert Denis
11080 N.W. 39th Street
Coral Springs, Fla. 33065

Indian River Computer Society
FIT Electrical Engineering Dept.
Country Club Rd.
Melbourne, Fla. 32901

Jacksonville Computer Club
Regency East Office Park
9951 Atlantic Blvd., Suite 326
Jacksonville, Fla. 32211

Miami Area Computer Club
c/o Terry Williamson
P.O. Box 430852 S.
Miami, Fla. 33143

Miami Computer Club
c/o John Lynn
13431 S.W. 79th St.
Miami, Fla. 33183

Microcomputer Society of Florida
P.O. Box 3284
Downtown Station
Tampa, Fla. 33604
OR
c/o Donald A. Marsh
5405B
Southern Comfort Blvd.
Tampa, Fla. 33614

South Florida Computer Group
410 N.W. 117th Street
Miami, Fla. 33168

Space Coast Microcomputer Club
c/o Ray O. Lockwood

1825 Canal Court
Merritt Island, Fla. 32952

Tallahassee Amateur Computer Society
c/o Larry Hughes
Route 14
Box 351-116
Tallahassee, Fla. 32304

University of Florida Amateur Computer Society
Electrical Engineering Dept.
Larsen Hall, Rm # 234
Gainesville, Fla. 32611

Georgia

Atlanta Area Microcomputer Club
c/o Jim Dunion
421 Ridgecrest Rd.
Atlanta, Ga. 30307

Atlanta Area Microcomputer Hobbyist Group
c/o Jim Stratigos
P.O. Box 33140
Atlanta, Ga. 30332

Hawaii

Aloha Computer Club
94-360 Hokuala St., Apt. 187
Mililani Town, Hawaii 96789

Idaho

Coeur d'Alene Society for the Prevention of Cruelty to Computers (CSPCC)
205 Foster, Apt. 2
Coeur d'Alene, Idaho 83814

Illinois

ALTAIR-CHICAGO
517 Talcott Rd.
Park Ridge, Ill. 60068

Chicago Area Computer Hobbyist's Exchange (CACHE)
c/o Bill Precht
P.O. Box 36
Vernon Hills, Ill. 60061

Chicago Micro Users Group
c/o Bill Precht
1102 S. Edison
Lombard, Ill. 60148

Chicago Users Group
c/o Robert Schwartz
195 Ivy Lanes
Highland Park, Ill. 60035

ICE-NINE, Inc.
P.O. Box 291
Western Springs, Ill. 60558

Microcomputer APL Enthusiasts
MAPLA
P.O. Box 574 NUMS
303 E. Chicago Ave.
Chicago, Ill. 60611

Quad City Computer Club
4211½ Seventh Ave.
Rock Island, Ill. 61201

SCCS 5063
c/o Roy Emerson
14904 S. Calis Ave.
Oosen, Il. 60469

Indiana

BETA IOTA TAU (Computer Fraternity)
c/o Richard A. Petke
RHIT
P.O. Box 420
Terre Haute, Ind. 47803

The Floyd County Computer Enthusiasts
c/o Nathan Engle
RR2, P.O. Box 466A
New Albany, Ind. 47150

Hoosier Amateur Computer and Kluge Society
HACKS
c/o Ray Borrill
111 S. College Ave.
Bloomington, Ind. 47401

Indianapolis Small Systems Group
4719 Squire Dr.
Indianapolis, Ind. 46241

Purdue University Computer Hobbyist Club (PUNCH)
Electrical Engineering Bldg. Rm. 67
Purdue University
West Lafayette, Ind. 47907

Iowa

Davenport Iowa and Rock Island Area
c/o Bill Bangasser
P.O. Box 4133
Davenport, Iowa 52808

The Eastern Iowa Computer Club
6026 Underwood Ave. S.W.
Cedar Rapids, Iowa 52404

Kansas

The Computer Network of Kansas City
968 Kansas Ave.
Kansas City, Kan. 66105

South Central Kansas Amateur Computer Assoc.
1504 N. St. Clair
Wichita, Kan. 67203

Kentucky

Louisville Area Computer Club
c/o Andy Ehalt
115 Edgemont Dr.
New Albany, Ind. 47150

Louisville Area Users of Cybertronics Computers
c/o Steve Roberts
P.O. Box 18065
Louisville, Ky. 40218

Louisiana

Crescent City Computer Club
P.O. Box 1901
University of New Orleans
New Orleans, La. 70122

New Orleans Computer Club
c/o Emile Alline
1119 Pennsylvania Ave.
Slidell, La. 70458

Maryland

Chesapeake Microcomputer Club, Inc.
c/o Philip Hisley
236 St. David Crt. #4
Cockeysville, Md. 21030

Massachusetts

Alcove Computer Club
230 Main Street
Route 28
North Reading, Mass. 01864

Boston Area Group
c/o John Vullo
21 Sunset Ave.
North Rearding, Mass. 01864

Boston Computer Club
c/o Jonathan Rotanberg
17 Chestnut St.
Boston, Mass. 02108

Boston Computer Society
c/o Donald Bradley
123 Commonwealth Ave.
Boston, Mass. 02116

Greater Boston Computer Users Group
c/o Steven Hain
40 Wilshire Dr. (Door 2)
Sharon, Mass. 02067

New England Computer Society
P.O. Box 198
Bedford, Mass. 01730

Richard F. Brown
730 Boston Post Rd.
Sudbury, Mass. 01776

Michigan

Ann Arbor Computing Club
c/o Roger Gregory
1485 Newport Rd.
Ann Arbor, Mich. 48103

Computer Hobbyists Around Lansing
c/o Joyce Church
4307 Mar-Moor Dr.
Lansing, Mich. 48917

Detroit Area Club
c/o Dennis Siemit
45466 Cluster
Utica, Mich. 48087

Detroit Areas Users Group
c/o Dana Badertscher
18300 Ash
E. Detroit, Mich. 48021

Jackson Hams and Hackers
Commonwealth Assoc., Inc.
209 East Washington St.
Jackson, Mich. 49201

C.J. Lamesfield
Box 271
Davison, Mich. 48423

Mid-Michigan Computer Club
15151 Ripple Dr.
Linden, Mich. 48451

Mid-Michigan MicroGroup
c/o William T. Serviss
13121 Tucker Dr.
DeWitt, Mich. 48820

Southeastern Michigan Computer Organization
SEMCO
c/o Dick Weir
20000 Great Oak Circle South
Mount Clemens, Michigan

Minnesota

Advanced Technology Research Association
ATRA
P.O. Box 456
Minneopolis, Minn. 55440

Minnesota Computer Society
P.O. Box 35317
Minneapolis, Minn. 55435

Small Computer Engineering Assoc. of Minnesota (SCEAM)
Resource Access Center
c/o Richard B. Koblow
3010 Fourth Ave. S
Minneapolis, Minn. 55408

Southwest Minnesota Amateur Computer Club
2122 N.W. 17th Ave.
Rochester, Minn. 55901

XXX-11 Users Group
c/o Dick Corner
514 Ninth Street
Moorhead, Minn. 56560

Missouri

St. Louis Area Computer Club
c/o Lou Elkens
P.O. Box 1143
St. Louis, Mo. 63188

Montana

Flathead Computer Society
c/o Ernest G. Brooner
B236
Lakeside, Mont. 59922

Nebraska

Mid-America Computer Hobbyists (MACH)
c/o Lt. Tom Smith
2708 Calhoun St.
Bellevue, Neb. 68005

Nevada

Northern Nevada Amateur Computer Club
UNSCC
P.O. Box 9068
Reno, Nev. 89507

SCCS
Quentin C. West
13 Ballerine
Henderson, Nev. 89015

New Hampshire

Nashua N.H. Area Computer Club
c/o Dwayne Jeffries
181 Cypress Lane
Nashua, N.H. 03060

New England Computer Club
c/o *BYTE* Magazine
70 Main St.
Peterborough, N.H. 03458

New Jersey

Amateur Computer Group of New Jersey, Inc.
c/o Sol Libes
Union City Technical Institute
1776 Raritan Rd.
Scotch Plains, N.J. 07076

Computer Group of South New Jersey
c/o David Jones
503 W. New Jersey Ave.
Somers Point, N.J. 08244

Holmdel Microprocessor Club
c/o Fred Horney
Rm. 3D317
Bell Telephone Labs
Holmdel, N.J. 07733

New Jersey Club
c/o Bruce C. Dalland
37 Brook Drive
Dover, N.J. 07801

Northern New Jersey Amateur Computer Group
c/o Murray P. Dwight
593 New York Avenue
Lyndhurst, N.J. 07071

SCCS
c/o William Staatse
Box 947
McGuire AFB, N.J. 08641

William Paulus
510 Nectar Ave.
Pine Hurst, N.J. 08201

New Mexico

Albuquerque Area Computer Club
c/o Gary Track
P.O. Box 866
Corrales, N.M. 87048

U.S. Robotics Society
Box 26484
Albuquerque, N.M.

New York

Buffalo Group
c/o Chuck Fischer
355 S. Creek Dr.
Depew, N.Y. 14043

Computer and Electronics Hobbyists Assoc. of America (CEHAA)
P.O. Box 13
Flushing, N.Y. 11352

Ithaca Computer Group
c/o Steve Edelman
204 Dryden Rd.
Ithaca, N.Y. 14850

Long Island Computer Assoc.
P.O. Box 864
Jamaica, New York 11431

Long Island Computer Club
c/o Popular Electronics
One Park Ave.
New York, N.Y. 10016

Microcomputer Club of Rochester
University of Rochester
Computing Center
727 Elmwood Ave.
Rochester, N.Y. 14620

N.Y. Amateur Computer Club
106 Bedford St.
New York, N.Y. 10014

New York City MicroHobbyist Group
c/o Bob Schwartz
375 Riverside Drive 1E
New York, N.Y. 10025

Niagara Regional Computer Group (NRCG)
c/o Chuck Fischer
355 S. Creek Drive
Depew, N.Y. 14043

Pacesetter's Users Group
1457 Broadway Rm. 305
New York N.Y. 10016

Rochester Area Microcomputer Society (RAMS)
P.O. Box D
Rochester, N.Y. 14609

Stony Brook Home-Brew Computer Club
c/o Ludwig Braun, Prof, of Engineering
SUNY
Stony Brook, N.Y. 11794

Students Cybernetics Lab
16 Linwood Ave.
Buffalo, N.Y. 14209

Westchester Amateur Computer Society
c/o Harold Shair
41 Colby Ave.
Rye, N.Y. 10580
or
300 Tarrytown Road
Elmsford, N.Y. 10523

Westchester Fairfield Amateur Computer Society
RR 1, Box 198
Pound Ridge, N.Y. 10576

North Carolina

Charlotte Microcomputer Club
Dr. Michael Allen
704-597-2303 (days)
Allen Grayson
704-366-7897 (nights)

Fayetteville–Fort Bragg Area
c/o Robert G. Lloyd
7554 Southgate Rd.
Fayetteville, N.C. 28304

Triad Amateur Computer Society
c/o Doug Drye
3202 Winchester Dr.
Greensboro, N.C. 27406

Triangle Amateur Computer Club
c/o Russell Lyday, Jr.
P.O. Box 17523
Raleigh, N.C. 27609

Ohio

Amateur Computer Society of Columbus
c/o Walter Marvin
408 Thurber Dr. West #6
Columbus, Ohio 43215
or
c/o Fred Hatfield K8 VDU
Computer Data Systems
1372 Grandview Ave.
Columbus, Ohio 43212

Cleveland Digital Group
c/o Gary Coleman
14058 Superior Ave., #8
Cleveland, Ohio 44116
OR
8700 Harvard Ave.
Cleveland, Ohio 44105
OR
c/o John Kabat, Jr.
1200 Seneca Blvd. #407
Broadview Heights, Ohio 44147

Compute, Evaluate, Trade
P.O. Box 104
Tipp City, Ohio 45317

Dayton Microcomputer Assoc. (DMA)
c/o Doug Andrew
8668 Sturbridge Dr.
Cincinnati, Ohio 45236

Goodyear Computer Club
c/o J.F. Derry
D-109 Plt 1
The Goodyear Tire and Rubber Co.
Akron, Ohio 44316

KIM Users Group
c/o Eric Rehnke
7656 Broadview Rd., Apt. 207
Parma, Ohio 44134

The Midwest Affiliation of Computer Clubs
c/o Gary Coleman
P.O. Box 83
Brecksville, Ohio 44141

North Central Ohio Computer Club
c/o Bill Hicks
618 Teakwood Ct.
Galion, Ohio

SR-52 Users Club
9459 Taylorsville Rd.
Dayton, Ohio 45424

Universe Unlimited Group
11981 Forest Ave.
Cleveland, Ohio 44120

Oklahoma

Central Oklahoma Amateur Computer Society (CENOACA)
c/o Lee Lilly
P.O. Box 2213
Norman, Okla. 73069

Oklahoma City Club
c/o Bill Cowden
2412 SW 45th Street
Oklahoma City, Okla. 73119

Tulsa Computer Society
P.O. Box 1133
Tulsa, Okla. 74101

Oregon

Portland Computer Club
c/o Bill Marsh
2814 NE 40th Street
Portland, Ore. 97212

Portland Computer Society
1003 Garland St., Apt. 4
Woodburn, Ore. 97071

Southwest OMSI Computer Club
Southwest Oregon Museum of Science and Industry
27 East Fifth Ave.
P.O. Box 1052
Eugene, Ore. 97401

Pennsylvania

Gene Beals
PET Users Group
POB 371
Montgomeryville, Pa. 18936

Delaware Valley Chapter—SCCS
c/o Martin Simmerman
1228 Barrowdale
Rydal, Pa. 19046

Northeast Computer Assoc.
834 Lawler Street
Philadelphia, Pa.

Philadelphia Area Club
404 Quince Street
Philadelphia, Pa. 19147

Philadelphia Area Computer Society (PACS)
POB 1954
Philadelphia, Pa. 19105

Pittsburgh Area Computer Club
c/o Fred Kitman
OPUS-1
400 Smithfield St.
Pittsburgh, Pa. 15222

St. Thomas District HS Computer Club
1025 Braddock Ave.
Braddock, PA 15104

Wilkes College Computer Club
c/o Eric Jansen, Math Dept.
Wilkes College
Wilkes-Barre, Pa. 18703

Rhode Island

Rhode Island Computer Hobbyist Club
c/o Computerist
Box 3
Chelmsford, Mass. 01824

Texas

Central Texas Computer Association
508 Blueberry Hill
Austin, Texas 78745

Computer Hobbyist Group—North Texas
c/o Bill Fuller
2377 Dalworth Apt. 157
Grand Prairie, Texas 75050

El Paso Computer Club
c/o Jack O. Coats, Jr.
213 Argonaut, Apt. 27
El Paso, Texas 79912

Houston Amateur Microcomputer Club (HAMCC)
c/o David M. Fogg
4223 S.W. Fwy. #203
Houston, Texas 77027
OR
c/o Al Corry, Librarian
Box 1644
Pasadena, Texas 77501
OR
6513 Jackwood
Houston, Texas 77074

Microcomputer Tinkers and Bug Busters
MITI BuBus—Mighty BooBoos
3845 Le Bleu St.
Beaumont, Texas 77707

NASA-JSC Computer Hobbyist Club
c/o Marlow Cassetti
1011 Devonport Lane
Seabrook, Texas 77586

Northside Computer Group
2318 Town Breeze
San Antonio, Texas 78238

Panhandle Computer Society
c/o Tex Everett
2923 S. Spring
Amarillo, Texas 79103

Permian Basin Computer Group
c/o John Rabenaldt
P.O. Box 3912
Odessa, Texas 79760

Texas A&M Microcomputer Club
P.O. Box M-9
Aggieland Station, Texas 77844

Texas Computer Club
c/o L.G. Walker
Route 1, Box 272
Aledo, Texas 76008

Theater Computer Users Group
Theater Sources Inc.
4712 Northway Dr.
Dallas, Texas 75206

Utah

Salt Lake City Computer Club
2925 Valley View Ave.
Holladay, Utah 84114

Virginia

Amateur Radio Research and Development Corp.
AMRAD
1524 Springvale Ave.
McLean, Va. 22101

Charlottesville Computer Hobbyists Club
P.O. Box 6132
Charlottesville, Va. 22906

Chesapeake Microcomputer Club, Inc.
c/o Richard A. Kuzmack
1435 Layman Street
McLean, Va. 22101

Andrew Convery
2315 Freetown Ct., Apt 110
Reston, Va. 22091

Dyna-Micro Users Group
c/o Dr. Frank Settle, Jr.
Box 1053
Lexington, Va. 24450

IBM 5100 Users Club
c/o Richard Easton, MD
5541 Parliament Dr. #104
Virginia Beach, Va. 23462

Peninsula Computer Hobbyist Club
c/o Larry Polis
2 Weber Lane
Hampton, Va. 23663

Roanoke Valley Computer Club
c/o Lee Yosafat
2026 Wynmere Dr. S.W.
Roanoke, Va.

Washington-Baltimore Computer Hobbyist Group
c/o R. Rubinstein
7711 Elba Rd.
Alexandria, Va. 22306

Washington

Northwest Computer Club
Box 242
Renton, Wash. 98055

West Virginia

West Virginia Computer Society
c/o Bill England
167 Iroquois Trl.
Ona, West Va. 25545

Wisconsin

Durant Club
c/o James White
901 S. 12th Street
Watertown, Wis. 53094

Wisconsin Area Tribe of Computer Hobbyists (WATCH)
c/o Don Stevens
P.O. Box 159
Sheboygan, Wis. 53085

Australia

Community Computer Communication
P.O. Box 268
Niddrie 3042, Australia

Canada

Amateur Microprocessor Club of Kidchener-Waterloo
Reading Room
Electrical Engineering
University of Waterloo
Waterloo, Ont. Canada N2L 3G1

British Columbia Computer Society
c/o Karl Brackhaus
203-1625 W. 13th Ave.
Vancouver. B. C., Canada V6J 2G9

Canadian Computer Club
c/o G. Pearen
861 11th Street
Brandon, Man., Canada R7A 4L1

Canadian Computer Club
c/o Ian MacLean
203 Seventh Street
Saskatoon, Sask., Canada S7H OW9

Montreal Area Computer Society (MACS)
P.O. Box 613
Stock Exchange Tower
Montreal, Quebec, Canada

Montreal Micro-8 Computer Club
Case Postale Al Succur Sale
Montreal, Que. Canada H4Y 1A2

Ottawa Computer Group
P.O. Box 13218
Kanata, Ont. Canada K2K 1X4

Societe d'Informatique Amateur de Quebec
c/o Ricardo Talbot
IRISCO du Quebec, Inc.
376 du Roi, Suite 304
Quebec, Canada PQ 2W6

Toronto Amateur Computer Users Society (TACUS)
c/o Kevin Crowston
3 The Wynd
Islington, Ont., Canada M9A 2L8

Toronto Region Association of Computer Enthusiasts (TRACE)
c/o Harold G. Melanson
P.O. Box 545 Streetsville PO
Mississauga, Ont., Canada

England

Amateur Computer Club
7 Dordells
Basilson, Essex, England

British Amateur Electronics
c/o J. G. Margetts
11 Hazelbury Dr.
Warmly, North Bristol, England

Computer Workshop
174 Ifield Rd.
London SW10 9AG, England

Japan

Japan Microcomputer Club
First Ohkura Bldg.
4f 2-1 Nikoubashi
Chuoku, Tokyo, Japan

Prof. Haruhisa Ishida
Univ. of Tokyo
2-11-16 Yayoi Bunkyoko
Tokyo, Japan

Mexico

Carlos de Leon
Avenue Chapultepec 318-603
Mexico City 7, DF, Mexico

New Zealand

Info-File
P.O. Box 27-206B
Mt. Roskill,
Aukland, New Zealand

Puerto Rico

Caribbean Computer Club
52 Kings Ct. 4A
Santurce, Puerto Rico 00911

Appendix H:

Home Computer Stores

Alabama

ACK Radio Supply Co.
3101 Fourth Ave.
Birmingham, Ala. 35233

James W. Clary Co.
1713 Second Ave.
Birmingham, Ala. 35233

Arizona

Complete Elect. Supply
3232 N. Third St.
Phoenix, Ariz. 85012

Bits & Bytes Computer Shop
6819 N. 21st Ave.
Phoenix, Ariz. 85015

Byte Shop—Phoenix West
12654 N. 28th St.
Phoenix, Ariz. 80529

Byte Shop—Phoenix East
813 N. Scottsdale Rd.
Tempe, Ariz. 85282

Byte Shop—Tucson
2612 E. Broadway
Tucson, Ariz. 85711

Desert Data
P.O. Box 1334
Tucson, Ariz. 85711

ALTAIR Computer Center
4941 E. 29th St.
Tucson, Ariz. 85711

Arkansas

Westark Comp Systems Inc.
2803 Rogers Ave.
Ft. Smith, Ark. 72901

Computer Products Unlimited
2412 S. Broadway
Little Rock, Ark. 72206

California

Heathkit Elec. Center
330 E. Ball Rd.
Anaheim, Cal. 92805

Amco Electronic Supply
635 E. Arrow Hwy.
Azura, Cal. 91702

Byte Shop—Berkeley
1514 University Ave.
Berkeley, Cal. 94703

Computer Kits Inc.
1044 University Ave.
Berkeley, Cal. 94710

Kentucky Fried Computers
2465 4th St.
Berkeley, Cal. 94710

Byte Shop—Burbank
1812 W. Burbank Blvd.
Burbank, Cal.

C & A Elect Enterprises
P.O. Box 5232 2529 E. Carson
Carson, Cal. 90749

Sunshine Computer Co.
20700 S. Alameda
Carson, Cal. 90745

Microbyte
584 Rio Lindo-Suite 4
Chico, Cal. 95926

Byte Shop—Sacramento
6041 Greenback Ln.
Citrus Heights, Cal. 95610

Action Audio Elect
323 S. Mayfair Ave.
Daly City, Cal. 94015

Elec. Brain Computer Str.
7000 Village Pkwy. Ste. L.
Dublin, Cal, 94566

Heathkit Electronic Ctr.
1541 S. 56th St.
El Cerrito, Cal. 94530

Computerware
830 1st St.
Encinitas, Cal. 92024

Cyberdux Micro Appl.
1210 Santa Fe Dr.
Encinitas, Cal. 92024

Byte Shop—Long Beach
11220 Talbert Ave.
Fountain Valley, Cal. 92708

Mircro Computer Store
9323 Warbler Ave.
Fountain Valley, Cal. 92708

Byte Shop—Fresno
4131 E. McKinley Ave.
Fresno, Cal. 93703

Custom Computer Services
1650 L St.
Fresno, Cal. 93721

Bits N Bytes
1216 W. Wilshire Ave.
Fullerton, Cal. 92633

Save on Electronics
13225 Harbor Blvd.
Garden Grove, Cal. 92643

The Data Center
136 N. Maryland Ave.
Glendale, Cal. 91206

Rainbow Computing Inc.
10723 White Oak Ave.
Granada Hills, Cal. 91344

Byte Shop—Hayward
1122 B St.
Hayward, Cal. 94541

Computer Land
22634 Foothill Blvd.
Hayward, Cal. 94541

Computer Systems Unlimited
18886 Hesperian Blvd.
Hayward, Cal. 94541

Computer Way Inc.
15525 Computer Ln.
Huntington, Cal. 92649

Computerland
6840 LaCienega Blvd.
Inglewood, Cal. 90302

Byte Shop—Lawndale
16508 Hawthorne Blvd.
Lawndale, Cal. 90260

Bargain Electronics Center
2018 Lomita Blvd. 1
Lomita, Cal. 90717

A-Vid Electronics Co.
1655 E. 28th St.
Long Beach, Cal. 90806

Ancrona Corp.
6060 Manchester Ave.
Los Angeles, Cal. 90045

Heathkit Electronic Center
2309 S. Flower St.
Los Angeles, Cal. 90007

Henry Radio
11240 W. Olympic Blvd.
Los Angeles, Cal. 90064

Computerland
24001 Via Fabricante
Mission Viejo, Cal. 92675

Byte Shop—Mt. View
1063 W. El Camino
Mt. View, Cal. 94040

Computer Store
17353 Citronia St.
Northridge, Cal. 91325

The Computer Mart
625 W. Katella 10
Orange, Cal. 92667

Byte Shop—Palo Alto
2233 El Camino Real
Palo Alto, Cal. 94306

Microprocessor Marketing
943 Industrial Ave.
Palo Alto, Cal. 94303

Zack Electronics
654 High St.
Palo Alto, Cal. 94025

Byte Shop—Pasadena
496 S. Lake Ave.
Pasadena, Cal. 91101

Lafayette Radio Elect
1252 E. Colorado Blvd.
Pasadena, Cal. 91106

Byte Shop—Placentia
123 E. Yorba Linda
Placentia, Cal. 92670

Electronics Warehouse
1603 Viation Blvd.
Redondo Beach, Cal. 90278

California Radio & TV
2537 Del Paso Blvd.
Sacramento, Cal. 95815

Selectronics
2204 Del Paso Blvd.
Sacramento, Cal. 95815

Zackitt Stores
1831 J St.
Sacramento, Cal. 95814

Digi Tronix
600 S. Main
Salinas, Cal. 93901

James Electronics
1021A Howard Ave.
San Carlos, Cal. 94070

Byte Shop—San Diego
8250 Vickers H.
San Diego, Cal. 92111

Computerland
4233 Convoy St.
San Diego, Cal. 92111

The Computer Center
8205 Ronson Rd.
San Diego, Cal. 921111

IV Dimension Inc.
7060 Miramar Rd. 104
San Diego, Cal. 92121

Electronics Emporium Inc.
7895 Claire Mont Mesa Blvd.
San Diego, Cal. 92111

Byte Shop—San Francisco
321 Pacific
San Francisco, Cal. 94111

Comp Store San Francisco
1093 Mission
San Francisco, Cal. 94103

Small Business Computer Co.
400 Dewey Blvd.
San Francisco, Cal. 94116

Zack Electronics
1444 Market St.
San Francisco, Cal. 94102

Byte Shop—San Jose
155 Blossom Hill Rd.
San Jose, Cal. 95123

Byte Shop—Campbell
2626 Union Ave.
San Jose, Cal. 95124

Amco Electronics
414 S. Bascom Ave.
San Jose, Cal. 95128

Computerland Inc.
1922 Republic Ave.
San Leandro, Cal. 94577

Computers & Stuff
664 Via Alamo
San Lorenzo, Cal. 94580

Proko Electronics
439 Marsh St.
San Luis Obispo, Cal. 93401

Westcom
831 C Grand Ave.
San Marcos, Cal. 92069

Byte Shop—San Mateo
1200 W. Hillsdale Blvd.
San Mateo, Cal. 94403

Byte Shop—San Rafael
509 B Francisco Blvd.
San Rafael, Cal. 94901

Byte Shop—Santa Barbara
4 W. Mission
Santa Barbara, Cal. 93101

Byte Shop—Santa Clara
3400 El Camino
Santa Clara, Cal. 95051

The Computer Store
820 Broadway
Santa Monica, Cal. 90401

D Curtis Serendipity Cours
Bay Haven Gate 5
Sausalito, Cal. 94965

Peoples Computer Shop
13452 Ventura Blvd.
Sherman Oaks, Cal. 91423

Byte Shop—Stockton
7910 N. Eldorado St.
Stockton, Cal.

Computer Power & Light
12321 Ventura Blvd.
Studio City, Cal. 91604

Sunnyvale Electronics
548 S. Murphy
Sunnyvale, Cal. 94086

Byte Shop—San Fernando
18424 Ventura Blvd.
Tarzana, Cal. 93156

Byte Shop—Thousand Oaks
2707 Thousand Oaks Blvd.
Thousand Oaks, Cal. 91360

Computerland
104 W. First St.
Tustin, Cal. 92680

Upland Computer Labs
75 E. 9th St.
Upland, Cal. 91786

Zackit Corp.
1815 Sonoma Blvd.
Vallejo, Cal. 94590

Computer Components
5848 Sepulveda Blvd.
Van Nuys, Cal. 91411

Byte Shop—Ventura
2409 Main St.
Ventura, Cal.

CNC Electronics
2126 E. Thompson Blvd.
Ventura, Cal. 93003

Byte Shop—Diablo Valley
2989 N. Main St.
Walnut Creek, Cal. 94596

Byte Shop—Westminster
14300 Beach Blvd.
Westminster, Cal. 92683

Colorado

Byte Shop—Boulder
2040 30th St.
Boulder, Colo. 80301

J.B. Saunders
3050 Valmont Rd.
Boulder, Colo. 80301

Bill Newman & Co.
1440 S. Santa Fe Dr.
Denver, Colo. 80223

Computer County
2200 W. Alamedia
Denver, Colo. 80233

Electronic Lollipop
3643 Broadway
Denver, Colo. 80216

Gateway Electronics
2839 W. 44th St.
Denver, Colo. 80211

Heathkit Electronic Center
5940 W. 38th Ave.
Denver, Colo. 80212

Smith System Assoc.
1221 S. Clarkson, Suite 122
Denver, Colo. 80210

Byte Shop—Arapahoe City
3464 S. Acoma
Englewood, Colo. 80110

Connecticut

Heathkit Electronic Center
395 W. Main St.
Avon, Conn. 06110

Kaufman Electronics
73 Frank St.
Bridgeport, Conn. 06604

JRV Computer Store
3714 Whitney Ave.
Hamden, Conn. 06518

The Computer Store
63 S. Main
Windsor Locks, Conn. 06096

Delaware

Artificial Intelligence
3308 Altamont Dr.
Wilmington, Del. 19810

Florida

Byte Shop—Cocoa Beach
1325 N. Atlantic Ave.
Cocoa Beach, Fla. 32931

Sunny Computer Stores, Inc.
138 S. Dixie Hwy.
Coral Gables, Fla. 33146

Byte Shop—Fort Lauderdale
1044 E. Oakland Park Blvd.
Fort Lauderdale, Fla.

Electronics for Yachting, Inc.
2001 SW 20th St.
Fort Lauderdale, Fla. 33315

BMC Electronics
320 Racetrack Road NE
Ft. Walton Beach, Fla. 32548

Computer Hut, Inc.
6737 Red Rd.
Hialeah, Fla. 33012

Heathkit Electronic Center
4705 W. 16th Ave.
Hialeah, Fla. 33012

Williams Radio & TV
2062 Liberty St.
Jacksonville, Fla. 32206

Amateur Radio Center, Inc.
2805 NE 2nd Ave.
Miami, Fla. 33142

Byte Shop—Miami
7825 SW 40th
Miami, Fla. 33155

Computer Assoc., Inc.
6900 N. Kendall #A103
Miami, Fla. 33156

Electronic Equipment Co., Inc.
4027 NW 24th St.
Miami, Fla. 33142

Computer Stores, Inc.
3804 N. 9th Ave.
Pensacola, Fla. 32503

Grice Electronics
320 E. Gregory St.
Pensacola, Fla. 32502

Elecon Corp.
4921 72nd Ave. N.
Pinellas Park, Fla. 33565

J & H Electronics Co.
1615 W. Waters Ave.
Tampa, Fla. 33604

Microcomputer Systems
144 S. Dale Mabry Hwy.
Tampa, Fla. 33609

Marsh Data Systems
54058 Southern Comfort Blvd.
Tampa, Fla. 33614

Georgia

Heathkit Electronic Center
5285 Roswell Rd.
Atlanta, Ga. 30305

The Computer System Center
3330 Piedmont Rd. NE
Atlanta, Ga. 30305

REC Computer Systems
5730 Glenridge Dr.
Atlanta, Ga. 30328

Atlanta Computer Mart
50918 Buford Hwy.
Atlanta, Ga. 30340

Illinois

Computerland
50 East Rand Rd.
Arlington Heights, Ill. 60004

Klaus Radio, Inc.
905 S. Neil St.
Champaign, Ill. 61820

The Numbers Racket
518 E. Green St.
Champaign, Ill. 61820

Heathkit Electronic Center
3462-66 W. Devon Ave.
Chicago, Ill. 60645

Howard Electronic Sales, Inc.
4573 Archer Ave.
Chicago, Ill. 60632

ACRO Electronics Corp.
1101 W. Chicago Ave.
E. Chicago, Ill. 46312

Heathkit Electronic Center
224 Ogden Ave.
Downer Grove, Ill. 60515

Itty Bitty Machine Co.
1316 Chicago Ave.
Elmhurst, Ill. 60201

MPU Shop Semiconductor Spec.
195 Spangler Ave.
Elmhurst, Ill. 60126

Data Domain
42 W. Roosevelt
Lombard, Ill. 60148

Joseph Electronics, Inc.
8830 Milwaukee Ave.
Niles, Ill. 60648

Spectronics
1009 Garfield St.
Oak Park, Ill. 60304

Chicago Computer Center
517 Talcott Rd.
Park Ridge, Ill. 60068

Klaus Radio, Inc.
8400 N. Pioneer Pkwy.
Peoria, Ill. 61614

American Microprocessors
241 Indian Creek, Box 515
Prairie View, Ill. 60069

Lillipute Co.
4446 Oakton St.
Skokie, Ill. 60076

Indiana

Electronic Supply of Anderson
2228 Columbus Ave.
P.O. Box 1178
Anderson, Ind. 46014

Data Domain
406 S. College Ave.
Bloomington, Ind. 47401

Hobbytronic Distributors
1218 Prairie Dr.
Bloomington, Ind. 47401

Castrups Radio Supply
1014 W. Franklin St.
Evansville, Ind. 47710

Ft. Wayne Electronics Supply
3606 E. Maumee
Fort Wayne, Ind, 46803

Quantum Computer Works
6637 Kennedy Ave.
Hammond, Ind. 46323

Data Domain
7027 Michigan Rd.
Indianapolis, Ind. 46268

Graham Electronics
133 S. Pennsylvania St.
Indianapolis, Ind. 46204

Heathkit Electronic Center
2112 E. 62nd St.
Indianapolis, Ind. 46220

Home Computer Shop
10447 Chris Dr.
Indianapolis, Ind. 46229

Data Domain
219 Columbia
W. Lafayette, Ind. 47905

Kansas

Heathkit Electronic Center
5960 Lamar Ave.
Mission, Kansas 66222

Amateur Radio Equipment Co.
1203 E. Douglas
Wichita, Kansas 67211

Computer Hut
521 N. Hillside Ave.
Wichita, Kansas 67214

Kentucky

Data Domain
506½ Euclid Ave.
Lexington, Ky. 40502

P.I. Burks Co.
842 S. 7th St.
Louisville, Ky. 40203

Data Domain
3028 Hunsinger Lane
Louisville, Ky. 40220

Heathkit Electronic Center
12401 Shelbyville Rd.
Louisville, Ky. 40243

Cybertronics
312 Production Crt.
Louisville, Ky. 40299

Computerland
813 B. Lyndon Lane
Louisville, Ky. 40222

Louisiana

Baxter TV
7924 Jefferson Hwy.
Baton Rouge, La. 70809

Heathkit Electronic Center
1900 Veterans Memorial Blvd.
Kenner, La. 70062

Trinonics
725 Focis
Metairie, La. 70005

Computer Shoppe
344 Camp St.
New Orleans, La. 70130

Maryland

Amateur Radio Center
1117 W. 36th St.
Baltimore, Md. 21211

Heathkit Electronic Center
1713 Joppa Rd.
Baltimore, Md. 21234

Surplus Electronics
9600 Baltimore Blvd. Rear
College Park, Md. 20740

The Comm Center
9624 Ft. Meade Rd.
Laurel, Md. 20810

Computerland
16065 Frederick Rd. (Rt. 355)
Rockville, Md. 20850

The Computer Workshop
5709 Frederick Ave.
Rockville, Md. 20852

Heathkit Electronic Center
5542 Nicholsen Lane
Rockville, Md. 20852

Baynesville Electronic, Inc.
1631 E. Joppa Rd.
Towson, Md. 21204

Massachusetts

American Used Computers
712 Beacon St.
Boston, Mass. 02155

Computer Warehouse Store
584 Commonwealth Ave.
Boston, Mass. 02215

The Computer Store
120 Cambridge St.
Burlington, Mass. 01803

Tufts Radio Electronics
386 Main St.
Medford, Mass. 02155

Heathkit Electronic Center
242 Andover St.
Peabody, Mass. 01960

Computer Mart, Inc.
1097 Lexington St.
Waltham, Mass. 02154

Heathkit Electronic Center
165 Worchester St.
Wellesley, Mass. 02181

Hamilton Avnet
100 E. Commerce Way
Woburn, Mass. 01801

Abbott Electronics Co.
902 Main St.
N. Woburn, Mass. 01801

Michigan

Compu-Mart
245 S. Wagner Rd.
Ann Arbor, Mich. 48103

The Computer Store
310 E. Washington St.
Ann Arbor, Mich. 48108

Purchase Radio Supply
327 E. Hoover
Ann Arbor, Mich. 48104

Newman Computer Exchange
1250 N. Main St.
Ann Arbor, Mich. 48104

Hobby House
1035 W. Territorial Rd.
Battle Creek, Mich. 49015

Heathkit Electronic Center
18645 W. 8 Mile Rd.
Detroit, Mich. 48219

Top Radio Supply Corp.
17885 Mt. Elliott
Detroit, Mich. 48212

Heathkit Electronic Center
18149 E. 8 Mile Rd.
E. Detroit, Mich. 48021

Midway Electronic Supply
990 W. 8 Mile Rd.
Ferndale, Mich. 48220

Radio Parts, Inc.
542-548 S. Division Ave.
Grand Rapids, Mich. 49502

Northwest Electronics
33610 Plymouth Rd.
Livonia, Mich. 48150

Electronic Distributors
1960 Peck St.
Muskegon, Mich. 49441

Computer Mart, Inc.
1800 W. 14 Mile Rd.
Royal Oak, Mich. 48073

General Computer Co.
2011 Livernois
Troy, Mich. 48084

Minnesota

Byte Shop—Eagan
1434 Yankee Doodle Rd.
Eagan, Minn. 55121

Heathkit Electronic Center
101 Shady Oak Rd.
Hopkins, Minn. 55343

Electronic Center Comm. Div.
127 Third Ave.
Minneapolis, Minn. 55401

Missouri

Computer Systems Center
13461 Olive Blvd.
Chesterfield, Mo. 63017

The Computer Workshop
6903 Blair Rd.
Kansas City, Mo. 64152

Gateway Electronics, Inc.
8123 Page Blvd.
St. Louis, Mo. 63130

Montana

Montana Computer Center, Inc.
2512 Grand Ave.
Billings, Mont. 59102

Electric City Radio Supply
2315 Tenth Ave.
Great Falls, Mont. 59405

Nebraska

ALTAIR Computer Center
2801 Cornhusker Hwy.
Lincoln, Neb. 68504

Heathkit Electronic Center
9207 Maple St.
Omaha, Neb. 68134

Nevada

Johnson TV Micro Computer
2607 E. Charleston
Las Vegas, Nev. 89104

New Hampshire

G. Paulsen Co.
27 Sheep Davis Rd.
Concord, N.H. 03301

Worldwide Electronics, Inc.
10 Flagstone Dr.
Hudson, N.H. 03051

Brynn Corp.
393 West St.
Keene, N.H. 03431

Computer Mart of N.H.
Route 3
Merrimack, N.H. 03054

Microcomputers, Inc.
538 Amherst St.
Nashua, N.H. 03060

Aircon, Inc.
Route 168
Union, N.H. 03887

New Jersey

Lashen Electronics Inc.
21 Broadway
Denville, N.J. 07834

William Electronics Sup.
1863 Woodbridge Ave.
Edison, N.J. 08817

Heathkit Elec. Center
35-07 Broadway Rt. 4
Fairlawn, N.J. 07410

Hoboken Computer Works
20 N. Hudson Pl.
Hoboken, N.J. 07030

Computer Mart of N.J.
501 Rt. 27
Iselan, N.J. 08830

Computerland
2 DeHart St.
Morristown, N.J. 07960

S. Rachles, Inc.
364 Oak St.
Passaic, N.J. 07055

Nidisco Inc.
2812 Kennedy Blvd.
Union City, N.J. 07087

Midwest Enterprises Inc.
815 Standish Ave.
Westfield, N.J. 07090

New Mexico

Electronics Parts Co., Inc.
2620 Rhode Island St. NE
Albuquerque, N.M. 87110

Computer Shack
3120 San Mateo
Albuquerque, N.M. 87110

Mannie's Elect & Photo
802 S. Soilano Dr.
Las Cruces, N.M. 88001

New York

Heathkit Electronic Ctr.
3476 Sheridan Dr.
Amherst, N.Y. 14226

Adirondack Radio Sup.
185 W. Main St.
Amsterdam, N.Y. 12010

Bronx Wholesale Radio
542 E. Fordham Rd.
Bronx, N.Y. 10458

Computer Land
1612 Niagara Falls Blvd.
Buffalo, N.Y. 14150

Summit Distributors Inc.
916 Main St.
Buffalo, N.Y. 14202

The Computer Mart
2072 Front St.
East Meadow, N.Y. 11554

Harison Radio
20 Smith St.
Farmingdale, N.Y. 11735

Computer Microsystems
6 Wooleys Ln.
Great Neck, N.Y. 11023

Synchro Sound
193-25 Jamaica Ave.
Hollis, N.Y. 11423

Computer Land
225 Elmira Rd.
Ithaca, N.Y. 14850

Heathkit Elec. Center
15 Jericho Tpke.
Jericho, N.Y. 11753

Byte Shop—Levittown
2721 Hempstead Tpke.
Levittown, N.Y. 11756

Aldelco
2281A Babylon Tpke.
Merrick, N.Y. 11566

Audio Design Electronics
487 Broadway Ste. 512
New York, N.Y. 10013

Computer Mart of NY Inc.
118 Madison Ave.
New York, N.Y. 10016

The Computer Store of NY
55 W. 39th St.
New York, N.Y. 10018

Dale Electronics
244 W. 14th St.
New York, N.Y. 10011

Heathkit Electronic Ctr.
937 Jefferson Rd.
Rochester, N.Y. 14623

Minimicromart
1618 James St.
Syracuse, N.Y. 13203

Trojan Electronic Sup., Co.
15 Middleburgh St.
Troy, N.Y. 12181

Computer Corner
200 Hamilton Ave.
White Plains, N.Y. 10601

Heathkit Electronic Ctr.
7 Reservoir Rd.
N. White Plains, N.Y. 10603

Ohio

Digital Design
7696 Camargo Rd.
Cincinnati, OH. 45243

Els System Engineering
2209 N. Taylor Rd.
Cleveland, OH. 44112

Heller Electronics
2189 Lee Rd.
Cleveland Heights, OH. 44118

Winteradio Elec. Supply Corp.
1468 W. 25th St.
Cleveland, OH. 44113

Amateur Radio Sls. & Svc., Co.
2187 E. Livingston Ave.
Columbus, OH. 43209

Heathkit Electronic Ctr.
2500 Moorse Rd.
Columbus, OH. 43229

Altair Computer Center
45 Murry Hill Dr.
Dayton, OH. 45403

Byte Shop
19524 Center Ridge Rd.
Rocky River, OH.

Heathkit Electronic Ctr.
10133 Springfield Pike
Woodlawn, OH. 45215

Oklahoma

High Technology
1020 W. Wilshire
Oklahoma City, OK. 73116

Radio Inc.
1000 S. Main
Tulsa, OK. 74119

Altair Computer Center
110 Annex 5345 E. 41st St.
Tulsa, OK. 74135

Oregon

Altair Computer Center
8105 SW Nimbus Ave.
Beaverton, OR. 97005

Byte Shop—Beaverton
3482 SW Cedar Hills Blvd.
Beaverton, OR. 97005

Real Oregon Computer Co.
205 W. 10th Ave.
Eugene, OR. 97401

Byte Shop—Portland
2033 SW 4th St.
Portland, OR. 97201

Portland Radio Supply
1234 SW Stark St.
Portland, OR. 97205

Pennsylvania

Byte Shop—Bryn Mawr
1045 W. Lancaster Ave.
Bryn Mawr, Pa. 19010

Kass Electronics Dist.
2502 Township Line Rd.
Drexel Hill, Pa. 19026

Heathkit Electronic Ctr.
630 Lancaster Pike
Frazer, Pa. 19355

Personal Computer Corp.
Frazer Mall
Frazer, Pa. 19355

Marketline Systems
2337 Philmont Ave.
Huntingdon Valley, Pa. 19006

Heathkit Elec. Center
6318 Roosevelt Blvd.
Philadelphia, Pa. 19149

Lectro Media Ltd.
22 New Market
Philadelphia, Pa. 19147

Heathkit Electronic Ctr.
3486 William Penn Hwy.
Pittsburgh, Pa. 15235

Caravan
116 S. Garner
State College, Pa. 19711

Hamtronics
4033 Brownsville Rd.
Trevose, Pa. 19047

Ham Buerger Inc.
68 N. York Rd.
Willow Grove, Pa. 19090

Rhode Island

Heathkit
558 Greenwich Ave.
Warwick, R.I. 02886

Computer Power Inc.
M24 Airport Plz. 1800 Post
West Warwick, R.I. 02886

South Carolina

Dixie Radio Supply Co.
1900 Barnwell St.
Columbia, S.C. 29201

Byte Shop—Columbia
2018 Greene St.
Columbia, S.C. 29205

Tennessee

Radio Electric Sup., Co.
961 E. Sullivan
Kingsport, Tn. 37662

Byte Tronics
1600 Hayes St. Ste. 103
Nashville, Tn. 37203

Texas

Arlington Electronics
915 E. Park Row
Arlington, Tx. 76010

Computer Shops Inc.
Northcentral Expwy.
Dallas, Tx. 75231

Electronics Center Inc.
2929 N. Maskell
Dallas, Tx. 75204

Heathkit Electronic Ctr.
2715 Ross Ave.
Dallas, Tx. 75201

KA Electronic Sales
1220 Majesty Dr.
Dallas, Tx. 75247

Tannei Electronics
11423 Harry Hines
Dallas, Tx. 75229

AMT Electronics Parts Co.
500 S. Charles St.
Elm Mott, Tx. 76640

KA Electronics Sales
1117 S. Jupiter Rd.
Garland, Tx. 75042

Radiohut
3449 Kingsley Rd.
Garland, Tx. 75041

Altair Computer Center
5750 Bintliff Dr. Ste. 206
Houston, Tx. 77027

City Electronics Supply
5074 Richmond Ave.
Houston, Tx. 77027

The Communications Ctr.
7231 Fondren Rd.
Houston, Tx. 77036

Electrotex
2300 Richmond
Houston, Tx. 77006

Madison Elect.
1508 McKinney
Houston, Tx. 77002

Microtex Inc.
9305 N.E.S.W. Harwin Dr.
Houston, Tx. 77036

Polaris Computer Systems
3311 Richmond Ste. 200
Houston, Tx. 77006

The Bit Bam
1111 Burke 313
Pasadena, Tx. 77506

Martin Wholesale Elect.
Box 588 6 Terrace Shop Ctr.
Richardson, Tx. 75080

The Micro Store
634 S. Central Expwy.
Richardson, Tx. 75080

The Computer Shop
6812 San Pedro
San Antonio, Tx. 78216

Utah

Central Utah Elec. Supply
735 S. State St. Box N
Provo, Utah 84601

The Computer Room
1455 S. 1100 East
Salt Lake City, Utah 84105

Byte Shop—Salt Lake City
261 S. State St.
Salt Lake City, Utah 84111

Manwill Supply Co.
2780 S. Main St.
Salt Lake City, Utah 84115

Ballard Supply Corp.
2430 S. 900 W.
Salt Lake City, Utah 84119

Virginia

Sasco Electronics
1009 King St.
Alexandria, Va. 22314

Arcade Electronics Inc.
7048 Columbia Pike
Annandale, Va. 22003

Electronic Sales Inc.
100 W. Mercury
Hampton, Va. 23669

The Computer Co.
1905 Westmoreland St.
Richmond, Va. 23230

Computer Hobbies Unlimited
9601 Kendrick Rd.
Richmond, Va. 23235

Computers To Go
4503 W. Broad St.
Richmond, Va. 23230

Microsystems Computer Corp.
6605A Backlick Rd.
Springfield, Va. 22150

Heathkit Electronic Ctr.
1055 Independence Blvd.
Virginia Beach, Va. 23455

Washington

Byte Shop
14701 NE. 20th Ave.
Bellevue, Wa. 98007

Pacific Computer Store
410 W. Champion St.
Bellingham, Wa, 98225

Micro Comp. Applications
6009 B 13th Way SE
Olympia, Wa. 98503

KBC Computer Shop
2735 152 Ave. NE
Redmond, Wa. 98052

Almac Stroum Elec.
5811 6th Ave. S.
Seattle, Wa. 98108

Amateur Radio Supply Co.
6213 13th Ave. S.
Seattle, Wa. 98108

American Mercantile Co.
2418 1st Ave. S.
Seattle, Wa. 98134

Heathkit Elec. Center
2221 3rd Ave.
Seattle, Wa. 98121

Retail Computer Store
410 NE. 72nd St.
Seattle, Wa. 98115

The Computer Shop
621 W. First Ave.
Spokane, Wa. 99204

West Virginia

Business Computer Svc.
1027 Virginia St. E.
Charleston, W. Va. 25301

The Computer Store
1114 Charleston Natl. Plz.
Charleston, W. Va. 25301

Wisconsin

Microcomp
785 S. Main St.
Fond du lac, Wi. 54935

Chester Elect. Supply Co.
1220 60th St.
Kenosha, Wi. 53140

Satterfield Elect. Inc.
1900 S. Park St.
Madison, Wi. 53713

Amateur Elect. Sup., Inc.
4828 W. Fond Du Lac Ave.
Milwaukee, Wi. 53216

Heathkit
5215 Fond du lac Ave. W.
Milwaukee, Wi. 53216

Milwaukee Computer Store
6916 W. North Ave.
Milwaukee, Wi. 53213

Itty Bitty Machine Co.
2221 E. Capitol Dr.
Shorewood, Wi. 53211

Wyoming

Computer Radio Workshop
120 El Dorado Ct.
Cheyenne, Wy. 82001

Houge Radio & Supply Co.
1108 Logan Ave.
Cheyenne, Wy. 82001

Canada

The Computer Shop
3515 18th St. SW
Calgary, A.B. Canada

Computer Hobby Shop
4812 16th St. SW
Calgary, A.B. T2T 4J5 Canada

Microtronics
1202 525 75th Ave. SW
Calgary, A.B. T2V 1R8 Canada

C M Peterson Co., Ltd.
575 Dondus St.
London, OT. Canada

Computer Store Div. of Harts
6000 Bourassa E. No. 25
Montreal, Canada

Payette Radio Ltd.
730 St. Jacques
Montreal, PQ H3C 1G2 Canada

B W Klatt
Microtronics
R R 1
Oliver, B.C. V0H 1T0 Canada

Focus Scientific
160 Elgin St.
Ottawa, OT. K2P 2C4 Canada

Microcomputer Devices Ltd.
46 Selkirk Crescent
Regina, SK. S4S 6J4 Canada

Microcomputer Sys. of Canada
4 Bendrama Crescent
Scarborough, OT. M1H 1K7
Canada

Computer Mart Ltd.
1543 Bayview Ave.
Toronto, OT. M1K 4K4
Canada

Computer Master Sys. Ltd.
69 Gloucester St.
Toronto, OT. M4Y 1LB
Canada

The Computer Place
186 Queen St. W.
Toronto, OT. M5V 1Z1
Canada

First Canadian Computer Str.
44 Eglinton St. W.
Toronto, OT. M4R 1A1
Canada

First Canadian Computer Str.
66 Castlefield Ave.
Toronto, OT. M4R 194
Canada

Gladstone Elec. Supply Co.
1736 Avenue Rd.
Toronto, OT. N5M 3Y7
Canada

Byte Shop—Vancouver
2151 Burrard St.
Vancouver, B.C. Canada

Heathkit Elec. Center
3058 Kingsway
Vancouver, B.C. V5P 5J
Canada

The Pacific Computer Str.
4509-4511 Rupert St.
Vancouver, B.C. VSR 2J4
Canada

Rendell Paret Elect. Ltd.
2048 W. 4th Ave.
Vancouver, B.C. V6J 1M9
Canada

Electro Sonic
1100 Gordon Baker Rd.
Willowdale, OT. M2H 3B3
Canada

Byte Shop—Winnipeg
665 Century St.
Winnipeg, Canada

SDS Technical Devices Ltd.
1138 Main St.
Winnipeg, MB. R2W 3F3
Canada

Foreign

Dick Smith Elec. Pty. Ltd.
24 Carlotta St.
Artarmon, NSW Australia

Hughes Electronics
120 Tamboora Ave.
Baulkham Hills, NSW Australia

Computer Resources
Chaussee De Charleroi 80
1060 Brussels, Belgium

Computer Workshop Ltd.
174 Ifield Rd.
London, SW 10 9AG England

Entryphone Co. Ltd.
172 Ifield Rd.
London, SW 10 9AG England

Byte Shop—Tokyo
2-9-9 Sotokanda
Chiyodaku, Tokyo, Japan

Microsistemas Sa.
Travesera De Gracia 48
Barcelona, 6 Spain

Comicro Ag.
Badenstrasse 281
Zurich, Switzerland

Pan Atlantic Computer Sys.
Frankfurter Strasse 78
D61 Darmstadt, W. Germany

Appendix I:

The History of the Computer and the Home Computer

The history of calculating machines and of cybernetics, the study of automated electronics, provides an insight into the origins of the development of microprocessors and home computers. There are many excellent books which provide a thorough history of the subject; this appendix offers a brief and succinct description for your understanding of the processes that resulted in the development of the home computer.

It is useful to look at the history of the computer in terms of three factors: (1) ideas about counting; (2) the building of tools to count with; and (3) the development of a means to record what has been counted.

Man's first means of counting was the process of corresponding "natural objects" with other objects to count them. In this way, man could use the fingers of his hands to count (to correspond to) objects up to 10. Beyond 10, there was no readily available correspondence. It had to be invented. The invention was the sand table in which pebbles were placed in columns in furrows of sand. The Latin word for pebbles is *calculi,* from which we get the word *calculate.* The recording of the quantities counted by this method were scratched into stone, imprinted in clay, or noted in sticks.

The problem with the sand tables was their impermanence. You could not prove something if the wind blew. They were not really "hardware." They could be reproduced, but could not be moved or made permanent. The first permanent and portable hardware for counting was developed in China around 2600 B.C. It was called an abacus, and was the first digital computer. This invention found its way to the West via Egypt, the Etruscan civilization, and Rome.

The abacus is made up of a frame on which parallel wires are strung. On each wire are a certain number of beads which represent digits or numbers. Wires represent "places" of ones, tens, hundreds, thousands, etc.; the accuracy of this tool depends upon its size. The recording of information was done externally to the abacus. For example, Romans used the abacus to calculate and then recorded the results of their calculations somewhere else, using "numerals." Such recording continued until the 12th century, when the Roman "numerals" were replaced by Arabic "numerals" brought to the European continent. The use of Arabic numerals for recording calculations was imperative by the time of the industrial revolution in the 18th and 19th centuries because they were neater and allowed for recording numbers of infinite variety.

The Coming of Calculating Devices

The idea of a calculating device did not appear until Arabic numerals had displaced Roman numerals.

Two men outstanding for their influence on the concept of handling numbers were the 17th-century scientists Gottfried Wilhelm Leibnitz and Sir Isaac Newton.

Leibnitz is responsible for the invention of calculus, for which he created the symbols that are used today. He developed two kinds of calculus: differential calculus, in which if you know quantities in a certain context, you can discover the ratio among the quantities as they change; and integral calculus, in which if you know the rates of change among quantities in a given context, you can discover the quantities.

Newton's work focused on changing the measurements of physical quantities so that they could be seen in relationship to each other, and that relationship could be established as a basis for viewing them in changing circumstances. For example: force seen as a function of mass and acceleration, or F = MA. The invention of calculating devices was also a function of the available technology.

17th-Century Calculating Devices

In 1664, the French mathematician Blaise Pascal invented a machine to help his father calculate taxes. La Pascaline, as the device was called, operated by the turning of wheels on which the numbers 0–9 were engraved (rows of wheels represented places—e.g., ones, tens, hundreds, etc.). However, La Pascaline was not efficient to produce because it was expensive to build, maintain, and repair.

In 1671, Leibnitz built a calculating device using the same principle as that behind La Pascaline, which Leibnitz had studied. This machine employed the rotation of a drum which turned wheels to operate counters based on the decimal system. It could perform the basic operations to aid mathematicians: add, subtract, multiply, divide, and extract roots. Leibnitz recognized (not necessarily as a result of having developed his calculating device) that a mechanical means to count correlates with the logical processes of thought such as man's ability to reason. (In this regard, Norbert Wiener, at a much later date, called Leibnitz the "patron saint" of cybernetics.)

The reason both Pascal and Leibnitz spent so much time and effort on developing calculating devices was their shared disdain for time-consuming hand calculations. As Liebnitz said: "It is unworthy of excellent men to lose hours like slaves in the labor of calculation which could safely be relegated to anyone else if machines were used."

19th-Century Calculating Devices

There were few notable achievements made in the improvement of calculating devices during the 18th century. One exception to this was the mechanical logic device created by Charles Earl Stanhope in 1777. Called the Logic Demonstrator, this machine would influence the work of Charles Babbage in the 19th century. Another exception was the Arithmometer invented by Charles Xavier Thomas, the first calculating device to be commercially produced.

It remained for the English mathematician Charles Babbage (1792–1871) to create the basic format for the modern computer. Babbage financed the construction of his calculating engines using his own resources and an almost equal amount from grants. Of Babbage and his contribution, B. V. Bowden writes: "He was one of the first men to appreciate the potentialities of the scientific method as applied to the problems of modern industry. He lamented the way in which ordinary scientists neglected their social obligations and industry was deaf to the claims of scientific ideas. He was probably one of the most farsighted men of his generation, but almost everything he did provoked derision and the scorn of nearly all his contemporaries. . . . He must have been one of the queerest fish that ever lived."

Babbage originally wanted to build a device that would aid in the calculation of mathematical tables. He was concerned with the same issue as Leibnitz. In a letter to Sir Humphrey Davies, president of the Royal Society in London, requesting funding for the construction of his first device, he wrote: "The intolerable labor and fatiguing monotony of a continued repetition of similar arithmetical calculations first excited the desire, and afterwards suggested the idea, of a machine, which . . . should become a substitute for one of the lowest operations of the human intellect."

Babbage was also interested in the idea that a calculating device could communicate to itself to operate rather than be wholly dependent on the intervention of a human operator. In addition, he was concerned with the speed and accuracy with which mathematical tables, and especially astronomical tables, could be calculated.

In order to construct his engines, Babbage had to invent practically all the tools used in the process as well as to invent the graphic language used in the drawings for them.

The Difference Engine

Babbage's first calculating device was the Difference Engine (1822), on which all mathematical tables could be calculated and recorded. Basically an adding machine made of columns of wheels and gears, the Difference Engine also had a printing mechanism for recording the results of calculations.

The Difference Engine was only partially built when work on it was halted in favor of the development of a second calculating device.

The Analytical Engine

Babbage worked on the Analytical Engine until his death in 1871. However, the machine was never successfully launched, as the technology required to mass produce it was too precise. As a result, its significance was not recognized until later when others copied it.

The Analytical Engine was intended to perform arithmetic operations, string those operations together, and solve arithmetic problems. The operation of the machine was mechanical, involving gears and cranks run by steam power. A key to the machine was the store where, according to Babbage, "all the variables to be operated upon, as well as those quantities which have arisen from the result of other operations, are placed." The store was composed of columns of wheels, each of which was engraved with the numbers 0 through 9. The machine had a mill "into which the quantities about to be operated upon are always brought," according to Babbage. The mill was operated by rotation of gears and wheels.

The purpose of one part of the Analytical Engine was to transfer numbers from the mill to the store and from the store to the mill. Another part of the engine was the place where numerical data was put in, and from where it issued out. The input-output was in the form of punch cards. This idea was taken from the available technology in the method invented by Joseph Marie Jacquard (1804) for controlling a loom. The input was to be close to the output so that the machine would have an easier time controlling itself. The Analytical Engine was to carry out operations on cue from two kinds of punch cards which were strung together in each case: (1) the operation card, which would tell the machine the operation it was going to perform; and (2) the variable card, which would tell the machine the variables on which the operation was to be performed. Babbage's conception of the punch card included the idea that the cards could be reused and therefore always accessible.

The storage of information in the Analytical Engine met the requirements for the amount that had to be stored to solve arithmetical problems and do arithmetical calculations. It had a device to print the results of operations on paper and a device to punch cards with the results of these computations. Error was detected in the machine in the instance where information to be used by the machine was absent from the store and the machine rang a bell to tell the operator the problem. It also had a decision-making capacity so that the machine's operations could be changed in accordance with previous operations. It operated in cycles and was capable of branching.

For its time, the Analytical Engine had amazing speed. According to Babbage, it was capable of 60 additions in a minute both calculated and printed; one multiplication of two 50-figure numbers in a minute; or a division of one 100-place number by a 50-place number in a minute. Babbage's constant concern was with increasing the machine's speed, and he revised his designs accordingly. Of his engine, he wrote: "This machine surpasses its predecessors, both in extent of the calculations which it can perform, in the facility, certainty, and accuracy with which it can effect them, and in the absence of all necessity for the intervention of human intelligence during its performance of calculations."

Babbage understood the importance of his contribution: "The great principles on which the Analytical Engine rests have been examined, admitted, recorded, and demonstrated. The mechanism itself has now been reduced to unexpected simplicity. Half a century may probably elapse before any one without those aids which I have behind me, will attempt so promising a task. If, unwarned by my example, any man shall undertake and shall succeed in really constructing an engine embodying in itself the whole of the executive department of mathematical analysis upon different principles or by simpler mechanical means, I have no fear of leaving my reputation in his charge, for he alone will be fully able to appreciate the nature of my efforts and value their results."

Key-Driven Adding Machines

A rise in business and commercialism paralleling the industrial revolution created the need for faster data entry than was provided by the punch cards. In 1850, D. D. Parmalee patented a machine in which key-punch operation supplied the input to the machine. From 1851 to 1857, key-driven adding machines were produced which could add single columns of numbers at once. In 1857, Thomas Hill patented a multiple-order key-driven adding machine that could add groups of columns of numbers; this machine was unsuccessful, however, because of its technological inadequacies.

The Comptometer

The Comptometer was invented in 1884 by Dorr E. Felt. A machine with a controlled carrying mechanism, it could do the four basic operations, plus square and cube roots, and could calculate interest, discounts, etc. Recording was done with a device which printed numbers on paper as the keys were pressed. Power was supplied by a hand lever, which also served to advance the paper.

The Paper Roll Machine

The first "cash register" was invented in 1878 by James Ritty. It was the Paper Roll Machine. Paper was punched in the proper place by pins as keys were pressed. The paper then advanced and acted as a record of the calculation.

This machine was developed so that business transactions could be calculated and recorded in a brief time. Ritty began to produce the machine. Eventually, the company came under the ownership of John Patterson, who founded the National Cash Register Company.

Automatic Governor

In the late 1800s, William Burroughs created a machine that had an automatic governor to control the lever action which controlled the operation of the machine. Burroughs' machine was created for bank use.

Development of Recording Information

Hans Hollerith (1885) created a system for recording information superior to that of Babbage. Hollerith devised a technique for recording data using punch cards in connection with the invention of a tabulating machine for compiling census figures. From 1880 to 1890 the population of the United States had increased much more than it had from 1870 to 1880; it took seven years to tabulate the figures for this. By using an electric tabulating machine with punch cards, Hollerith compiled the 1880–1890 census in one-third the time it had taken to tabulate the previous decade's census figures.

In his system, punch cards recorded census information in terms of age, job, etc. The improvement of the system over Babbage's was threefold: (1) electrical contacts sensed holes in cards as they passed through the machine (input); (2) the cards were coded so they would fall into the right place in the sorting boxes (output); (3) the cards had 24 columns into which data could be punched (this facet was developed by IBM in later years, the result being a 96-column card by 1969).

The company that Hollerith established to produce his tabulating machines later became IBM. The machines initially made by the company were used to compile costs, analyze payrolls, keep inventories, analyze railway operations, do accounting, etc. At about the same time, another company was being formed by James Powers to make tabulating devices for the Census Bureau. This organization later became the Sperry-Rand Corporation.

Development of Mathematical Logic

During the 19th century, George Boole (1815–1864), an English logician, developed the algebra of logic. In 1854, Boole published "An Investigation of the Laws of Thought on which are Founded the Mathematical Theories of Logic and Probabilities." Boole's algebra of logic expresses the logical relationships among groups in symbols rather than words. The impact of his work on the technology of calculating machines was not felt until 1938, when Claude Shannon of MIT demonstrated how Boolean principles could be applied to the design of electronic circuitry. This revolutionized the design of the calculating device and transformed it into a computer.

The 20th Century

The early part of the 20th century can be viewed as a transition period, first of mechanics to electronics and the parallel formulation of ideas in response to the changing technology. In this regard, new uses were devised for automatic machines. For instance, between 1925 and 1945, automatic calculators were developed for scientific uses—calculation of tables of mathematical functions such as sines, cosines, logs, etc.

In 1931, Vannevar Bush of MIT created the Differential Analyzer. This machine was a large-scale analog calculator. The numbers computed corresponded to the angles of gears within the machine, which was completely mechanical except for the electric motors that powered it. The original machine had a limited capacity in that it could not handle equations of many variables. This problem was corrected by Bush on later models that included electrical methods for measuring the angles of the gears, a programming method using pre-punched paper tape, information storage transmission using electrical connections to the machine, and an amplification process for increasing the power to lift the gears.

Bush's work attracted the attention of the Ballistics Research Lab at the Aberdeen Proving Ground. Eventually, one of the later models of the Differential Analyzer was used in World War II to compute artillery firing tables.

The Turing Machine

In 1937 a major development occurred. Alan M. Turing (1912–1954), an English mathematician, introduced the idea of a general-purpose computer, called the Turing Machine, in a paper entitled "Can a Machine Think?"

The Turing Machine is a theoretical device which, when analyzed, proves that there are definite processes by which certain similar kinds of mathematical problems can be solved. The machine consists of a tape on which 1's and 0's can be written and erased and arranged in a specific order to represent numbers to be operated upon. The tape is scanned in order to be read; the scanner sends signals to an electronic device after each motion of the tape so that the machine can be told what to do next. This is the concept upon which the control unit in a computer is constructed.

Turing observed the limits to which nature could be explained using mechanical terms. He believed that analysis of the Turing Machine would contribute to the explanation of human behavior and the functioning of the brain. Turing's work contributed to the work of cyberneticians Warren McCulloch, a psychiatrist at the University of Illinois, and Walter Pitts, a logician at Chicago University, who worked together exploring the neural network of the brain as a defining element in the brain's logical functioning.

In his paper, Turing mentioned the universality of digital computers indicating that they would eventually have the capacity to become general-purpose machines and therefore could handle many kinds of problems. He wrote: "This special property of digital computers, that they can mimic any discrete state machine, is described by saying that they are *universal* machines. The existence of machines with this property has the important consequence that, consideration of speed apart, it is unnecessary to design various new machines to do various computing processes. They can all be done with one digital computer . . . all digital computers are in a sense equivalent."

Mark I

In 1937, Howard Aiken recognized the necessity for general-purpose computers and their feasibility in terms of the fact that all general-purpose digital computers could be structured using the same logic. He saw a gradual phasing in of electronics. Aiken, with Thomas Watson, introduced the electromechanical computer: the Automatic Sequence Controlled Calculator, Mark I. This machine was designed to operate by following a series of instructions via paper tape without being interrupted by a human operator. The instructions were broken down into many simplified steps. The machine operated at a speed of 200 steps of instructions per minute.

Mark I consisted of numerous registers for adding and storage, separate units for multiplication and division, and special registers for calculating logs, sines, etc. Input via punch cards triggered positions of internal switches. Output was issued by punch cards or printed by electrical typewriter. Mark I produced mathematical tables for 15 years after it went into operation in 1944. There were later models: Mark III used vacuum tubes for storage; and Mark IV used solid-state electronics, replacing the cumbersome technology of vacuum tubes.

World War II

One of the great spurs to computer development occurred during World War II as a result of the need to develop devices to handle the information necessary to avoid air attacks. This involved obtaining knowledge of positions of aircraft in the air at any given moment. The schedules of commercial, military, and private aircraft all had to be computed and compared with the information being received via radar so that enemy aircraft could be detected. Specifically, this meant that special electronic circuitry had to be designed for integration into the computer to be used with radar tracking devices. An example is the SAGE development by the Air Force built at MIT to be used in case of an air attack.

ENIAC

As a result of the work done during World War II, the modern computer and computer science began to emerge. From 1944 to 1946, the first electronic computer was developed by Dr. J. Presper Eckert and Dr. John Maunchly at the Moore School of the University of Pennsylvania, which would become a central institution for computer development. It was called ENIAC: Electronic Numerical Integrator and Computer. ENIAC was intended to compensate for the shortage of people available to handle the vast amount of information required by the military. This computer was used for the computation of ballistics tables for newly designed shooting weapons. For example, ENIAC could determine types of shells, their trajectories, how the latter were affected by wind conditions, etc.

ENIAC used 20,000 vacuum tubes and operated faster than Bush's machine or the Mark I. However, many design problems had to be ironed out. For instance, at first a vacuum tube would go out every 7½ minutes. Eventually, the machine was altered so that the tubes would have a life of two days.

ENIAC processed information using the decimal system. Its logic was based on AND/OR elements and included a high-speed logic device for storage and control. Its electronic circuits applied in number manipulation and operation. Instructions were stored internally via certain wiring configurations of particular circuits.

EDVAC

The development of the first stored-program computer occurred at the Moore School from 1947 to 1950. This computer was the result of the work of Jon von Neumann, Eckert, and Maunchly. EDVAC, as it was called, was moved to the Aberdeen Proving Ground in 1950.

IAS Computer

The next step was the development of a stored-program and binary-use computer. This took place at the Institute for Advanced Studies at Princeton University from 1946 to 1952 in the work done by Jon von Neumann according to a model described in a paper written with Dr. Herman Goldstine and Arthur Burks in 1946 entitled "Preliminary Discussion of the Logical Design of an Electronic Computing Instrument."

The machine, known as the IAS computer, was copied many times; versions included ILLIAC at the University of Illinois, and the IBM-701, among others.

The Transistor

A major step in the miniaturization of computers was the invention of the transistor at Bell Labs in 1948. For their part in this work, John Bardeen, Walter H. Brattain, and William B. Shockley received the Nobel Prize in Physics in 1956.

UNIVAC

In 1951, Eckert and Maunchly developed the first commercial stored-program computer for Sperry Rand Corporation. This followed by one year the introduction of WHIRLWIND by Jay Forrester, in which a memory core replaced storage in vacuum tubes.

UNIVAC I (Universal Automatic Computer) consisted of 5,000 vacuum tubes and thousands of semiconductor diodes for logic circuits. It had an instructions set of 45; the program was stored in 6-bit code, and the I/O (input/output) medium was magnetic tape. Because of the automatic programming techniques designed for UNIVAC, the practice of designing programming languages was initiated. An example is FORTRAN, which was developed by IBM in 1954.

A total of 48 UNIVACs were constructed. The original machine operated continuously for 12 years at the Census Bureau. In 1953, it was disassembled and some of its parts were placed in the Smithsonian Institution in Washington, D.C.

Developments of the 1950s

One turning point in the 1950s was the creation of a commercial market for computers because of the need of science and industry to deal with increasingly staggering amounts of information. For example, in the sciences, huge quantities of information were being provided through the telescope and microscope.

In 1958, as a result of the work of Jack Kilby of Texas Instruments, the transistor became a part of the integrated circuit (IC). The IC is imprinted on a single silicon chip and assumes an important role in the family of semiconductors. It contains the electronic functions of logic components as well as the functions of the transistor for storage and programming. The IC houses the heart of the computer. Its application reduces the size and cost of computer electronics.

The adaptation of the transistor into full use took 10 years from inception. The adaptation of the IC took five years from inception. Such devices made computers ever more accessible and available. This radical change in the technology proved to be a turning point in changing attitudes towards computers and their application in society.

Cybernetics

One of the major contributing factors to the change in the attitude of society toward computers was the work of Norbert Wiener. Wiener had been introduced to computer technology during the 1940s. In 1948, he published *Cybernetics,* a landmark work which is a technical exposition on how technology molds human evolution. The book was updated and revised in 1950 so that the general reader would have a clearer understanding of it.

Cybernetics (the word was coined by Wiener) developed as the science of man interacting with machine. In Wiener's words: "The interaction between man and machine is the aspect of cybernetics which most directly enters our daily life. Whether driving a car, using a computer, operating a factory or sending a satellite into orbit, man assumes the role of ultimate controller in deciding how the machine will operate. We communicate with the machine, and in so doing use it as an amplifier of our own abilities, either by direct operation, as in steering a car, or through automatic systems which we can instruct and from which we receive results in return. This man/machine interface allows complex control situations which man alone could not handle . . ."

In cybernetics, society is modeled as a growing entity which changes its relationship to communication of information and control of the environment. "Society can only be understood," wrote Wiener, "through a study of the messages and communication facilities which belong to it: that in the future development of these messages and communications facilities, messages between man and machines, between machines and man, and between machine and machine, are destined to play an ever increasing part." In explaining the basic concepts of cybernetics, he continued, "It is the purpose of cybernetics to develop a language that will enable us indeed to attack the problem of control and communication in general but also to find the proper repertory of ideas and techniques to classify their particular manifestations . . . under certain concepts."

Concepts of cybernetics are useful and necessary to a proper understanding of computers and their role in our society, not only in terms of how the computer works, but also in terms of how we can perceive our role within the society of human/computer interaction.

Basic Cybernetic Concepts

In addition to the ideas of Norbert Wiener presented above, the following cybernetic concepts are of interest.

Machine: In 1945, Ross Ashby defined a "machine" as "that which behaves in a machine-like way, namely that its internal state, and the state of its surroundings, defines uniquely the next state it will go to."

Systems: This concept assumes that systems have the ability to aim toward a goal and that when conditions change surrounding the system, the goal will change or there will be a change in the activity of the system which will allow it to remain stable (adaptation); and that given these facts, prediction about the effects of change in the system can be made.

Feedback: This is a function of the transmission of information from one place to another in a way that allows uncertainty about the predictability of a system's behavior to be minimized. An example is the case of negative feedback, where desired behavior of a system is automatically compared with the actual behavior of the system and the system works to make the desired behavior and actual behavior one and the same, like the action of a thermostat. The computer can be seen in this light as an automatic control system which can handle many factors in determining a system's behavior. Another way of defining feedback is as a function of the recognition of change in a system so that change can be recognized and communicated to the system.

Servomechanism: This is defined by Arthur Porter in *Cybernetics Simplified* as "an automatic feedback control system in which the motion of an output member . . . is constrained to follow closely the motion of an input member, and in which power amplification is incorporated." Such servomechanisms are required of systems that operate beyond human capacity in terms of power and speed.

Models: A cybernetic model of a system can be in physical or mathematical terms, and can simulate the behavior of a biological, physical, or chemical system. Depending on the accuracy of the model, one can predict the system's behavior and see how it would change as a whole in response to internal/external changes.

Stability: Controlling a system means maintaining its stability. Such stability requires the appropriate information to be input to the system.

John von Neumann

John von Neumann was one of the great cybernetic theorists. In his paper "The General and Logical Theory of Automata," he explored the correspondence between machines and living organisms, a biological model of technology and its uses. He was also interested in the correlation between the functioning of the computer and the functioning of the human brain. In *The Computer and the Brain* (1958), an anthology of lectures, he dealt with both the computer and the brain as automata. He showed that there was "control within the machine" and that the logic of the nervous system and the logic of the computer would always "differ widely." Von Neumann made a digital analogy: he correlated nerve-pulse functioning of the brain with the logic-gate functioning of the computer processor. He made the analogy between the response of muscles as the measure of reaction to nerve pulses and the action of an analog computing machine.

Artificial Intelligence

Today, computer engineers hope to develop machines which can simulate human intelligence so that computers can actually demonstrate "artificial intelligence." This implies that computers can begin to perform some of the functions performed by humans. Joseph Weizenbaum makes the following comments about such suggestions: "What could be more obvious than the fact that whatever intelligence a computer can muster, however it may be acquired, it must always and necessarily be absolutely alien to any and all authentic human concerns? . . . Computers can make judicial decisions . . . psychiatric judgments, they can flip coins in much more sophisticated ways than can the most patient human beings. The point is that they *ought* not to be given such tasks. They may be able to arrive at 'correct' decisions in some cases, but always and necessarily on bases no human being should be willing to accept."

This is a negative point of view in an area where many different and valid points of view have been expressed. Looking inside a computer means recognizing it as an electronic device. Using a computer means supplying it with the information that is appropriate for the improvement of operating machines which support human activity—for example, using the computer in the home to regulate all those activities which no longer need human intervention for control; using the computer to allow learning to happen faster; using the computer to allow what is learned to be applied in the prudent regulation of larger systems of which we are a part.

Technological Evolution

The 1950s saw the beginnings of the development of peripherals to be interfaced with the computer once the basics of computer technology had been established. In this regard, there was a strong need for faster I/O devices because processing capability of computers was becoming faster. Some of those new developments are described below.

The early cathode ray tube display unit (CRT) necessitated that the computer memory hold the information being displayed because the display had to be constantly refreshed in order to retain the image.

In 1955, the alphanumeric display generator in the

CRT was developed to relieve the computer's memory. This acted as a memory for the CRT so that the computer would send information only once.

The stand-alone CRT was developed in 1968. This allowed the CRT to be utilized without placing demands on the main computer because the display unit could be either directly interfaced with a computer or placed in a remote location. This necessitated that it contain a refresh memory.

Alphanumeric display units replaced typewriters and teletypewriters. Such units are now in use throughout the country for hotel, airline, and car reservation systems.

Computer output recording devices allowed the photographing of output from CRTs on microformat. This is known as computer output microfilming (COM). In 1970, the Memorex 1603 used light-emitting diodes (LEDs) to print on microfilm. Holography is now used in memory storage because a larger amount of information can be stored in the computer than can be supplied by magnetic modes of memory; the laser beam records information on a photo medium that can be repeatedly referred to.

The optical character reader (OCR), first introduced in 1954 by Intelligent Systems Research, allows for more efficient inputting of information into the computer. The OCR can deal with information rapidly and it codes it outside of the computer so that it can be processed immediately. Its applications are in the area of billing, handling charges and accounts, etc. In the 1970s, its use is still limited, as documents fed into it have to be absolutely flawless, not smudged or dirty. In the last few years, the price of the OCR data entry device has been reduced to about $1,500 because of microprocessor control of the recognition and read unit. This can either be a hand-held wand that scans documents or like the device now used in many supermarkets at checkout counters to scan package markings.

In the 1960s there was a turning point in the price, and therefore the availability, of electronics and computers. In 1964 and 1965, the production of minicomputers began. The PDP-8 by Digital Equipment Corporation was introduced at a price of $50,000. This was made possible through the use of large-scale integration in the computer processor, the result of changing technology in integrated circuits such that the ICs have more capacity and therefore more capabilities.

In 1969, Datapoint Corporation contracted Intel and Texas Instruments to make a logic device on a single silicon chip to be used in Datapoint's newly designed computer. This machine, called the Intel 8008, did not meet the specifications of Datapoint, so Intel decided to market the product independently. This particular device became the model for the development of other microprocessors.

The microprocessor demonstrates the shrinking of the electronics of the computer, the capacity for the computer to be reduced in cost, and, because of the advances used in the production of the microprocessor, the maximization of efficiency in computer production. The Intel 8008, as a programmable logic device, began the microprocessor revolution.

The development of calculating machines and the development of cybernetics together created the new world of home computers. The review of this history is interesting in that it reveals that the process of imagination linked with the practical needs of counting produced a new technology. And because of this technology, a new way of dealing with information, learning, and the control of activities has been placed within reach of everyone.

ABOUT THE AUTHORS

EDWIN SCHLOSSBERG received Ph.D. degrees in Science and Literature from Columbia University. He has taught at Columbia University, M.I.T., and the University of Illinois, and designed the Learning Environment for the Brooklyn Children's Museum. He is the author of *Wordswordswords, Einstein and Beckett,* and coauthor of *Projex*. He and John Brockman are the coauthors of *The Pocket Calculator Game Book, The Pocket Calculator Game Book #2, The Kids' Pocket Calculator Game Book, The 1977/78 CB Guide* and *The Home Computer Handbook* (with Lyn Horton). Dr. Schlossberg lives in Chester, Massachusetts.

JOHN BROCKMAN is the author of several works of contemporary philosophy. His books, *By the Late John Brockman, 37,* and *Afterwords,* are the subject of a collection of essays, *After Brockman*. Mr. Brockman is the editor of *Real Time 1* and *Real Time 2*. He lives in New York City.

LYN HORTON received an MFA degree from California Institute of the Arts. She was Research Associate for *The Psychology Today Omnibook of Personal Development* by Katinka Matson and assisted in the development of the games for *The Pocket Calculator Game Book #2* and *The Kids' Pocket Calculator Game Book* by Edwin Schlossberg and John Brockman. She lives in Chester, Massachusetts.

INDEX